Praise for Hunter S. Thompson

"Thompson should be recognized for contributing some of the clearest, most bracing, and fearless analysis of the possibilities and failures of American democracy in the past century."

—*Chicago Tribune*

"Thompson's voice still jumps right off the page, as wild, vital, and gonzo as ever."

—*The Washington Post*

"[R]ollickingly funny throughout, Thompson's latest proves that the father of gonzo journalism is alive and well."

—*Publishers Weekly*

"Thompson gives another side to every story, another wall to cast your view of reality against. In doing so, he adds something often lacking or poorly executed in modern journalism. He makes it fun"

—*South Bend Tribune*

"Thompson's wicked humor, mixed with characteristic hubris, offers leaps of insight that it seems only he could unleash. He writes what others would fear to think, let alone lay down in such an unbridled manner."

—Denver *Rocky Mountain News*

"Hunter Thompson is the most creatively crazy and vulnerable of the New Journalists. His ideas are brilliant and honorable and valuable—the literary equivalent of Cubism: all rules are broken."

—Kurt Vonnegut, Jr.

"His hallucinated vision strikes one as having been, after all, the sanest."

—Nelson Algren

"He amuses; he frightens; he flirts with doom. His achievement is substantial."

—Garry Wills

"There are only two adjectives writers care about anymore—'brilliant' and 'outrageous'—and Hunter Thompson has a freehold on both of them."

—Tom Wolfe

"What we have here is vintage Hunter S. Thompson, a literary orgy of wicked irreverence."

—*The Boston Globe*

"Thompson is a spirited, witty, observant, and original writer."

—*The New York Times*

"Obscene, horrid, repellent . . . driving, urgent, candid, searing . . . a fascinating, compelling book!"

—*New York Post*

"No one can ever match Thompson in the vitriol department, and virtually nobody escapes his wrath."

—*The Flint Journal*

"While Tom Wolfe mastered the technique of being a fly on the wall, Thompson mastered the art of being a fly in the ointment. He made himself a part of every story, made no apologies for it, and thus produced far more honest reporting than any crusading member of the Fourth Estate. . . . Thompson isn't afraid to take the hard medicine, nor is he bashful about dishing it out. . . . He is still king of beasts, and his apocalyptic prophecies seldom miss their target."

—*Tulsa World*

GENERATION
OF
SWINE

**Tales of Shame and Degradation
in the '80s**

HUNTER S.
THOMPSON

Simon & Schuster

New York   London   Toronto   Sydney   Singapore

SIMON & SCHUSTER
Rockefeller Center
1230 Avenue of the Americas
New York, NY 10020

To Maria Khan and David McCumber,
   the other two legs of the tripod

Earth receive an honored guest;
William Yeats is laid to rest:
Let the Irish vessel lie
Emptied of its poetry.

Time that is intolerant
Of the brave and innocent,
And indifferent in a week
To a beautiful physique,

Worships language and forgives
Everyone by whom it lives;
Pardons cowardice, conceit,
Lays its honors at their feet.

Time that with this strange excuse
Pardoned Kipling and his views,
And will pardon Paul Claudel,
Pardons him for writing well.

—W. H. Auden
from "In Memory of W. B. Yeats"

Contents

Contents

6   *Contents*

GENERATION
OF
SWINE

Author's Note

"And I will give him the morning star."

That is from Revelation—once again. I have stolen more quotes and thoughts and purely elegant little starbursts of *writing* from the Book of Revelation than anything else in the English language—and it is not because I am a biblical scholar, or because of any religious faith, but because I love the wild power of the language and the purity of the madness that governs it and makes it music.

And there is also the fact that I spend a lot of my time on the road, renting typewriters and hustling FAX machines in strange hotels and always too far from my own massive library at home to get my hands on the wisdom that I suddenly realize—on some sweaty night in Miami or a cold Thanksgiving Day in Minneapolis—I need and want, but that with a deadline just four or five hours away is utterly beyond my reach.

You cannot call the desk at the Mark Hopkins or the Las Vegas Hilton or the Arizona Biltmore and have the bell captain bring up the collected works of Sam Coleridge or Stephen Crane at three o'clock in the morning. . . . In some towns Maria has managed to conjure up a volume of H.L. Mencken or Mark Twain, and every once in a while David McCumber would pull a rabbit like Nathanael West's *Cool Million* out of his hat or his own strange collection in his office at the *Examiner*. . . .

But not often. Fast and total recall of things like page 101 from *Snowblind* or Marlowe's final judgment on Lord Jim, or what Richard Nixon said to Henry Kissinger when they were both on their knees in front of Abe Lincoln's portrait in the White House on some crazed Thursday night in July of 1974 are just about impossible to locate after midnight on the road, or even at noon.

It simply takes too much time, and if they've been sending bottles of Chivas up to your room for the past three days, they get nervous when you start demanding things they've never heard of.

That is when I start bouncing around the room and ripping drawers out of the nightstands and bed-boxes and those flimsy little desks with bent green blotters that they provide for traveling salesmen—looking for a Gideon Bible, which I know will be there somewhere, and with any luck at all it will be a King James Version, and the Book of Revelation will be intact at the end.

If there is a God, I want to thank Him for the Gideons, whoever they are. I have dealt with some of His other messengers and found them utterly useless. But not the Gideons. They have saved me many times, when nobody else could do anything but mutter about calling Security on me unless I turned out my lights and went to sleep like all the others. . . .

I have spent half my life trying to get away from journalism, but I am still mired in it—a low trade and a habit worse than heroin, a strange seedy world full of misfits and drunkards and failures. A group photo of the top ten journalists in America on any given day would be a monument to human ugliness. It is not a trade that attracts a lot of *slick* people; none of the Calvin Klein crowd or international jet set types. The sun will set in a blazing red sky to the east of Casablanca before a journalist appears on the cover of *People* magazine.

It is always bad business to try to explain yourself on paper—at least not all at once—but when you work as a journalist and sign your name in black ink on white paper above everything you write, that is the business you're in, good or bad. Buy the ticket, take the ride. I have said that before and I have found, to my horror, that it's true. It is one of those half-bright axioms that can haunt you for the rest of your life— like the famous line Joe Louis uttered on the eve of his fight with Billy Conn: "He can run, but he can't hide."

That is a thing you want to remember if you work in either journalism or politics—or *both,* like I do—and there is no way to duck it. You will be flogged for being right and flogged for being wrong, and it hurts both ways—but it doesn't hurt as much when you're right.

There are times, however—and this is one of them—when even being right feels wrong. What do you say, for instance, about a generation that has been taught that *rain is poison* and *sex is death*? If making love might be fatal and if a cool spring rain on any summer afternoon can turn a crystal blue lake into a puddle of black poison scum right in front

of your eyes, there is not much left except TV and relentless mastur-
bation.

It's a strange world. Some people get rich and others eat shit and die. A
fat man will feel his heart burst and call it beautiful. Who knows? If there
is, in fact, a Heaven and a Hell, all we know for sure is that Hell will be a
viciously overcrowded version of Phoenix—a clean well-lighted place
full of sunshine and bromides and fast cars where almost everybody
seems vaguely happy, except for the ones who know in their hearts what
is missing. . . . And being driven slowly and quietly into the kind of
terminal craziness that comes with finally understanding that the one
thing you want is not there. Missing. Back-ordered. No tengo. Vaya con
Dios. Grow up! Small is better. Take what you can get. . . .

Heaven is a bit harder to figure. And there are some things that not
even a smart boy can tell you for sure. . . . But I can guess. Or wonder.
Or maybe just think like a gambler or a fool or some kind of atavistic
rock & roll lunatic and make it about 8-1 that Heaven will be a place
where the swine will be sorted out at the gate and sent off like rats. With
huge welts and lumps and puncture wounds all over their bodies. Down
the long black chute where ugliness rolls over you every 10 or 16 minutes like waves of boiling asphalt and poison scum. Followed by sergeants and lawyers and crooked cops waving rule books. And where
nobody laughs and everybody lies and the days drag by like dead animals and the nights are full of whores and junkies clawing at your windows and tax men jamming writs under your door and the screams of the
doomed coming up through the air shaft along with white cockroaches
and red stringworms full of AIDS and bursts of foul gas with no sunrise
and the morning streets full of preachers begging for money and fon-
dling themselves with gangs of fat young boys trailing after them. . . .

Ah . . . but we were talking about Heaven . . . or trying to . . . but
somehow we got back into Hell.

Maybe there is no Heaven. Or maybe this is all pure gibberish—a
product of the demented imagination of a lazy drunken hillbilly with a
heart full of hate who has found out a way to live out there where the *real*
winds blow—to sleep late, have fun, get wild, drink whiskey and drive
fast on empty streets with nothing in mind except falling in love and not
getting arrested. . . .

Res ipsa loquitur. Let the good times roll.

HST
Paradise Valley

Saturday Night in The City

I dropped Maria off in front of the tattoo parlor just before midnight. There was no place to park on the street, so I sent her inside and found a place on the sidewalk, in front of a house with no lights.

Why not? I figured. Black car, dark sidewalk, nothing but cranked Chinese teen-agers on the street . . . and we did, in fact, need the story. The week had been too long and fast for wise and considered reflection. I had lectured for something like 166 straight hours on morals and manners and politics, in addition to drugs and violence. I had been awake for too long.

We had located the Picture Machine Tattoo Parlor in the Yellow Pages, only an hour before it closed. It was time to get the story.

Fortunately, it was only a few blocks away from the hotel, on the corner of Third and Geary, in the same lonely doorway as Suicide Prevention Inc. The whole front of the building was shrouded by thick steel accordion screens, like the ones they have in Beirut.

The suicide clinic was closed, but Maria rang the bell to the tattoo parlor and then disappeared inside.

By the time I got there, she was already staring dolefully at a small white card from the Key and Cohn Dermatology Clinic. It said, "Tattoo Removals by Laser Surgery," prices and fees on request.

Another card, which the tattoo man had given her, said, "DO NOT PICK SCAB. . . . I WILL NOT THEREFORE BE HELD RESPONSIBLE FOR ANY TATTOO AFTER YOU LEAVE MY PREMISES. THANK YOU."

The proprietor was a giant Swiss named Mark, whose arms and shoulders looked like something out of a Fabulous Furry Freak Brothers cartoon. He had knives and snakes and scorpions and skulls full of Hell's Angels slogans: Live Fast, Die Hard . . . Live to Ride, Ride to Kill . . . I Should Have Killed You Yesterday . . . I'd Rather See My Sister in a Whorehouse Than See My Brother on a Jap Bike . . .

There were many other options, displayed all over the walls and ranging from dainty four-color florals to monstrous full-body murals depicting scenes like The Rape of Nanking and six-legged Gorgons eating fire and gnawing the skulls of their enemies.

"Eagles and panthers," he said. "Those are still the most popular. . . . But, you see, ladies get more flowers and stuff. The guys get the eagles and panthers."

The man seemed nervous. He had wanted to close by midnight, but now he saw shadows in his life. It is not good business, on the dark end of Geary Boulevard at two minutes to midnight on Saturday, to entertain two strangers with glittering eyes and no apparent motive.

"We need something fast," I told him. "I have a deadline at noon tomorrow. How long will it take to put a tattoo on this woman?"

He eyed me warily, then took another long look at Maria. "Where do you want it?" he asked.

"Never mind that," I shouted. "We'll put it on her back." I scanned the walls for a suitable design, but most of the good ones required too much time. Some took two or three minutes, but others needed eight or 10 hours.

"What about that panther?" I said finally, pointing to a raging black beast about the size of a volleyball. It was large, but the lines were not complex. It was mainly a matter of black ink and blood, from the sting of the hideous needle.

Maria stretched out on the gurney and I pulled her sweater up, to expose both shoulder blades. The unhappy Swiss took a long time cleaning his high-powered electric needle in a pan full of alcohol and ether. It hummed and whined like a huge dentist's drill, and then he plunged it into her flesh.

Sunday morning is calm on Geary Boulevard. A huge orange sign that says STORAGE is the only living thing on the horizon. After that it is only The Avenues, a bleak vista of fogbound caves stretching all the way out to the beach. Strange vans in the driveways and huge motorcycles chained to the fireplugs.

I understand The Avenues. I know them like the veins in my neck. I can drive at top speed all the way to the Beach Boy cafe in fog so thick that even the streetcars can't operate.

There were nights, in the old days, when we drove big bikes in tight packs through the park, like a thundering herd of wild pigs. We would scream and drink whiskey and light our joints with Zippos as we zoomed through the darkness like rats, leaning crazily into the long curves around the lakes and the polo field . . . just a gang of nice guys and athletes, out for a ride in the weather.

But things are different now. I am living in a penthouse suite in the Miyako with wraparound balconies and a deep ginzu bathtub, looking down through long black binoculars on the alleys and rooftops of Japantown. I have egg rolls from room service and a new black Camaro in the hotel parking lot.

They know me here. When I came back last night I saw the hotel bell captain standing out in the middle of Post Street in a sleazy black kimono, jabbering blankly at oncoming traffic . . . so I stomped on the gas and swerved left at him, just to test the basic reflexes.

He leaped back and cursed me as I veered off into the hotel parking lot. Maria ran quickly inside, taking the satchel of otter furs, along with the records and evidence from our recent burglary trial.

"Did you have fun?" asked the bell captain, as he opened the driver-side door for me.

"Are you crazy?" I said. "I have a serious deadline to meet. We've been at the tattoo parlor all night. It was the only way to do it."

"What?" he said. "You got yourself tattooed?"

"Oh no," I told him. "Not me." I pointed to Maria, who was already far into the lobby. "She's the one who got the tattoo," I said. "A huge black and red panther between her shoulder blades."

He nodded slowly, but I could see that his face was tense. "What do you mean?" he said. "You made that poor girl get tattooed? Just for a newspaper story?"

"It was the right thing to do," I said. "We had no choice. We are, after all, professionals."

December 9, 1985

Showdown in the Pig Palace

"This generation may be the one that will face Armageddon."

—Ronald Reagan, *People* magazine, December 26, 1985

It was just after three when my phone rang. I stared at it for a moment, then jerked it off the hook and said nothing. Three o'clock in the morning is not a late hour for some people, but they are usually not the calm ones. People who work the long distance lines at the darkest hour of the morning tend to be a special breed. When the phone rings at three it will not be the Culligan man, or anybody else with a straight job.

There was no sound on the other end of the line, but I could hear a person breathing. "Speak up!" I screamed finally. "What do you *want*?"

"Hello," said the voice. "Are you busy?"

It was my friend the political strategist, calling from Washington. His nerves were getting away from him, he said. He wanted to talk about almost anything except politics.

"Call a priest," I said. "I'm in the politics business, and tonight I need some numbers."

"On what?" he said. "The Senate?" He laughed harshly. "Don't bother. It makes no difference. The Democrats might gain control, but Reagan will still have the veto. Our only hope is to stonewall him until 1988. That's when the deal will go down."

"You fool!" I said. "I warned you to stay away from that Crack. One of these days they're going to put you in a cage. Your children will come around on Sundays and poke you through the bars with sharp sticks."

"So what?" he replied. "We will all be in jail pretty soon. I will be worshiped like Walt Whitman."

"Never mind that," I said. "Get a grip on yourself. There are 34 seats up for grabs. All the Democrats need is a net gain of four. What are the numbers for Georgia? I also need Missouri and California. And what about that quack in Alaska? Does he have a chance?"

"Are you kidding?" he said. "That's Doc Olds. He's a sleeper. He might even win."

"Maybe," I said. "How about seven to one?"

He agreed, and we spent the next two hours fixing numbers on the other 33 Senate races. More than half were locked up, but we shook the list down to a dozen or so that looked interesting enough to gamble on.

Alaska—Presumed safe for Republican Frank Murkowski. . . . But Alaska's economy has crashed worse than Texas, and unknown Demo challenger Dr. Glenn Olds might pull off an upset. Odds: 7-1 *against*.

Missouri—Tom Eagleton is giving up a safe Demo seat here, and former GOP Gov. Kit Bond has a huge name recognition advantage over current Lt. Gov. Harriet Woods, who might possibly win. Odds: 3-1 *against*.

Louisiana—Russell Long gives up another safe Demo seat here, probably to Republican Rep. Henson Moore, a heavy favorite to win 50 percent of the vote against four Democrats in the *open primary* Sept. 27. . . . But if Moore fails to get 50 percent, odds against Demos will drop from 8-1 down to 5-2. A very long shot, but possible.

California—There is no reason why Alan Cranston should be in trouble here, but some of the smart money says he is—against standard-brand millionaire GOP Rep. Ed Zschau, a yellowjacket Party Animal who in any normal year would consider himself fortunate to be allowed to shine Cranston's shoes. Odds: 3-2 Cranston.

Colorado—Another Demo seat vacated, this time by Demo presidential front-runner Gary Hart. His friend and ally Tim Wirth, a high-profile congressman and proven Kennedy-style vote-getter in House races, is said to be in trouble from GOP Rep. Ken Kramer. Don't bet on it. Odds: 7-5 against Kramer.

Nevada—Even the boys in the back room are wringing their hands about this one. Two-term GOP Sen. Paul Laxalt, the gray eminence and key strategist of the Reagan dynasty, is giving up a seat that is currently rated 50-50 between Republican Jim Santini and Demo Rep. Harry Reid. Laxalt is too much a classic Party man to give up a Senate seat unless he thought he could guarantee his successor. But he may be wrong. He is running his own high-tension big-stakes presidential candidacy for 1988, lurking in the weeds behind George Bush, and he might have lost his touch on the local scene. Remember Oscar Bonavena. He thought he was safe while strolling through the grounds of a local whorehouse called Mustang Ranch—but he was mysteriously slain when a sniper put a 30.06 bullet through his neck. Odds: 6-5 Reid.

North Carolina—Former governor and Hubert Humphrey clone Terry Sanford is overdue to win an election, and recently appointed GOP incumbent James Broyhill is not. Broyhill is serving out the term of former Sen. John East, who recently committed suicide under sad and morbid circumstances. The natives are still uneasy about it. Odds: 3-2 Sanford.

Florida—Reagan family favorite Paula Hawkins is in serious trouble here. Gov. Bob Graham is a finely organized political hot rod with major ambitions and a blue-chip staff with few weak links. He will beat her like the family mule. Odds: 5-2 Graham.

Georgia—GOP incumbent Mack Mattingly is the easy favorite here, but Atlanta Congressman Wyche Fowler is feeling uppity after flogging former Carter best boy Hamilton Jordan in the Demo primary. Mattingly is a Barbie Doll with no clear constituency and is not resting easy as the front-runner. As a 2-1 underdog, Fowler is one of the best bets on the board.

Alabama—We are looking at two pigs in a poke, here—but some pigs are more equal than others, and hard-edge fundamentalist fanatic Jeremiah Denton is a genuine dingbat who will seize almost any opportunity to make a fool of himself and perhaps even blow his big lead over Demo Congressman Richard Shelby. But probably not. Odds: 7-1 Denton.

With eight weeks to go until Election Day, the numbers are holding comfortably at just over 50-50, or maybe 51-49 to the Democrats, depending on whose numbers you like. My own figure is 52-48.

The '86 Senate elections will be critical. A Democratic victory would not change the world, but it would at least slow the berserk white-trash momentum of the bombs-and-Jesus crowd. Those people have had their way long enough. Not even the Book of Revelation threatens a plague of vengeful yahoos. We all need a rest from this pogrom. Ronald Reagan is an old man. It will be the rest of us who will face Armageddon.

September 1, 1986

Nixon and the Whale Woman

I was not in a mood for idle conversation. The day had been ugly and my heart was full of hate for everything human. I had spent the morning hours at the Hall of Justice, grappling with lawyers and thugs, and the afternoon was wasted by chasing a humpback whale that had somehow got loose in the Sacramento River, creating what is known in the trade as a "media circus," which my cruel and ambitious associate, Maria Khan, forced me to join.

In Rio Vista, a small riverside town about an hour's drive east of San Francisco, I met an elderly Chinese woman who claimed to be the former mistress of Richard Nixon. She lived on a houseboat that was moored in a slough near Antioch, she said, and the ex-president had often visited her there when he came to California.

"Sometimes he came in a helicopter," she said, "with a bunch of Secret Service agents. They would sit on the dock and drink long-neck Budweisers while we went below decks and played cards. That's all he wanted to do. People said he drank too much gin, but I never saw him that way. We did it for 13 years and nobody ever found out."

We were sitting on the balmy deck of a restaurant with a view of the river, where the 40-ton whale was lurking like some kind of a Loch Ness monster.

Nobody knew what it meant, but hundreds of curious whale-watchers had come from as far away as Hollywood and Oregon and Winnemucca to chase the beast in fast cars along the narrow dirt roads on the riverbank. Local fishermen were outraged. The whale was a menace to boating, they said, and besides that it was probably diseased. A marine biologist from Sausalito came up with a theory that the mammal was crazed by a terminal parasite called "Brain Fluke," which might cause it to wallow hysterically in shallow waters and eventually beach itself in some local farmer's back yard, where it would die in a horrible frenzy of howling and spouting that would be seen all over the country on network TV. . . . Others feared it would bloat and go belly-up in the channel, blocking the river all winter with a mountain of floating grease.

This has not happened yet, but it probably will in a week or so, according to the marine biology people, and there is nothing anybody can do about it. A tugboat captain from Pittsburg tried to put a harpoon in the animal and drag it backward down the river, but on the night before he was scheduled to do battle with the whale he was arrested for aggravated sodomy in a parking lot behind the Stamm Theatre in Antioch.

In fact the whale was not much to see, anyway—just a log the size of a 727 that surfaced every two or three minutes on some days and rarely or never on others.

I had a bottle of gin that I'd planned to drop off with Nixon's Chinese woman on my way out of town. The press was still on the whale-watch—but not me; I delivered the gin and fled.

Sometime around midnight I stopped in Novato to pay my respects at a bachelor party for a male stripper who was marrying a lap dancer from the O'Farrell Theatre. Some of the guests were shocked when the bride appeared in a set of 100-year-old cowboy chaps and went wild like a minx in heat, but I had worked long enough in The Business to appreciate the subtlety of it.

It was almost three in the morning by the time I screeched into the parking lot at the hotel. The cavernous hotel lobby was empty except for a group of degenerate-looking yuppies who were waiting for the late-night elevator. There were six or seven of them, all about 30 years old and dressed like they'd come from a disco.

The men wore slick-leather jackets and new white Reeboks that squeaked on the tile floor as they paced around nervously and cursed the hotel for fouling the pattern of the elevators.

"They're all stalled up there on the 35th floor," said one. "That's where they keep the girls. You can't get there without a special key."

"Who cares?" said his friend. "We can get anything we want out of this newspaper." He was thumbing through a tabloid sheet called "Spectator," which had a dim gray photo of what looked like a naked woman and two dogs on the cover. On the back page was a sepia-tone ad for something called the "Euphoria Unlimited" Escort Service—"Outcall Only, Now Hiring Class Ladies."

One of the women snickered. She was carrying a handful of 20-dollar bills in one hand and a shopping bag from the Dynasty Massage Parlor in the other. Her companion had a cardboard box full of high-heel spike shoes.

It was clear that these people were swingers of some kind, sodomites up from L.A. for the weekend. There was talk of orgies and flogging, and also of calling the baby sitter and getting back in time for the Rams game. One of the women asked me what I thought about Ed Meese, the new attorney general.

"He'll get you," I said. "You'll all be in jail before long."

She backed away and stared at me. "What are you?" she muttered, "Some kind of creep?"

"I am the night manager of the O'Farrell Theatre," I said, "the Carnegie Hall of public sex in America. I am the final authority on these things. I know the face of decadence."

October 21, 1985

The Hellfire Club

How long, O Lord, how long? Are these TV preachers *all* degenerates? Are they wallowing and whooping with harlots whenever they're not on camera? Are they *all* thieves and charlatans and whoremongers?

Another of the shameless buggers got whacked last week. Jimmy Swaggart, a 52-year-old howler from Baton Rouge known in some quarters as "the Mick Jagger of TV evangelism," got nailed in a nasty little sting operation down in New Orleans and was forced to resign his $145 million-a-year ministry for the same kind of sex crimes that his old rival Jim Bakker got busted for last year.

There were those, in fact, who said it was Swaggart himself who hatched the plot to disgrace Bakker and have him labeled for life as a brutal sodomite and a flagrant embezzler with a dope fiend for a wife and the IRS for a new partner, instead of Jesus.

Then Swaggart, crazed by hubris, tried to take out yet another of his rivals—Preacher Gorman from New Orleans—by calling him a sot, a pervert and a dangerous child molester who couldn't help himself.

So it was Gorman who turned up, last week, in possession of a set of malicious photographs of Big Jim slinking into one of those "third-rate romance, low-rent rendezvous"-style motels with a known prostitute, or at least a woman of ill repute.

It reminded a lot of people of the naked lunacy that blew Gary Hart out of the '88 presidential race.

It was a shame, they said. But you know how these people are. . . . The semen finally backs up into the brain; the eyes get too bright, and the synapses start fusing into each other. Instead of secret love-nests, they begin strutting into the Holiday Inn and going to orgies on the outskirts of town. . . .

Not much has changed with these powermongers since Caligula's time. Sex and power have a long history of feeding on each other. In 18th-century England, the king and half his ministers were involved in a whole network of strange and violent sex clubs, whipping parlors and half-secret cults that embraced everything from Satanism and human sacrifice to flagrant white slavery and public bestiality.

In the early years of the century, there were a large number of "Rakes' Clubs" in London, where the high point of most evenings was hitting the streets in a drunken, brainless frenzy and raping, beating and maiming every human being they could get their hands on.

Bargo Partridge in his classic *History of Orgies* said, "The Bucks and Gallants roamed the streets terrifying the elderly, beating up the watch [police], breaking windows, committing rape and sometimes even murder. Young girls were stood on their heads in the gutter, and elderly ladies popped into barrels and sent rolling down hills. . . . There were clubs called the Mohawks and the Man-Killers, which tried to out-do each other in the hideous game called 'tipping the Lion.' This consisted in crushing the nose, and simultaneously gouging out the eyes of the victims unfortunate enough to be waylaid by them. They also carried a piece of apparatus for distending mouths and slitting ears."

These were not *lower class* thugs, as in *Clockwork Orange,* but the sons of the aristocracy. There was no law for them. Only the rich and powerful were allowed to carry swords or ride horses—which put the poor at a certain disadvantage when gangs of rich drunkards swooped down on them in some dim-lit street after midnight. . . .

That was the Golden Age of what they used to call "gentlemen's clubs" in London. . . . But it couldn't last. There were too many losers wandering around with their noses crushed, their eyes gouged out and their mouths so stretched that they could take in a whole cantaloupe and still make idle conversation in a pub. Public opinion turned on the "wild boys," and their clubs were banished.

By the second half of the century, there was a whole new focus for the gentlemen's clubs—the worship of sex and extravagant public decadence. This was the time of the infamous Hellfire Club, which included among its inner circle the Prince of Wales, the Lord Mayor of London, Benjamin Franklin, the crazed Earl of Sandwich, the monstrous Earl of Bute, then prime minister of England.

These people didn't fool around. They raised the orgy to an art form unknown since Caligula or even the fiendish Mongol hordes of Genghis Khan, who begat a long line of rapists and treacherous sex maniacs who were said to lament the fact that the human body had so few orifices to penetrate that they were forced to create new ones with their own daggers in order that the whole clan could swarm on a victim at once.

Dilettantes like Hart, Bakker and Swaggart would have been turned away at the door of the Hellfire Club, rejected as humorless churls and cheap masturbators. . . . Their only "crimes," after all, have involved low rumors and innuendo and being seen in public with sluts and half-naked bimbos.

The Earl of Sandwich would have taken great pride in being accused of these things. He was so constantly involved in orgies that he had little time for his duties, which included running the British Navy and entertaining the Empire on five oceans. . . . And one of his main accomplishments during that time—in addition to inventing the sandwich—was to sell off the Hawaiian Islands, which cost England control of the whole Pacific Ocean for the next 200 years.

King George III, meanwhile, was so crazed with his own warped fantasies that he had little time to deal with a nasty little colonial insurrection that would come to be called the "American Revolution."

These were no *amateur* degenerates, like the ones we sneer at today. They put the whole British Empire on the road to ruin and thought nothing of it—nor cared, for that matter. . . . When the famous English navigator, Capt. Cook, sent word back to London that he had Hawaii and all of Polynesia in the palm of his hand—if only Sandwich would authorize a new mast for his crippled flagship—the earl ignored the request. A few weeks later, Capt. Cook was murdered by angry natives—but Sandwich never noticed.

So much for Empire. These boys liked their orgies, and *nothing* was going to interfere. These were giants. They had standards—not like these whimpering mashers who keep fouling our headlines today.

Maybe Alphonse Karr was wrong.

February 22, 1988

Gary Hart Talks Politics

I called my old friend Gary Hart the other morning. It was Friday and he was at his law office in Denver, hard at work on a speech to the Foreign Affairs Council in Philadelphia later this week, and also on his major confrontation with Ted Koppel on a special edition of "Nightline" Tuesday night, when he will have to make a major statement about whether or not he would get back into the presidential race.

"Never mind that stuff. Save it for the gossip columns," I told him. "What I need from you now is help for my winter book numbers this week. I know that you don't gamble, but now that you're out, I figured you'd be the one person who could tell me who's going to get the nomination."

He laughed sardonically. "You know I can't be quoting numbers for gamblers on anything as serious as the presidential campaign." He paused. "Are you going to quote me?"

"Of course not," I said. "You know me, Gary. We've been in this business together for 15 years. Why would I want to quote you? I just needed a little help in readjusting my odds. . . . I can't make any sense of it."

GH: I can't either. I think everybody's kind of 12-1. . . . It's so wide open and it's unprecedented in so many ways. There's no front-runner.

HST: Why did Nunn drop out? I thought he had a lock on the South.

GH: Well, I don't know. . . . He couldn't sell it to the big boys on the (Democratic) National Committee, and also he knew he couldn't get the nomination. It's still a left-centered nomination process. He knows that. And the big boys in Washington couldn't guarantee him a clean sweep on Super Tuesday, which he had to have.

HST: Who, then?

GH: What will happen is, between Iowa and New Hampshire the race will narrow from six or seven to two or three. Not including Jesse. You've got to treat Jesse separately. Two or three white guys. They'll go to the South and one of them will dominate down there and go forward and win the nomination. The only way it will be a brokered convention is if they—the two or three—just keep swapping states around.

HST: Ye gods, it didn't occur to me that we would at this point be looking at—if you had to make book—a Republican in the White House.

GH: But part of the problem is our party doesn't have any policies.

It doesn't have any direction. People know that. They'd rather go with a Republican they know than a Democrat, a devil that they don't know.

HST: I look at a guy like Paul Simon. He appeals to me in an odd way. . . .

GH: Paul isn't a hound for publicity. He's a great guy. His campaign platform is, "I care about people, and I'm the next Harry Truman." That's it. You know the problem is these guys will not take the trouble to go out and find a foreign policy or a military policy or an economic policy. It's hard work. And it took me 10 years to do it. . . . They're all backing away from the serious problems. They've got to do the hard work. It bores people and it's dull, but the only reason I was able to emerge as a serious national candidate was because people thought I was a serious man. There was an impression created that I had done the work necessary to know where the country ought to go. And you can't stand up and say that. You can't say, "Vote for me because I've done the work." You've got to demonstrate it. You've got to get articles out, you've got to make speeches.

HST: Can any of them win?

GH: Yeah, they could, but not the way they're doing it now. Several of my supporters went to work for this one and that one. They kept asking me what they should do. I said they should take the summer off, not go to New Hampshire, not go to Iowa. Get together with the smartest people, not the Washington or New York crowd, but really thoughtful people. Come up with six blockbuster speeches and hit the country right between the eyes in September or October. That person would jump up in the polls. None of them has done it.

HST: What kind of time frame do you see on it?

GH: Now there's another window. The last window was the summer. Now all the reporters are going to start odds-making in September. And nothing will change. Now Dukakis looks good, Gephardt's looking better, Biden not. All that's horse manure. I think these guys all have a chance in the next 60 to 90 days to redefine themselves in bigger terms. . . . It's not that they're bad guys. They're not bad guys. They're good guys. It's simply a question of scope and dimension and size. It's not good or bad, it's just size. That's what's missing is size. It's not left or right or any of that ideological crap. . . . The field is still wide open. There may be more entries. Any handicapping right now is going to be folly.

HST: You've still got some control. Even in your hideous shame, there are people who wouldn't vote for you before because you didn't wear the right kind of tie who have said, well, yeah, now they'd vote for you. I think there's a huge kind of backlash vote out there.

GH: Oh, I do too.

HST: What do we call it, Gary? What kind of vote is it? The adulterer's vote? The sex fiend's vote?

GH: The victim's vote. The first time in my life, Hunter, that black people come up to me on the street and want to shake hands with me. It's amazing. It's a sense of us and them.

HST: We really can't afford to lose this one, Gary. Four more years of these vengeful half-bright rich boys in the White House will drive a whole generation out of politics. It's time to win, Gary. It's necessary to maintain the bloodlines.

GH: You're right. But there just aren't any more heroes on white horses around, Hunter.

HST: The hell with white horses. They can ride mules or Harley-Davidsons for all I care. We're talking about winning. And save that talk about no more heroes until we have more time, like 16 straight hours on my porch with a case of beer. Let's not forget, sport, that a few months ago you were a hero. You were the closest thing we've had to a president-in-waiting that anybody in this generation will ever see.

GH: OK, Hunter, OK—I'll get there to Woody Creek in a few weeks, and we'll talk about it then. I could use some time on your porch.

I hung up with a twinge of sadness. Gary is still the brightest and shrewdest of all the presidential candidates, and he will make a run at it. I like Gary and wish him well, but the gambler in me puts him at about 44-1. We are, after all, professionals.

September 7, 1987

A Generation of Swine

Home medicine is a big industry these days. A recent network survey by one of the major evangelical organizations indicates that one out of every three Americans will experiment this year with a variety of do-it-yourself home cures and quack remedies ranging from self-induced vomiting kits to alpha/beta brain wave scans and multihead, blood-magneto suction-drums to measure percentage of true body fat.

Others will test themselves daily, in towns and ghettos all over the republic, for potentially fatal levels of blood glucose, or use strange and expensive litmus tests to screen each other for leg cancer in the femurs and the ankles and knees.

We are all slaves to this syndrome, but in some ways it is a far, far better thing. . . . Last Saturday night I went out to the snack bar at the Geneva Drive-In near the Cow Palace and performed tests on a random selection of customers during the intermission period between "Rocky IV" and "Pale Rider."

The results were startling. . . .

Huge brains, small necks, weak muscles and fat wallets—these are the dominant physical characteristics of the '80s . . . The Generation of Swine.

"Rocky IV" runs about 91 minutes, but it seems more like 19 or 20. We had barely settled in—with a flagon of iced Near Beer and a full dinner of Spicy Hot nuggets from the Kentucky Fried Chicken people in lower Daly City—when a series of horrible beatings climaxed abruptly in a frenzy of teen-age political blather from Sylvester Stallone, and then the movie was over.

The only excitement came when Sly beat the huge Russky like a mule and the whole crowd of fog-windowed cars in the audience, as it were, came alive with a blast of honking horns and harsh screams.

I joined in, leaning heavily on the horn of my fully loaded Camaro, but when I tried to get out of the car and speak seriously with the other patrons I was menaced by a pack of wild dogs that had gathered around my car to gnaw on the fresh chicken bones.

I kicked one in the throat and seized another by the forelegs and bashed it against a nearby Datsun pickup with three women in the front seat. One of them rolled down the window and cursed me as the truck roared suddenly into action and screeched off in low gear, ripping the cheap metal speaker out by the roots. . . .

I moved the Camaro a few rows away and fled back through the darkness to the snack bar, where I found the heart-rate machine.

The directions were clear enough: "Deposit 25¢ and insert middle finger. As a rule, the lower your heart rate, the better your physical condition."

It had the look of state-of-the-art medical technology, a complex digital readout with ominous red numbers on a scale from 60 to 100. Anything under 60 was "athletic"; 60 to 70 was "well-conditioned"; 70 to 85 was "average"; and after that it got grim.

Between 85 and 100 was "below average," and over 100 said, "Inactive—consult your physician."

I tested Maria first, and she came in at 91, which shocked even casual onlookers. She wept openly, attracting the focus of a large crew-cut uniformed cop who said his name was Ray and asked me for some "personal or professional ID."

I had none. My attorney had run off, the night before, with all my credentials and press cards.

"Never mind that, Ray. Give me your hand," I said to him. "I need some human numbers for the baseline."

Meanwhile, I had laid my own middle finger into the slot and came up with a reading of 64, which visibly impressed the crowd. They moaned and jabbered distractedly as Ray moved into position, looking as spiffy and bristly and confident as a middle-aged fighting bull. I slapped another quarter into the slot and watched the test pattern seek out his number.

It was 105, and a hush fell over the crowd. Ray slumped in his uniform and muttered that he had to go out and check the lot for dope fiends and perverts and drunks.

"Don't worry," I called after him. "These numbers mean nothing. It could happen to anybody."

He eyed me sullenly and moved away, saying he would be back soon for another, more accurate reading. The crowd was thinning out; Maria had locked herself in the ladies' room and now I had nothing to work with except a few vagrant children.

I grabbed a small blond girl who said she was 10 years old and led her up to the machine. "I'm a doctor," I told her. "I need your help on this experiment."

She moved obediently into position and put her finger into the slot. The test pattern whirled and sputtered, then settled on 104. The child uttered a wavering cry and ran off before I could get her name. "Never mind this!" I shouted after her. "Children always run high on these things."

Her little sister spat at me as they backed away like animals.

I grabbed another one, a fat young lad named Joe, who turned out to be the son of Maggie, the night manager, who arrived just in time to keep Ray from calling in a SWAT team to have me locked up as a child molester.

Little Joe registered 126, a number so high that the machine offered no explanation for it. I gave him a quarter to go off and play the Donkey Kong machine on the other side of the aisle.

Ray was still hovering around with a worried look on his face. I was beginning to feel like the night stalker, a huge beast running loose in the neon swamp of the suburbs. Ray was still asking about my credentials, so I gave him one of my old business cards from the long-defunct National Observer.

"Not yet," I said. "I want to take another reading on myself." By that time I had loaded up on hot coffee and frozen my right index finger in a Styrofoam cup that Maggie had brought from the office.

Ray stood off, still confused by my relentless professional behavior, as I dropped my last quarter into the well-worn slot. The test pattern locked into a freeze pattern, unlike anything else we had seen to this point. The numbers rolled and skittered frenetically on the screen; people stood back and said nothing . . . and finally the test pattern settled on a number that nobody wanted to read.

It was double zero. I had no pulse. It was official—as final as some number carved in white granite on a tombstone on the outskirts of Buffalo.

The children stared blankly. I finished my hot dog and scurried off into the night . . . back to The City, back to the weird and sleazy streets where questions like these are not asked.

December 16, 1985

Buffalo Gores a Visitor

TO: The Editor.
SUBJECT: Ideas for my new column.

My friend Skinner was trapped and mauled by a rogue buffalo while traveling in Wyoming to visit his ex-wife on Labor Day. Nobody knows what happened. On the front seat of his 300 h.p., aluminum-body Land Rover, found three days later in a roadside rest area near the Montana state line, authorities found a yellow printed "WARNING" notice from the U.S. Dept. of the Interior saying: "NEARLY A DOZEN VISITORS HAVE BEEN GORED BY BUFFALO THIS SUMMER. Bison can weigh 2,000 pounds and can sprint 30 mph, three times faster than you can run. All the animals in the park are wild, unpredictable and dangerous. Stay in or near your car."

Skinner ignored these warnings, and he paid a terrible price. According to hoofprints taken at the scene, the beast chased him for 2,000 yards across muddy pastures and razor-sharp mesquite bushes and finally ran him down and crushed him like a dumb animal against a rusty hurricane fence. He still is in critical condition in a cowboy hospital on the outskirts of Cody, and when I drove up there and talked to him recently he said he remembered nothing.

His ex-wife, however, currently working as a lap dancer in Gillette, said Skinner had come to Wyoming on a fact-finding mission regarding the Aryan Nations Church, a relentlessly violent white supremacist sect with links to the Ku Klux Klan, the Moral Majority and the Shiite Terrorist underground—with headquarters in Idaho not far from the Wyoming border.

Skinner's previous history of contract employment with the CIA in Egypt and Indochina did not go unnoticed by local police, who confiscated his vehicle and all its contents, for reasons they refuse to explain.

This is only one of the many unsettling stories I think we should have a look at, now that we've officially opened the can and let the first wave of snakes out. I have many more that I want to deal with when we get the equipment in place and the research staff assembled.

We will want to pay these people well—or at least as well as the Aryan Nations Church pays its own operatives, which is said to be upwards of $20,000 a year. Please forward all applications for these positions to me, c/o my associate, Maria Khan, who will compile the final list.

Regarding electronics, I understand the earth station will be in place out here at Owl Farm before I get socked in by the Colorado snow and that your people will arrive to install a modem, printer and other hardware by the first Tuesday in October.

Thank you very much for the elegant weekend at the Mark Hopkins Hotel and the perfect beauty of our $50,000 picnic at the Presidio pistol range. I always enjoy the use and handling of weapons, and the Mexican lunch was exquisite. Please convey my condolences to the staff and the film crew. I am genuinely sorry about having to chop the arm off that poor woman's Alaskan parka that you made me wear, but I was only doing my job. We are, after all, professionals.

Due to the erratic behavior of the production crew, however, I'm sure it's as clear to you as it is to me that we will be forced to make another, more creditable TV commercial advertising my new job as "media critic" of the new and revitalized *Examiner*.

But never mind that ugliness. I am more concerned now with getting my schedule in order, at least until Groundhog Day. I am, after all, a farmer and my crop has just come in—a brace of snow peacocks, born at 8,000 feet, and the third generation of a huge and virile breed I established some 10 years ago, in the throes of a profound psychotomimetic hubris.

In any case, I will be in Colorado for most of the football season, ram-feeding the strange little buggers for the winter season and exorcising predators with a 10-gauge Savage goose gun. The breeding of peacocks is an extremely rare occurrence at this altitude, and I feel that it is one of my special accomplishments. They are tropical birds, jungle beasts. I bred a strain so strong and weatherproof that I recently sold a pair to a golf course in Nome for $5,500 each.

Which is interesting, but not real close to the bone in the context of hard news and media analysis.

So let's ponder some column ideas. I will, of course, have to go to Washington and speak at length with my old friend Patrick Buchanan, who was recently hired on as director of communications at the White House. We will want to get a leg up on the winter book for the 1988 elections and also ask why the president appears to be 129 years old.

There is also the phenomenon of "gold fever" in Key West, which I want to check on A.S.A.P. if only because Boog Powell is about to sell my boat for overdue dock fees and I left a suitcase full of Spanish doubloons from the wreck of the galleon Atocha in a bat tower on Sugar Loaf Key.

That will fit nicely with a visit to the set of "Miami Vice," where my friend Don Johnson has arranged for me to test-fire and evaluate the whole spectrum of weaponry in the arsenal of the South Florida Strike Force . . . and also to the Super Bowl in New Orleans in January.

In March I am scheduled to run the Elephant Rapids on the Zambezi River for 12 days, and after that to South Africa with Vanessa Williams to do the Saturday night in Johannesburg story that we discussed last week at The Waterfront restaurant in San Francisco.

What is Charles Ng telling the Mounties?

Will Richard Nixon be the next president?

Why did agents of the French intelligence service bomb the Greenpeace boat in New Zealand?

GOP sex clubs in Georgetown and East St. Louis.

And this: A woman from Pacifica wrote recently to complain that her fiancé, a Venezuelan national, had been confined for two years by federal marshals in a huge underground salt cavern in Louisiana.

Indeed, there is no end to this madness, and the yahoos never sleep. But this is the Year of the Ox, and the Roundheads are pushing their luck. Halley's comet will signal the end for THE TIME OF THE WHITE TRASH. Trust me. I understand these things.

September 23, 1985

The Geek from Coral Gables

The tube was alive Thursday night with news of Hurricane Gloria, said to be menacing the whole Eastern seaboard with disaster and destruction on a scale unknown since the time of Noah's Ark, or at least since the earthquake in Mexico City. The networks were reporting that "the eye of the hurricane, with peak winds of 130 mph and mountainous seas with waves up to 40 feet high," was about to come ashore somewhere on the cold and dirty beaches of New Jersey—or maybe Long Island, or perhaps even as far north as Cape Cod and Sag Harbor.

"Tides are high, schools are closed, energy shelters are full," said CBS News, following ABC's lead on the "Hurricane Gloria" coverage, much as it did two weeks ago when "Hurricane Elena" more or less hit the Gulf Coast after hovering offshore for five or six days and then dissipating somewhere in Arkansas, after 2 million angry and bewildered people were repeatedly evacuated from their homes along a crescent from New Orleans to St. Petersburg for reasons that were never made clear, except in constant TV warnings from "the National Hurricane Center" in Coral Gables, Fla.

It is an ominous story but there is something elusive about it—something "soft," as they say in the trade, and after 33 long hours of watching and brooding on the news, I think I know what it is. The news department of ABC-TV, in its relentless pursuit of hired reliable sources, has signed up a dingbat named Dr. Neil Frank, the "director of the National Hurricane Center," as the network's on-camera final authority on all hurricane coverage . . . which has been considerable, of late, and a generally shameful episode.

Ted Koppel's "Nightline" has sold more hurricane insurance the last six weeks than all the agents from Allstate and Lloyd's of London.

No casualties were ever reported from Elena—only high waves in Biloxi and the hellbroth of disputed insurance claims from places like Pensacola and Dauphin Island off Mobile where many people maintain flimsy board and batt–style beach homes that normally would be expected to blow apart in any wind over 50 mph, which is not even a hurricane, but only a Force One "tropical storm."

Nonetheless, it went into the record books as "the fourth costliest hurricane ever, in terms of insured property," according to the American Insurance Service Group—with claimed damages of $543.3 million.

Indeed. And so much for Elena, which seemed more and more—as The Days of Dumbness rolled by—like some kind of paranoid bogeyman dream whipped up by Ted Koppel and "Nightline's" creature/consultant.

It came, it wandered, it made "Nightline" a winner in the ratings for five straight nights . . . and in the end it meant nothing at all except as a big-time insurance scam.

And now there was Gloria, which Ted and Neil managed, over the days, to crank up to a genuinely terrifying level of public fear and confusion. As "Nightline" opened last Thursday, on the eve of the storm's widely advertised landfall somewhere between Palm Beach and Boston, Koppel stared soulfully into the camera as he punched up a live feed from Coral Gables that showed Dr. Frank visibly distraught as he confirmed his own worst public and private fears by re-emphasizing on-camera his warning, issued earlier in the day, that "all 24 million residents of the Eastern seaboard are staring down the barrel of a gun" . . . and also that Hurricane Gloria "contains almost the same energy as one of our early atomic bombs."

Weird news for people in New York City, which is not a lot bigger than metropolitan Nagasaki, and where even smart people were driven to mindless panic by the fearful news reports. My bookie closed his office in Manhattan and fled like a rat to some greasy refuge in the mountains of Central New Jersey where he refused to write checks or even take calls from his family.

Sometime early Friday, with the storm still running offshore and aimed directly at New York City and the south coast of Long Island, I called my friend Terry McDonell, one of the most intelligent people I know, to get a true fix on what I now suspected was the essentially bogus nature of this so-called Force Five "killer hurricane." As of 10 o'clock Friday morning it had managed to avoid every town on the Eastern seaboard north of Key Largo, and Neil Frank was frantically adjusting his asimuths to account for the hideous disparity he'd created between Gloria's berserk reputation and her strangely quiet behavior.

McDonell, however, was still in a state of fear.

"The whole city is closed down," he said. "We expect it to hit in two hours. The streets are empty. People are afraid."

"That's ridiculous," I said. "You people are like pigs in the wilderness. Get a grip on yourself. There *is* no storm. That maniac down in Coral

Gables just ran another sick trip on us. He's blown two in a row now. And he looks like Ozzie Nelson on speed."

"Nonsense," said McDonell. "He's the director of the National Hurricane Center."

"So what?" I said. "He's a raving lunatic—a nice guy, maybe, but a hopeless hurricane junkie. Pay no attention to him. Go out and play golf. The links will not be crowded today."

September 30, 1985

666 Pennsylvania Ave.

"Here is wisdom. Let him that hath understanding count the number of the beast: for it is the number of a man; and his number is Six hundred threescore and six."

—Revelation 13:18

We were somewhere on the freeway near the San Diego Zoo when I mentioned to my friend Willis, a former political analyst now living in La Jolla, that I was worried about Ronald Reagan going to Geneva in six weeks to confront the wily Russian, Mikhail Gorbachev, at the most critical big-bore summit conference since Jack Kennedy got flogged by Khrushchev in 1961.

We had just watched Gorbachev on TV in the lounge at Lindbergh Field, and he was clearly on a roll, despite the ominous imprint of what appeared to be the Mark of the Beast on his forehead. He charmed the wig off Maggie Thatcher in England last winter, and his sleek red-headed wife was—even as we spoke—dazzling Parisians and arranging for a Pierre Cardin franchise in Moscow.

François Mitterrand, the French neo-socialist president, was resisting Mik's high-powered blandishments regarding arms control in Europe and nuclear disarmament by the U.S. and the U.S.S.R—but the weight of political opinion all over the world was not on Reagan's side.

There were rumors in the national press that Reagan was not intellectually prepared for it, that Gorbachev would beat him like a dog if they ever went one-on-one, and that Moscow has already won the presummit "propaganda war" by capturing the hearts and minds of the French and the British and even a few of our own high-strung, debtridden CIA people.

"It's all nonsense," said Willis, veering off on the shoulder to avoid a nasty rush-hour wreck in the slow lane. "Those people missed the whole point. Reagan is a religious determinist, like Jerry Falwell and Cap Weinberger. He believes in the Holy Bible, the Scriptures, the Book of Revelation—that Russia is the evil 'Land of Gog,' and that the end of the world is at hand."

"Exactly," I said. "That's Ezekiel 38, where it says that Armageddon will be on us when the Land of Israel comes under attack by the armies of the Ungodly Nations and that Libya will be among them."

"Right," Willis said. "And also Ethiopia. That is critical to the scheme."

We stopped at a red light on El Cajón Boulevard and a black man carrying a hookah rushed up to the car and grabbed me by the arm.

"Come with me, brother," he said. "The time has arrived. The Lord works in wondrous ways."

I bashed him away with a shot on the cheekbone with the edge of my stainless steel Rolex and we roared off toward the Alvarado Freeway. . . .

When we got to the hotel I ordered some whiskey and went out on the balcony overlooking Mission Bay and pondered a Gideon Bible. I wanted to have another look at the Book of Revelation.

Which is a serious piece of work, a thunderhead mix of Bolero, Sam Coleridge and the ravings of Cato the Elder. I was awed, once again, by the fearful intensity of the language . . . and also by the idea that this, the genuinely hideous Revelation of "St. John the Divine," is generally assumed in Washington to be the long-range personal blueprint that Ronald Reagan will take with him for guidance when he goes off to meet Gorbachev in Geneva. . . .

. . . Which would be admirable, perhaps, on some elderly dingbat's application to a writers' colony like Yaddo; but Revelation is extremely active language, and language is taken very seriously in Russia, especially when the fate of the Soviet peoples might depend on it.

The first few verses of Chapter 13 are a litany of doomsday gibberish:

1. And I stood upon the sand of the sea, and saw a beast rise up out of the sea, having seven heads and ten horns, and upon his horns ten crowns, and upon his heads the name of blasphemy.

2. And the beast which I saw was like unto a leopard, and his feet were as the feet of a bear, and his mouth as the mouth of a lion: And the dragon gave him his power . . . and great authority.

3. And I saw one of his heads as it were wounded to death; and his deadly wound was healed: and all the world wondered after the beast.

4. And they worshipped the dragon which gave power unto the beast: and they worshipped the beast, saying Who is like unto the beast? who is able to make war with him?

5. And there was given unto him a mouth speaking great things and blasphemies; and power was given unto him to continue forty and two months.

6. And he opened his mouth in blasphemy against God, to blaspheme his name, and his tabernacle, and them that dwell in heaven.

7. And it was given unto him to make war with the saints, and to overcome them: and power was given him over all kindreds . . . and nations.

8. And them that dwell upon the earth shall worship him, whose names are not written in the book of life of the Lamb slain from the foundation of the world.

9. If any man have an ear, let him hear.

10. He that leadeth into captivity shall go into captivity: He that killeth with the sword must be killed with a sword. Here is the patience and the faith of the saints.

October 7, 1985

Death to the Weird

"The mayor appeared to be drunk when the others got off the plane in Denver, so nobody paid much attention as he vomited once again and fell over against the greasy plastic window."

That is from my notes on the night of Monday, Oct. 7. Which was almost as bad as nights get. It was one of the worst and most humiliating episodes in the history of commercial aviation, a nightmare of failure and treachery that began as a routine 40-minute night flight from Denver to Aspen on a jam-packed plane carrying 44 unwary passengers across the Continental Divide in weather that was rumored to be menacing—a freakish early snowstorm was coming in from Montana, they said—but whoever was watching the weather for the airline that night had apparently sized up the menace and found it to be acceptable.

We left at 6:51 P.M., just as the Monday Night Football game between Washington and St. Louis was about to get under way. I had bet heavily on the game, taking the Redskins and two points, at home, against the Cardinals, who were 3-1 at the time and looking uppity. The Redskins were 1-3 and playing like winos. There were rumors of dissension in Washington: Quarterback Joe Theismann was said to be in the viscous grip of Cathy Lee Crosby, and all-pro running back John Riggins was allegedly suffering from the same drinking problem that caused him to sleep on the floor during a black-tie George Bush speech last January in Washington.

It was a sporting proposition, and I was not the only one on the plane who was eager to get home and watch the game on TV. The flight was due in at 7:30, which meant I could sprint off the plane to the ancient red Jeep I had left in the airport parking lot a few days earlier, and catch the last three quarters in the squalid comfort of the downvalley tavern where I normally watch these things.

Howard Cosell is gone now, but so what? I am a gambler, and if the games were called by Judge Crater, it would make no difference to me, as long as I have a clear view of the action and know the score at all times. Never mind the announcers. Somebody has to do it, and the best we can hope for is one who won't get in the way.

That was Howard. He has no more business in the ABC press box for Monday Night Football than I do. When you take the game seriously you want information, not gibberish, and the smooth gray call of a professional football creature like Frank Gifford.

John Madden can make a dull game vaguely interesting, in the same way he can no doubt spice up a long trip on Amtrak, as he rides the rails from town to town like some kind of Wandering Jew with a gold-plated potbelly and a stolen Xerox copy of his old Raiders playbook.

But Madden is not objective, like me. In his heart he is still in Oakland, lurking around the old practice field in the marshes of Alameda with the ghosts of other bedrock outlaws like Freddy Biletnikoff and Ted Hendricks and even a past wide receiver, who was arrested almost constantly during every season for extremely savage crimes. Rape was the least of them, as I recall, and it was not a one-time thing. The wide receiver had a real taste for crime, and he indulged it with an erratic kind of vigor that made him an albatross for Madden and a natural soulmate for my old friend, Al Davis, who remains the ultimate Raider.

They were serious people, and John Madden was definitely one of them, for good or ill. Living with the Oakland Raiders in those days was not much different than living with the Hell's Angels.

I was brooding on these things when the pilot came on the squawk-box and said we were turning back to Denver, because of either ice on the runway or failure of the plane's de-icing equipment, or maybe fog in the valley. The real reason was never made clear.

The mayor, meanwhile, had denounced me in public for daring to smoke a Dunhill on the plane, and the pig-eyed stewardess was threatening to have me "met," as they say, by an armed FAA inspector when the plane touched down in Aspen . . . or Montrose . . . or maybe even Parker, Arizona.

Madden was right about airplanes. We are all hostages once the wheels are up . . . and I was trying to explain this to the mayor, who was threatening me with jail if I smoked another cigarette. It was against the law, he said, but I knew he was lying. . . .

By this time we had botched our second aborted landing at the Aspen airport and we had been wallowing around in the sky for two hours. The long tin cabin smelled of fear and confusion and vomit. The stewardess had taken the names of at least six people who had tried to get back to the lavatory in the rear, but were harshly turned away because the "seat-belt" sign was on. The woman defended her turf like a wolverine. No smoking, no drinking, no moving about the cabin. . . .

Then the pilot announced on the intercom that we were preparing for yet another half-blind run at the Aspen airport. We had missed the first time, he explained, because he couldn't see the runway, and on the second pass he saw the lights but he was going too fast to land.

And now, as we rolled around crazily in the black October sky, he was jabbering nervously about "trying again," if we had enough gas. . . .

"No! No!" the mayor screamed. "We'll never make it!"

Which was true. It was sometime around midnight when he got back to Denver, where we'd started four or five hours ago. The night had been a monumental failure. We had taken the worst flight in the world and gone nowhere. The Redskins game was over and we didn't even know who won.

As I passed up the aisle, getting off the plane, I noticed that the mayor had fallen out of his classic brace position and his neck was oddly bent. Later, when goons dragged him into the terminal where angry passengers jeered him as he collapsed on a plastic bench, I put my cigarette out on his neck and took $100 out of his wallet—the price of two fares—and told him he was lucky to get off so easy. "This will teach you to lean on serious people," I said. "You body-Nazis have had your way long enough."

October 4, 1985

Bad Nerves in Fat City

"There was a vague, unpleasant manginess about his appearance; he somehow seemed dirty, though a close glance showed him as carefully shaven as an actor, and clad in immaculate linen."

—H.L. Mencken, on the death
of William Jennings Bryan

It was sometime around midafternoon on deadline day when the swine began pounding on my door. At first I thought it was the hotel security people, or maybe the real police, coming to seize me on charges of defrauding an innkeeper. The brainless editor had once again failed to cover my room-service bills for the week, and the desk was getting rude.

We had been through this before, in better days, when I was keeping a rooftop suite at the Mark Hopkins. They whined like curs every week when the bill came in. And then they put commercial announcements on the radio, saying I spent all the money for bullwhips.

It was nonsense, of course, but so what? Something like 366,000 people heard it on the radio at least once, and when I tried to cash a check at the concierge's desk in the lobby, she laughed and called me a pervert. "I know about you," she snapped. "You're crazy for guns and whips."

"Never mind that," I told her. "What I need now is cash. I'm going out to the Avenues to buy a hotel in the Yucatán."

That was a few nights ago, before the dog woman came and "CBS News" got my number. Strangers shoved envelopes under the door, and death threats came on the telephone. The hotel management became edgy with my situation.

All day long strange people had been knocking and clawing on my door . . . and now I had not just the Mitchell Brothers on my hands, along with a locked-out woman who had already called in two bomb threats the last time she clashed with the Mitchells . . . but I also had Warren Hinckle, who had just covered the final rites for one-time Supervisor Dan White, who had just committed suicide. Hinckle's obituary was as tough and relentless as anything written about a dead man since H.L. Mencken wrote the notice for William Jennings Bryan.

We were all edgy. I had been on the road for too long, constantly doing business for reasons that were never made clear. There were bills for expensive motorcycle parts and an Oldsmobile windshield in Birmingham. (I was frustrated by travel delays, and the University of Alabama—where I was supposed to lecture—had sent a car for me and I bashed in the windshield in a frenzy, and they deducted the $290 from my fee.)

By the time I started having trouble with the hotel accountants I was not in a mood to be reasonable. The government of Tanzania was offering me $1,000 a day to go there and help exterminate a herd of "killer crocodiles" that was threatening to turn the Ruvuma into a river of bones and blood, but day after day I was forced by a strange chain of circumstance to postpone my departure from San Francisco.

The pounding on my door on the day of the great expense account crisis was not, in fact, the cops or some vicious collection agency—but a blindly persistent geek from CBS-TV. He had a camera crew in tow, he said, and he was ready to do the interview.

It had something to do with The Examiner and new adventures in journalism, but I told him I wanted no part of it. I wanted no part of the New York Times story, or the Newsweek story, or McNeil-Lehrer, or all the other media pack rats who have been covering this newspaper to the point that it is interfering with our work.

I could see the CBS man through the warped convex glass of the peephole, and I yelled at him:

"Get away from here, you giddy little creep! Never bother the working press. Spiro Agnew was right. You people should all be put in a cage and poked with sharp bamboo sticks."

I called hotel security and complained that a drug dealer was hanging around in the hallway outside my door. They took him away within minutes, still jabbering about freedom of the press. I went back to bed and smoked Indonesian cigarettes until the evening news came on.

Hinckle and his animal had arrived about sundown, traveling nervous and semi-incognito in a white Mercedes sedan with the Mitchell Brothers and a woman from Oakland who said she was looking for work, and also that her husband wanted to stab me in the head if he ever got the chance.

The woman from Oakland was not a stranger to me, or to anyone else in the hotel. She had been prowling the hallways for days, spooking the maids and scrawling pentagrams on my door. A few months earlier she had lent me her husband's motorcycle, and he went wild with rage when he came home and found it was gone.

It was madness, but I felt I could handle it more or less by myself until she turned up at the hotel that afternoon in the same car with Hinckle and the infamous Mitchell Brothers. They sent her away for a while, but soon she was pounding savagely on the door, a wronged woman out of control.

We all cowered stupidly as the hammering on the door continued. Hinckle feigned sleep and Jim Mitchell called his wife on the phone.

Artie jabbered nervously about politics and morals in Utah. The dog started barking.

The woman eventually left, but not without slipping another menacing letter under the door, saying she would be back later, and next time she would come with her husband, a known knife-freak about the size of the monstrous William Perry.

Work was impossible. The geeks had broken my spirit. They had done too many things wrong. It was never like this for Mencken. He lived like a Prussian gambler—sweating worse than Bryan on some nights and drunker than Judas on others. It was all a dehumanized nightmare . . . and these raddled cretins have the gall to complain about my deadlines.

October 25, 1985

Full-time Scrambling

The TV business is uglier than most things. It is normally perceived as some kind of cruel and shallow money trench through the heart of the journalism industry, a long plastic hallway where thieves and pimps run free and good men die like dogs, for no good reason.

Which is more or less true. For the most part, they are dirty little animals with huge brains and no pulse. Every once in a while, they will toss up a token human like Ed Bradley or Edwin Newman or Hughes Rudd . . . and there are others, no doubt, like Studs Terkel in Chicago and the twisted Rev. Gene Scott, who works like a sleepless ferret in the maniac bowels of Southern California. . . .

But these are only the exceptions that prove the hideous rule. Mainly we are dealing with a profoundly degenerate world, a living web of foulness, greed and treachery . . . which is also the biggest real business around and impossible to ignore. You can't get away from TV. It is everywhere. The hog is in the tunnel.

I was reminded of all these things, once again, when I finally limped back home—after 15 days in the eerie confines of an airless cubicle in a high-rise on Market Street—to find the TV business working overtime in my front yard.

It was 9 o'clock at night, with a full moon, when we came up the driveway in Weird John's cab from the airport, and I felt the chill of winter. Daylight-savings time was over, the football season was half-gone, and there was frost on all the windshields.

The Jeep and the Volvo were almost hidden in a maze of frozen weeds, and a big blue peacock was squatting nervously on the trunk of the Bavaria. There was no sign of the Range Rover, which meant that Jay had probably gone off to Texas with the Nazis.

Years ago I made the decision to keep the whole place looking like an abandoned sawmill—which has worked out well for the trapping and disciplining of trespassers, but it is not a natural context for massive high-tech machinery. . . .

So it was a serious shock to see THE DISH, a huge white saucer that seemed suspended in midair and tilted up at the moon like a NASA receptor on Mars. It was the tallest thing on the ranch, a 16-foot electric white Birdview dish antenna, perched on a jagged, grassy knoll about 100 yards back from the main house and blocking my view of the mule pasture.

Motorcycle tracks led back through the snow in the direction of the cistern, then veered off sharply toward the raw mud and concrete base of the new installation—which was in fact the full-bore all-channels 19-satellite Earth Station that I'd ordered from the electric people, before I went to San Francisco.

I am, after all, the media critic; and TV falls into that category, so I thought I should have all the channels, including Spanish Reuters and the morning news from Bermuda, which is as far across the Earth's curvature as our commercial satellites can see.

This had been my problem, all along. I was living too far up in the Rockies, with atavistic technology. The local cable company had refused to even talk about running a line up Woody Creek—as a "special favor" they said—for me or anyone else. My two closest neighbors are Don Henley the musician and ABC sportscaster Bob Beattie . . . and we have our own professional reasons for needing total TV at all times, and especially on weekends for the games. But the cable company said "NO."

"Never," the man told Beattie. "You people are too far away, and there's not enough of you. We need a hundred hookups for every two miles of line. You only have seven. Forget it. You will never qualify."

Which was true. The cable had passed us by; the dish was the only hope, and eventually we were all forced to turn to it. By the summer of '85, the valley had more satellite dishes per capita than an Eskimo village on the north slope of Alaska.

Mine was one of the last to go in. I had been nervous from the start about the hazards of too much input, which is a very real problem with these things. Watching TV becomes a full-time job when you can scan 200 channels all day and all night and still have the option of punching Night Dreams into the video machine, if the rest of the world seems dull.

This was the situation I found at my house when I got back from San Francisco. My friend Cromwell had installed a whole galaxy of wires and motors and screens and stainless steel TVRO with red lights and green lights and baffling digital readouts to compute things like spatial polarity and the uplink angle from London. I had all the latest equipment to watch any channel I wanted.

"Not quite," said Cromwell, when he stopped by later that night to drink whiskey and give me his bill. "There's one more thing—the descrambler. It's going to run you about $500, plus at least $100 a month for the rest of your life."

"That's ridiculous," I said. "How can they charge me for signals I pick out of the sky with all this fantastic new equipment?"

"It's easy," he said. "They will scramble their signals, beginning on Jan. 15 of next year, and you will need a special 'decoding' machine to see anything that matters. The channels will cost you $12.95 a month each, and you will naturally want at least 10—or maybe 30 or 40, for a man with a job like yours."

"What are you saying?" I screamed at him. "That all this overpriced junk that you've installed in my house is useless?"

"Of course not. There's a whole raft of things that you'll still be able to get—the 700 Club, the Vast Brokers TV Auction," he said as he smiled in the manner of a raccoon. "And also Jimmy Swaggart and the big-time wrestling specials."

I smacked him on the side of the head with a rolled-up thick, wet towel from the Communications Club, on Turk Street, where I had recently been involved in a wedding. It would have croaked a weaker man, but Cromwell was still laughing as he staggered down the driveway to his power wagon. "Call me when you get smart," he yelled. "I could get all the machinery you need from Bob Arum."

November 4, 1985

The Worst People in the World

Memo to my editor: It was the morning after Election Day when I finally made the decision to apply for the journalist-in-space program. I stayed up all night and drove down to the post office at dawn to pick up the official application form. There was only one press seat, according to the people at NASA, and the competition would definitely be fierce.

Walter Cronkite was the natural choice, they said, but he was far too old for the weight training and his objectivity was suspect.

Ten years ago, or more, Walter had taken a profoundly personal interest in whatever he perceived at the time to be the "U.S. space program," and the boys at NASA had long since adopted him as a very valuable ally and in fact sort of a team mascot. Walter was a true believer: He was "on the team," as they say in places like Lynchburg, Va., and he was also the most trusted man in America.

I'm waiting for the phone call from the politicians of NASA. I know it will come at night. Most nights are slow in the politics business, but only lawyers complain. Never answer your phone after midnight, they say. Other people's nightmares are not billable time, and morning will come soon enough. Leave it alone, if you can; the slow nights are the good ones—because you know in your nerves that every once in a while a fast one will come along, and it will jerk you up by the roots.

There are many rooms in the mansion, and weirdness governs in most of them. Politics is not just elections, and telephones are not just for reaching out and touching someone.

If the telephone call doesn't come from NASA and they send Cronkite instead of me into space, then it will be time to deal with my notion of taking Vanessa Williams to Johannesburg for a casual Saturday night of dinner and dancing, which the *Examiner* contemptuously rejected for what I took to be blind-dumb reasons with roots in a classic psycho-expenso syndrome.

Which is not bad thinking, for a comptroller, but it is going to get in the way if we ever plan to start justifying the *Examiner*'s "next generation" format and the oft-implied promise of "a thinking man's newspaper" for the '80s.

That would be a major move in any decade, but in this one it makes a certain amount of at least theoretical sense because we have what looks to me like a genuine Power Vacuum on our side.

The *Washington Post* jumped *The New York Times* in the '70s, mainly on Watergate, but the chaos of success and the natural human weirdness of life at the Post (Janet Cooke, Bob Woodward, etc.) led to a kind of dysfunctional stalemate that is still a big factor in contemporary journalism, where the prime movers now are in television.

"Sixty Minutes" can rock your boat worse than the *Times* and the *Post* combined, and minute-to-minute judgments made at the CNN news desk in Atlanta have more effect on morning newspaper headlines all over the country than anything else in the industry except maybe a five-bell emergency bulletin on the AP wire.

The only other newspapers that have caused any functional excitement in the business are the *L.A. Times* and the *Boston Globe,* and I think we should pay attention to both of them. They are nothing alike, on the surface, but in some ways they share the same giddy instincts that we are just beginning to flirt with.

They are both stockpiling talent at top-dollar rates, and planning to amortize their investment by reselling their talent—and the leverage that supposedly comes with it—via national or even international syndication arrangements, which in theory is not bad business. It harks back to the basic difference between "vertical" and "horizontal" corporations: i.e., Ford and General Motors.

• • •

Jesus! And all I wanted to do here was make a pitch for going to South Africa, where TV cameras have suddenly become useless and print journalism has been elevated, by default, to a bizarre and critical level.

I assume you've been following these ominous developments on TV— (as I have, thanks to my recently installed TVRO "Earth Station")— which have effectively shut down all coverage of public violence in South Africa by our colleagues in the video press. The South African government has made it punishable by up to 19 years in prison (that's PRISON, in SOUTH AFRICA) for using a TV camera or even a sound recorder at any scene of violence.

It is an impossible situation for the kinds of people charged with TV coverage in what amounts, now, to a war zone. They are the storm troopers of journalism, for good or ill. And in the main, they are very tough-minded neo-dimensional people whose only link to the mandates of traditional journalism is to *get* the story and get the story *out*.

That is going to cause them trouble in South Africa. It is like telling fish to stay out of water, and the Afrikaners are serious. They are universally recognized—even among non-political travelers—to be The Worst People in the World.

November 11, 1985

The Beast with Three Backs

Montreal—All nights are cold in Montreal. The last time I was here was in the spring—for the first Duran-Leonard fight—and the downtown streets were like sheet ice. Harold Conrad was dancing crazily in an after-hours club on St. Catherine Street, and when we went outside for some air, a French whiskey sot in a Z-28 Camaro ran over two people in the narrow street outside the club and then tried to flee—but he panicked and crashed into a bread truck and an outraged mob chased him down and whipped him until he confessed. There was no need for police, until later.

I was part of the mob, for some reason, along with Bill Murray and Bob Arum and a dozen or so punk rockers shouting things like "Bastarde! Bastarde!" and "J'accuse!"

Nobody knows who did the actual beating, but I'm sure it was none of the fight crowd, although Arum later tried to take credit for it, and Murray had blood under his fingernails for the next two days. "I tripped on the curb," he explained. "All I remember is clawing at the legs of people running over me."

Nobody believed either one of them, but in the end it made no difference. All memories are gray when the time comes to start sorting out details of mob violence. The truth is that we had gone temporarily wild like the others, behaving like beasts and borne along by a frenzied crowd . . . and in fact there were no real injuries, not even to the original hit-and-run victims. The only certified loser was the driver of the bread truck, who had his whole load of croissants scattered like popcorn all over the street.

But that was a long time ago, and we have all become older and wiser since then—even Sugar Ray Leonard, who lost to Duran in Montreal, then redeemed himself in New Orleans a year later.

This time I was in town for very different reasons. The underlying theme was still violence, but now it had to do with Ronald Reagan and Mikhail Gorbachev and the threat of a nuclear war between the United States and Russia that seriously worries the Canadians—and whether Richard Nixon would become president in 1988.

This was the subject of a talk I was scheduled to deliver the next day at Concordia University, and I was met at the airport by a student committee of two—Doug and Terrence.

Terrence is bright and ambitious, but he is cursed with a dark and twisted curiosity that all too often characterizes Canadians. I'd forgotten that trait since my last trip across the northern border, but it only took a few minutes with Terrence to remind me.

In the course of our conversation on the way from the airport, I mentioned to him that I was on leave from my job as night manager of the O'Farrell. This piqued his interest more than anything I'd said, and he insisted we pay a visit to Montreal's foremost adult theater to compare style. Like any responsible administrator, I agreed to go and check out the competition.

Club Super Sexe is located at 696 St. Catherine, just down the street from the place where Conrad had spun into his dance frenzy on my last trip. According to my colleagues who run the Super Sexe, there are 80 dancers on the roster, but there were only about 20 still working this late on Thursday night.

There was something unsettling about the crowd, which consisted of major pimps and boyfriends—wild-looking Canucks with 14-karat gold chains and black biker sweat shirts with chopped-off sleeves and the dumb, nervous eyes of animals who sense they're in trouble but don't quite know where it's coming from.

There was also something unsettling about the dancers, which was so foreign I felt I should bring it up with the natives, just to be sure I wasn't ignorant about some bizarre Canadian tradition.

"Is it fatigue hysteria," I asked, "or does that woman have hairy legs?"

"Well . . . ah . . . yeah," Terrence said without much of his usual conviction.

Just about that time, a woman came to our table and offered to dance—Montreal's watered-down version of lap dancing. Terrence quietly declined, and when the woman was a safe distance from the table, I leaned over and in a desperate whisper said to him, "Ye gods! Another woman with hairy legs. . . ."

"No, you're mistaken . . . take off your dark glasses," he said.

"Don't lie to me, Terrence," I said. "The woman has hairy legs. I have not been in the business this long for nothing, and my eyes at this range are like those of a snow falcon. Do all Quebec women have hairy legs?"

He pretended not to hear, and it was just as well. It was 2:55 A.M.—the last dance—and I knew from my professional experience the girls were in the dressing rooms packing their things, eager to get home, and nobody was in the mood to discuss issues of hygiene.

Montreal is a strange city. It was built about 400 years ago on an ice-bound island in the St. Lawrence River by renegade Frenchmen who thought they had found the New World and would soon own it.

This has not come to pass—or at least not yet, according to the hard rockers who speak for the Free Speech Quebec Separatist Party who identify mainly with the I.R.A., Puerto Rican nationalists and the ghost of Chiang Kai-shek. But they say it will happen soon—that the long screw of history is still turning and the war is not over yet.

As far as the French Separatists are concerned, with any luck at all, Reagan will go belly up when he meets Gorbachev in Geneva this week and Washington will be seized by a cabal of crazed generals in the style of "Dr. Strangelove." The colossus to the South will be paralyzed by fear and greed, paving the way for a takeover by truffle-eating wine-sucking anarchists.

It was a hard and irascible attitude to deal with when I went up on stage the next day to answer all the obvious questions about the U.S.-Canadian political position vis-à-vis the Kremlin and the 1988 election.

It was a long afternoon, but finally a consensus emerged: Canada is doomed to the status of a nuclear chattel, regardless of what happens in Geneva. Reagan will use the summit conference as nothing more than a flag-waving update of his TV commercials for GE in the good old days, and the winter book favorite to win the 1988 election has to be Richard Milhous Nixon.

I left for the airport immediately, feeling lucky to get out of the country without being flogged.

November 18, 1985

The Doctor Will See You Now

"Call immediately. Time is running out. We both need to do something monstrous before we die."

—Message from Ralph Steadman

I don't get many letters from Ralph. He is not into small talk. But the few that eventually reach me are always serious. His recurrent themes are Death and Degradation, along with a lust for money so wild and raw that its intensity would shame the gamekeeper in *Lady Chatterley's Lover*.

Russell Chatham is the same way. Artists never write letters unless they are desperate, and by that time their brains have seized up. They lack the pure logic and focus of the literary life, and their eyes are rheumy with drink.

I have had trouble with Russell before, and with Ralph for most of my life. They are rich and famous artists, two of the major talents of their time—but they would have long since been legally put to sleep in any properly organized society.

Instead, they are paid huge fees for their twisted works and they are honored all over the globe. Ralph lives like a caliph in a 44-room castle about an hour south of London in the fashionable county of Kent, and rides now and then to the hounds.

Russell carries a platinum American Express card, drives a Cadillac, and lives generally in the style of Sam Coleridge—an existence that not even his friends understand.

They are both shameless Sybarites, far gone in wanton abuse, but who am I to make judgments? We all have weird friends. Some call from jail at four in the morning and others write ominous letters.

I drove down to the post office the other day and found only two envelopes in my box—Russell's and Ralph's, both of them crazy with anger. I turned Russell's over to the sheriff, but Ralph's had the tone of a serious medical bulletin, and it seemed to need a reply.

Dear Ralph. I finally got your letter from the intensive care ward at Maidstone Hospital, but it was dated 20 March 85 and that was a long time ago, considering that you mailed it from the very lip of the grave.

You sound like an old woman, Ralph. I'm tired of your bitching and whining. Just because you got drunk and almost died is no reason to come jabbering at me about royalties and the meaning of life.

Never mention either one of these things to me again, Ralph. Your questions are dumb and ugly, but so what? We will take them one at a time:

1) There are no royalties on anything and there never will be. It is an ugly situation. My attorney will be in touch with you about the money and the slander problem.

2) This gibberish about the meaning of life is a senile cop-out. You are a full-blooded country squire, Ralph, a man of tweeds and art. Your neighbors don't want to know what you do to those animals that you catch in the spring traps; and they certainly don't want to think—when

they see you roaming your hedgerows at night with something that looks like a shotgun—that you have six fingers on each hand and your mind is a raging inferno of contradictions.

They would have locked you up, Ralph, if they thought you were desperately crazy . . . and they will, if you can't get a grip on yourself.

Take my word for it. Don't give them a handle. I know that man Narley who runs the Maidstone Pub, and I've heard the crude gossip he spreads. He is definitely not on your side.

But don't worry, Ralph. I have the answer. My own life has been exceedingly strange, of late. I went through one of those giddy periods where I believed what people told me, and naturally it ended in grief. I went over there, as you know, to do the *Playboy*/feminist-porno story, but I ended up deeply involved and was arrested almost constantly, for reasons I can't explain to you now, due to the numerous pending court actions.

The Night Manager is running a bit behind schedule at this point, because of my weakness for journalism. In addition to all my other jobs, titles and responsibilities, I am now a sort of neo-syndicated columnist for the *San Francisco Examiner*, the once-proud flagship of what was known as "The Hearst Empire." Young Will, the heir, has decided to make it "a thinking man's newspaper for the '80s," and of course I am out on the point.

Why not? We have Warren on the night shift, whipping the police at all times, and I suspect there is life in the project . . . which means, of course, that you will have to fill one of the "Artists in Residence" slots, a high-powered four-week gig that will cause you to move to San Francisco and actually work for a living for a while. You will be sent out on routine assignments like an ordinary journalist and your work will be treated like offal, but I think you can overcome it and perhaps do some unusual work.

Let's look at Groundhog Day for your opening shot. We will get you a flat in the Avenues, my old neighborhood, and your first assignment will probably be the trial of Charles C. Ng, an alleged mass sex slayer from Calaveras County who will soon be deported from Canada to stand trial here in Fat City . . . or maybe in some rural jurisdiction where they will treat us like decent people when we roll into town like the Joad brothers.

You will have to trust me on this one, Ralph. I know it sounds strange, but in fact it might even be sane. I have an acrobat's sense of these things, a higher and finer touch.

So pack your bags and get ready to work on Groundhog Day. We will have a strategy conference at the Beach Boy Cafe and then we will creep out in the fog and do our filthy business. Welcome to the next generation.

November 25, 1985

Revenge of the Fish Heads

"And a thousand thousand slimy things lived on; and so did I."

—Sam Coleridge, "The Rime of the Ancient Mariner"

One of the things you have to deal with in this business is being whipped on by brainless freaks and special-interest pleaders. It never ends. On some nights they gnaw on your doorknob, and on others they plot rotten lawsuits and fondle themselves like chimpanzees in rooms lit by 25-watt bulbs.

These things happen. Not everybody lives like the Cleavers. Some people are bent like Joe Theismann's leg, but few of them work for the Redskins, and nobody takes them to a hospital when their bones erupt through their flesh.

We are all victims of this slime. They squawk on our telephones and clog all the court calendars and fill our mailboxes with gibberish that would get them indicted if people had time to press charges.

There is no cure for it. Some god with a sense of humor like Ed Winn made them that way, for his own reasons. Only a few are really dangerous—maybe 1 or 2 percent—but these are the ones who go over the edge and kill and slit and burn, or keep a hundred stray cats in their condos and worship yellowed photos of Susan Atkins.

• • •

They also write letters, and I have had a lot of them recently. They are all from Miami, from fish heads and Jesus freaks and Nazis—and they are all connected, in one way or another, to the strange and frenzied cult of Dr. Neil Frank, the infamous hurricane junkie who works for ABC News and was recently honored as 1985's "Communicator of the Year" by the National Association of Government Communicators in Washington, D.C.

It was a fitting honor for the man. He is nothing if not a communicator. His frantic late-night commentaries on the high spots of his recent hurricane season were the hottest thing on the airwaves since Orson Welles did "War of the Worlds" in 1938. He drove millions of people crazy with fear and confusion.

Frank is the on-screen director of something called the National Hurricane Center in Coral Gables, Fla., a once-fashionable suburb of Miami.

He is also—according to a man named Tex, from Coconut Grove—a lay preacher of some kind in the evangelical mode who once opened a crusade for Billy Graham. This may or may not account for his huge and rabid following in south Florida, where his doomsday-style warnings about impending hurricanes "with the energy of one of our early atomic bombs" has elevated him to the status of a holy man, a literal Messenger of God. More people have abandoned their homes and fled like rats to the high ground on the word of Neil Frank than ever ran blindly around the mountain and through the Red Sea with Moses.

All Frank really does is scare people to death and tell them to flee God's wrath. But the truth is that any baboon with a healthy heart and good diction and a contract with ABC's "Nightline" could do Neil Frank's job, and the same giddy people would worship him.

An outraged couple named Kempker (F.L. and Virginia) from Key Largo said—in a short, crisply typewritten note—"You have done Mr. Neil Frank a great disservice with your ignorant and vicious criticism."

"God will forgive you, if you ask him," said a man named Possiel from somewhere on the south end of Miami Beach, "No sin is too great except if you reject his son, Jesus. May the Lord have mercy on you."

Somebody called Pick Cotton from the Cathe L. Cotton-DeBoer South African massage organization called me a jackal with no feeling and said I was irrationally jealous of Neil. "Go back into the crevice you crept out of," he said. "You we can do without."

The Thanksgiving week was a slow time for news in the Rockies. The summit was over, the Broncos were beaten and the snow got deeper each day. Many animals died. But Russell Chatham ate most of them, and his mad-dog girlfriend got off with something like 600 cured hides, which she sold on the street in Hollywood.

Finally we had to put the Jeep in four-wheel low just to get over the long hill to the tavern. Frozen bulls blocked the road in front of Wayne's place, pissing and stomping on the terra. Some people stopped for the brutes, which is always a nasty mistake. The only way to move them is to whack the lever into compound low and stomp on the gas. Go straight at the buggers and give them a taste of the chrome.

Sometimes a long blast of the horn will panic the whole herd and you can chase them for miles at top speed.

The tavern is normally calm on weekdays. It is a cowboy place, a small roadhouse far out on a back road down valley, the only neon sign within 10 miles in any direction.

But the parking lot on this weekend was crisscrossed with Porsches and Range Rovers and an occasional new BMW 735i. The local manager of the "Friends of Robert Vesco" group drove a Ferrari 308, and his wife is a deputy sheriff. They claimed to be from Shelbyville, Ky., and said they raised purebred dingo dogs for a living. Australian animals, tan curs about 30 or 40 pounds with no brains at all and a serious killer instinct. A pair of them recently sold at a dog show in Denver for $22,000.

Which is hokum, of course—but that was the price they announced. The buying and selling of dogs, especially working purebreds like dingos and Dobermans, is a treacherous and unstable business.

None of these things mattered to the Friends of Robert Vesco. Most of them had dogs of their own, and they were here for their annual reunion. It was a mean crowd, by and large, in sheepskin parkas and eelskin cowboy boots, but they paid in cash and nobody had any trouble. One man stabbed his wife in the parking lot, but it was only a scrape and she was on the first plane to Denver on Monday.

December 2, 1985

Après Moi, le Déluge

"It don't mean nothing till you prove it all night."

—Richard Milhous Nixon

There was serious movement in Washington last week. Skinner called me from the senator's office late Thursday afternoon to say that he was no longer totally committed to his job as executive consultant with the Kennedy for President campaign.

"He is quitting the race," he said. "We just got the word. He's going on TV in Boston in 10 minutes to announce his final decision."

"You lying swine!" I shouted. "Why do you bother me with these cheap political rumors?"

"This one's true," he said. "The man is pulling out. The whole campaign staff is terminated as of 10 o'clock this morning. People are weeping and clinging to each other. I just lost $500 a day for the next two years."

"Never mind the money. What's happening?"

"Madness," he replied. "Our switchboard almost shorted out. By 4:30 P.M. all the phone lines were lit up. The first guy said he's either got AIDS or there was another body in the car. The second guy said it's some kind of scandal. The third guy was a friend of his and said there must be some family tragedy—his son has cancer again or something like that. The fourth person said he's getting remarried. It's that strong-willed Czechoslovakian woman he's going out with."

"Hideous," I muttered, "truly hideous."

"And in between, all these press calls are coming in. It's like when Nixon resigned. You'd pick up the phone to make a call and you couldn't get a dial tone because all the circuits on Capitol Hill were tied up. It was a bombshell."

"Are you serious? You didn't know?"

"*Nobody* knew," he said, "not even Pat Caddell. His new superpower consulting firm that broke up two days ago—they didn't even know. When he and Doake and Shrumm split up, Caddell was in the other room screaming, 'It's a Kennedy plot; it's part of the Kennedy for President thing.' That's how weird this has been."

"What does this do to the party?" I asked him.

"It's chaos. Jesse Jackson can be the nominee now. With the 15

Southern states combining for Super Tuesday, you've got nine whites in the race, and Jesse. So Jesse wins 15 primaries on Super Tuesday. That's it. I've got nothing else to say. No more stories on the Kennedy thing.''

"So," I said, "out of nowhere comes a strong-willed Czechoslovakian woman who is now credited by top-level Washington gossip as being perhaps the only legitimate reason that Sen. Edward M. Kennedy of Massachusetts has suddenly decided to drop out of the presidential race where he is a 2-1 favorite over all the other candidates?"

"Yep," Skinner replied. "That's what they'll be saying at Duke Ziebert's tomorrow, when Bob Strauss and Hamilton Jordan eat lunch."

"What about you?" I asked.

"Not me. I'm going to the race track tomorrow," he said. "There are more important things than who's going to be the next president of the United States."

Most nights are slow in the politics business, but every once in a while you get a fast one, a blast of wild treachery and weirdness that not even the hard boys can handle.

It is an evil trade, on most days, and nobody smart will defend it . . . except maybe Ronald Reagan, who seems dumber than three mules. But he is, after all, The President. He can drop bombs on any town in the world and have anybody who bothers him arrested.

That is not a bad gig, in this world, and it raises certain questions about dumbness. It is like calling Herschel Walker a fool for earning a million dollars a year for doing nothing at all.

There is no need for the president of the United States to be smart.

He can be hovering on the grim cusp of brain death and still be the most powerful man in the world. He can arrest the chief of the Mafia and sell the Washington Monument to Arabs and nobody will question his judgment.

These things happen . . . and he is, after all, our leader, a man widely admired by the public. Year-end polls show him always to be the "best-dressed," the most popular, and the most-desired donor to all sperm banks. They laughed at Thomas Edison, but they whimper like dogs when they come to the gate of the White House.

Frank Sinatra is said to be smart, but he was fired and cut off from every casino in New Jersey when he tried to play blackjack by rules he learned in Nevada.

Canceled. Get out of town by . . . We never really liked you anyway. . . . Not even Bruce Springsteen could help Frank in Atlantic City. They chased him out like a wino. It was an ugly thing to see.

Yet even Frank Sinatra worships The President. He croons love songs to The President's wife, and his friends take tea in the East Wing.

We live in troubled times. Bull fruits roam the streets of St. Louis and even the Secretary of State was threatened with being forced to submit to a lie-detector test for reasons of routine security. Mike Ditka is jailed for drunken driving in Chicago, on the day of the Bears' greatest victory since 1942. "I'm finished in this town," Skinner said. "I'm going back to Bangkok. The Year of the Rat never ended."

December 23, 1985

The Dim and Dirty Road

"Blot out his name, then, record one lost soul more,
One task more declined, one more footpath untrod."

—Robert Browning, "The Lost Leader"

Ted Kennedy was in the news again last week, but nobody seemed to be able to make sense of it. Even his own staff people were shocked by his apparently sudden decision to pull out of the 1988 presidential race, at a time when even the GOP national committee had polls showing him as a 2-to-1 favorite to finally win the Democratic nomination.

Winter book numbers, at the time, had Kennedy at 44 percent, Gary Hart at 22 percent and Mario Cuomo at 18. . . . But nobody in the business would have bet on those numbers; two years is a long time to live as a front-runner in this league.

Many were cynical, saying they'd heard it all before—four times in the last 15 years—and that probably it was just another evil Kennedy trick. He'll be lying out there in the weeds, they said, waiting for the right time to pounce.

Well . . . maybe so . . . but others called the move wise, then cursed The Senator in private for pulling them through 16 years of ruinous political agony for a flawed dream that was doomed from the start. "He should have emigrated to Australia 10 years ago," said a professional pol who once worked for him. "Once he put that woman in the water, it was all over."

Which is probably true. Chappaquiddick was hard to explain—except as a flagrant and genuinely hideous example of bad driving.

The details remain hazy, for reasons that were never made clear or even acceptable—but in the end it was mainly a matter of a grown man on his own turf in his own car, who couldn't drive in a straight line across a short bridge.

That was the nut of the problem. He could soar with the condors and crawl with the wildest of swine—but when the deal went down he was simply a bad driver. There are people in Washington who will tell you that Ted Kennedy would be president of the United States today, if he'd ever learned to drive.

I have had my own problems with bad roads and wrong cars, from time to time, and tonight it happened again.

The moon is full, and there is not a cloud in the sky. No stars are visible because of the deep white glow of the moonlight on the snow, which triples the ambient light and makes it possible to drive without headlights on these back roads. . . .

Which is a good thing for militants, Indians and dope fiends. Not everybody needs headlights. There are those among us who can race through the frozen mountains like slot cars, with no lights at all, and never even drift on a curve, or come up too fast on a bull elk.

Indeed. There is no need to mention this business of driving without headlights except that the lights suddenly went out on my recently rebuilt and totally overhauled Volvo tonight, and I had to run the last five miles to the ranch by nothing but the light of the moon.

It was one of those decisions that would probably make most people nervous. I was driving out from town, after dinner, with some people from Miami—and my first hint of trouble came when I sensed that the moon was brighter than my headlights. . . .

Which is wrong, as Mr. Nixon said, and it immediately raised questions in my own mind about the true credibility of my night vision. When your headlight beams start looking like the dim glow of some antique Aladdin's lamp—and then even dimmer, like votive candles—it is time to seek professional advice.

Never mind the unholy moonlight. What happens *next* week when it's gone? Not even Sitting Bull could drive at top speed in total darkness. Maybe the time has come to see an eye doctor; one of these quacks who runs ads on TV saying to come in and take all the tests . . . $49.95, guaranteed to correct all your blindness, make you see like a mountain goat.

I was flirting with these ominous notions—too many years on dark roads, too many scars on the retinas—when my headlights went out altogether and the road became like the ocean, as if I were driving a boat.

There are no street lights on the sea. We all drive by maps, or buoys and distant markers, and nobody has any headlights. I have run up on sandbars at night going 40 mph when I thought I was right in the middle of the channel.

It is an ugly feeling. First there is a bad hissing sound, as the bow runs up on the sand, and then the passengers start screaming. They are always worried about sharks, when you run them aground at midnight. It requires quick work on the power-tilt to get the prop out of the water before it destroys itself on the rocks.

After that, you just sit for a while, and nobody has much to say . . . because everybody knows what comes next. Does the radio work? Are we doomed? Can we call the Coast Guard for a tow?

Probably not. No answer on Channel 19. Get out in the warm salt-water, up to your knees and your neck, and drag the bugger off by yourself.

Even a small Mako, like mine, can weigh 3,000 pounds and that is an evil burden to be hauling around in the ocean at midnight. It will move about two inches every six minutes, depending on the rise of the tide. It is like dragging a Buick with four flat tires across a gravel parking lot.

These things happen to people who drive at night with no lights, on the ocean or anywhere else.

Ted Kennedy is in town this week, along with Donald Trump and Anand Kashoggi, with his squadron of black-shirted bodyguards. People are afraid. There is also Prince Faisal, who comes every Christmas with his brown-eyed, olive-skinned girls and eunuchs to guard the driveways.

The Arabs are curious people. They are not much for running at night on the ocean, but so what? That is not their gig. They have learned our highways well enough—with or without headlights. They don't drink whiskey so they can do whatever they want.

Where will it end? Mount Etna is erupting again, and George Shultz is about to be fired, for reasons of national security. There is no respect, and there is more than one hog in the tunnel. *Carpe diem.* Prepare to eat or be eaten.

December 30, 1985

Off With Their Heads

"The only way for a reporter to look at a politician is down."

—H.L. Mencken

Aspen—Ted Kennedy is gone now, and all his hoary ghosts have gone with him. He left town the day after Christmas, on the same plane with Barbara Walters and George Hamilton—or at least that's what they said at the airport. Another rumor had him hitting the road at midnight with two French girls and a half-gallon of gin in a modified four-wheel-drive Ferrari Boxer that he had borrowed from Anand Kashoggi, the richest man in the world.

Nobody knows, for sure. He either drove to Denver or flew to Dallas or checked into a private club on the outskirts of Salt Lake City. . . . The Mormons are tolerant people, in some areas, and Teddy is one of their favorites. He can do no wrong in Utah, with women or anything else. His big brothers are worshiped like half-living gods in places like Vernal and Provo, where whiskey is hated and the river is more mud than water.

But things are not like they were—even three weeks ago—when Teddy's movements were tracked by the national media like the wanderings of a bull snow leopard in the Himalayas. By Christmas, his press coverage had withered drastically and no reporters followed him anywhere.

He is "no longer a factor," as they say, in the 1988 presidential race. He had pulled out, with no warning, and left all the big boys jabbering. Even Pat Buchanan, in the White House, was said to be stricken with grief. The hardballers had lost a big target.

Gary Hart is the hot item now, the new and sudden front-runner in a field that was not impressive. They were rookies and amateurs, for the most part—Eastern senators and Western governors with a sprinkling of low-rent Southerners who would "give the ticket some balance," as they used to say at the Capitol Hill Hotel, in the good old days, when men were men and women worked on their shoulder blades.

That hotel is gone, now. It was a palace of shame and depravity. The back reaches of the bar were so dark that even Wilbur Mills and Rita Jenrette could work the room with impunity. Gene McCarthy had his office upstairs, the Chang sisters lived in the basement, and most of the other rooms were rented out permanently to lobbyists for things like Gotham Trucking and Siamese Oil and the International Concrete Brotherhood.

It was a crossroads of sorts, an international safe house for rich thugs and fixers and stateless pimps with false passports. The manager was cool, the staff was corrupt, and the rugs in the rooms were crusted with spilled whiskey and old marijuana seeds.

I was known there, and they always made me welcome. Some nights were strange and intolerable, but it was mainly a nice place to stay when I came to business on The Hill. Kennedy's office was next door and Hart's campaign headquarters was just a few blocks south on Third Street.

These memories are hazy, now. The hard rockers are gone—some to Lorton and others to Lompoc and Miami. Only a few ghosts remain: Bobby Baker, Tom Quinn, Richard Nixon and the girls from the Bop Kaballa . . . they prowl the hallways and wet alleys down by the train station, moaning for crab cakes and liquor, and a touch of the old human essence.

Kennedy has retired, more or less, and Hart has moved his act out to Denver, where he meets the press and drinks Perrier water at a Mexican lounge called the El Rancho near an exit on I-70.

He is there today, in fact, amusing a huge crowd of journalists with his genuinely curious decision to quit his job as the senior U.S. senator from Colorado, and campaign full time for the presidency in 1988. He is the certified front-runner, now—4 points over Mario Cuomo and 15 over anyone else except maybe Bernhard Goetz and Ronald Reagan, who is faced with mandatory retirement in two years, provided he lives that long.

There are those—Attorney General Ed Meese and CIA Director William Casey among them—who still call him "Dutch" and expect him to live forever—to change the law and rule for another four years, a third term and maybe a fourth.

But probably not. He is already the oldest president in the history of the United States—older than television or hamburgers—or even the invention of radio and the electric light bulb. Reagan is older than most parrots, which can live about 200 years.

My friend Cromwell, down the road, has a huge mottled green bird that still squawks "Off with their heads," a dim memory from the time of Madame DeFarge and the madness of the French Revolution. The filthy, ageless animal was hatched in the slums of Paris and came over on a boat with a servant who was indentured, at the time, to Benjamin Franklin.

It is weird to stare into the crazy black eyes of a savage yet well-spoken old bird who can remember snatches of conversation between Ben Franklin and Aaron Burr, and sometimes even George Washington. You never know for sure, with these beasts, but lying is not in their nature and most smart people take them seriously. When the thing starts screeching and babbling about a thunderstorm over the Hudson River on Wednesday night in 1788, it is probably telling the truth.

Nobody knows what it means. Old Ben had a queer sense of humor, but he definitely understood the weather. Thomas Jefferson kept ferrets, which gnawed on his body at night, and eventually poisoned his blood.

Hart will not be so lucky. He is already $3.5 million in debt from his charge on the White House in 1984, and the next one will cost about 10 times that much—which will not be easy to raise, even for a born-again front-runner with good teeth and a brand-new red Firebird and a big town house on Capitol Hill. His hard-core yuppie constituency will have to raise a serious bundle of money and make sense to people who despise them and live like winos and weasels, on the other side of the tracks.

There were not enough votes in the unions to elect Fritz Mondale, and there will never be enough yuppies to elect Hart. They are fickle and greedy, prone to panic like penguins, and naked of roots or serious political convictions. Jesse Jackson can crank more energy and loyalty and action out of 10 people on any street corner in East St. Louis than Gary Hart could ever hope to inspire in a week of huge rallies in New York and Chicago and Pittsburgh.

January 6, 1986

The American Century?

"Every American feels the aching temptation to bomb Libya back to the Stone Age from which its barbarous dictator springs."

—Denver Post editorial, January 9, 1988

The main noise in the media last week was an unlikely tale about a showdown between Ronald Reagan and some maniac criminal Arab named Khadafy or Gaddafi or even Moammar el-Qaddafi, the usage of *The New York Times*. Nobody in Washington seemed to know how to spell the man's name, despite his sudden emergence as the pivotal figure in a countdown to World War III.

Col. Khadafy—the accepted West Coast spelling—is the chairman of the Revolutionary Command Council of the Libyan Arab Republic and also commander-in-chief of all the Libyan armed forces. He lives, they say, with his wife and seven children behind thick stone walls in the Bab al Aziziya military barracks on the outskirts of Tripoli, where he spends most of his nights raving and plotting into a phalanx of microphones connected somehow to the International Cable and Wireless network, which allows him to speak at all times to every capital in the civilized world, and presumably to most of the others.

The colonel is not shy about communicating his night thoughts and broodings on the airwaves, even to people he may plan to kill—which is a long and varied list, these days, from Ronald Reagan and the queen of England to U.S. jet pilots on the *USS Coral Sea* and random civilian targets on any street in America. He will kill them all, he says, unless he is left alone.

This is the word we get out of Washington, where Khadafy is viewed as a mad-dog fiend worse than Hitler. Even smiling Jody Powell, former White House press secretary under former President Jimmy Carter, is now saying in print that "the time has come to punish Khadafy" for insane crimes of international terrorism. . . . And "punishment," in this situation, is generally understood to mean serious military action, such as hitting the beaches of Tripoli with U.S. Marines and B-52 bomber strikes on suspected "terrorist training camps" far out in the Libyan desert.

This is an interesting line of thought, with many loose ends, and both Reagan and Powell have been to this well before. The last time Reagan intervened in a violent Middle East situation, he got 264 Marines sent home from Beirut in body bags, for no good reason at all . . . and Jody Powell's last adventure with military leverage in the Pan-Islamic world resulted in a humiliating disaster—the failed and brainless 1980 "rescue mission" of U.S. hostages in Iran that ended in a fireball of death, dishonor and disgrace.

Our recent record is not good in that part of the world. The Arabs are no more afraid of our threats and bombs and technology than the North Vietnamese were. They seem to have other plans, for good or ill, and on some days you can get a strange feeling—despite the current chaos in the price pattern of OPEC oil—that we are not really included. They are looking beyond "The American Century," as Henry Luce called it, and even the Islamic calendar puts the year 2001 less than a dog's life away from today.

Col. Khadafy was born 43 years ago in a goatskin tent somewhere in the desert between the Mediterranean port city of Sirte and a bleak inland boom town called Sebha, capital city of the southern province of Fezzan. Libya was still a colony of Italy at the time, a war-torn primitive fiefdom on the useless shores of North Africa, boiling over with fear and confusion.

Moammar's father and his uncle were jailed for political crimes against the colonial administration, so he grew up hating Italians. At the age of 27, recently promoted to the rank of captain in the army signal corps, he seized control of the country with 60 young co-conspirators in a bloodless coup that toppled the hapless King Idris—who had a 20,000-man personal army at the time—and began a long and fruitful reign as leader of one of the world's leading oil producers.

So what? He has been there for 16 years now, which is longer than almost anyone else in the currently active political world except Alfredo Stroessner in Paraguay, Ferdinand Marcos in the Philippines and Fidel Castro in Cuba—none of them classical democrats.

Sixteen years is a long time in this league and this century. Ronald Reagan has the look of a man who has been at the helm forever, but in fact it has been just five years. John F. Kennedy was killed before he finished even three, and Winston Churchill was fired twice after less than five.

Tenure is short in the fast lane. Julius Caesar was dead after five years at the top, and the hideous pervert Caligula was gone just short of four, like a one-term U.S. president.

Not even Franklin Delano Roosevelt served as many years as Moammar Khadafy has already logged as the weird shepherd-king of Libya, and the man is still only 43 years old. He is said to have no living enemies, or at least not for long, and his regime is apparently more stable than anything in North Africa since Haile Selassie in Ethiopia, who was deposed after ruling for 44 years.

Selassie, the "Lion of Judah," deferred to no man or even to God, in his time, but he misjudged the ignorant thugs who deposed him and Mussolini years earlier.

Selassie's reign was chaotic and his legacy was worse, but his tenure was longer than that of anybody else in the century except Emperor Hirohito of Japan, who has been in for 59 years. It is a record that might last forever, given the nature and pace of the times . . . and if there is any conceivable challenger still alive and working these days, it is probably Col. Moammar Khadafy of Libya.

He is smarter than Reagan and dumber than Fidel Castro and he has a perfect understanding of the ethic of massive retaliation. Not even the Germans want to cross him, regardless of what crimes he's committed.

Col. Khadafy might be savage and treacherous and crazy, as Ronald Reagan says, but even our closest allies enjoy doing business with him, and he will probably be around for a long time, unless Reagan can have him killed.

January 13, 1986

Crank Time in Tripoli

There was a lot of violence in the news last week, but not much of it fit the mold. There were no major bombings or hijackings or massacres. Even South Africa was slow, for a change, and only a few hundred people were reported killed in Lebanon on Wednesday.

The *Washington Post* reported that the plane crash that killed pop singer Ricky Nelson last week in Texas may have been caused by a cocaine freebasing experiment that went wrong and set fire to the doomed DC-3 that carried the seven passengers to their deaths. This was said to be bad and shocking news for Ricky Nelson fans, who presumably still cling to the man as some kind of pure symbol and standard-bearer for the lifestyle and values of the all-American mid-'50s teen-age suburban way of life that he once represented on TV. It was too bad, they said, that Ricky let his people down by going out in a wild blaze of drugs.

Well . . . count me out on that one. I grew up with that newt and I have seen his lame type come and go like fruit flies, for longer than I want to remember.

He was a punk, but so what? Only his ex-wife called him a dope fiend, and then her lawyer called in the press. . . . But there was no evidence or reason or even a credible rumor that he was so deep into freebasing that he might go sideways at any moment and set drug fires of such brain-damaged magnitude that airplanes would melt in the sky, killing his fiancée and best friends.

The accusation traced back to a five-year-old divorce file, and even then it was all circumstantial—a nest of gibberish, as they say in the trade . . . and not entirely unlike the gaggle of wild charges laid by Ronald Reagan against Col. Moammar Khadafy of Libya.

The colonel was whooping it up in Tripoli last week with a fast round of bear-baiting, breast-beating and unsettling displays of what is beginning to look like a genuinely perverse sense of humor, although not everybody saw it that way.

There were those in Washington, including some prominent Democrats, who saw the colonel's behavior as the last stages of some deep and malignant craziness that might soon cause The End of The World. Sen. Howard Metzenbaum of Ohio, a traditionally flaky liberal with credentials suggesting some kind of awful mutation with the genes of Hubert Humphrey, Billie Sol Estes and a Stalinist camel driver from South Yemen, went on national TV to say that the time had finally come for Khadafy to be put to sleep. It was a call for a political assassination. "Maybe we're at that point in the world," said Metzenbaum, a longtime lobbyist for Israel, "where Mr. Khadafy has to be eliminated."

Not even Defense Secretary Caspar Weinberger was willing to go that far—not even after the colonel discussed his plans for destroying the U.S. 6th Fleet and perhaps every oil well east of Gibraltar in a lengthy personal discussion with Ted Koppel on "Nightline."

In almost the same breath, however, he assured Koppel that he was absolutely sincere about inviting Reagan to come and visit with him in his tent and hash things out like real men. Koppel responded by inviting Khadafy to the White House, for a long lunch without George Shultz, and *al Qaid* said, "Why not?" He has never been west of England—and only there for six months, long ago, which he spent hunkered down in some vile basement flat in Brixton—but when Koppel asked him to Washington he seemed gratified. It was an "encouraging exchange," as they say in the diplomatic business, and some even called it a "breakthrough."

Indeed. And so much for TV diplomacy. Within 24 hours the colonel had shifted back to his Mr. Hyde mode and was calling Reagan a Nazi pig who should be put on trial for international war crimes. He reverted to his earlier assessment of the president as "a stinking rotten crusader" and "an aging third-rate actor" who is even worse than his old movies, which are shown constantly on Libyan TV.

Khadafy also called for help in the form of a new International Brigade of volunteers to join terrorist "suicide squads" to wreak havoc all over the world, if the U.S. attacks Libya.

Koppel had no comment and Shultz laughed all night in his office in Foggy Bottom, and Khadafy claimed he got 10,000 applications in less than 48 hours.

My friend Skinner was not among these, but for reasons of his own he left for North Africa at once. He called from the airport in Seattle last night, saying he was leaving at midnight on a charter flight over the pole to Amsterdam and then Cairo, where he and his group—mainly young female American schoolteachers—would be met by "some of the colonel's people" and whisked off on a fast coastal freighter to the Libyan port of Benghazi.

The Egyptians were getting nervous, he said, about the sudden rush of strange air travelers to Tripoli. The transit lounge at Cairo International was swarming with ugly young men wearing Ray-Bans and hauling long Goretex duffel bags with Harley-Davidson locks and Soldier of Fortune I.D. plates. They smelled like wax and they paid in Swiss francs and many had Lebanese passports. It was clearly a bad situation.

"I won't be gone long," Skinner assured me. "This thing is a red herring. Once Khadafy gets a look at these harebrained thugs who say they want to fight to the death for him, he'll put them in prison—or at least try to, and that's when the trouble will start. Most of these people are murdering scum who couldn't even get work in South Africa."

He figured the whole thing would blow over in six weeks, and Khadafy would drop out of the headlines. "He's a stooge," he said. "All they have on him is that he talks too much—which is maybe the worst thing you can do in big-time Arab politics. They didn't worry about him when he was a terrorist, but when he started talking about it every night on international TV, they got nervous. He's a dingbat now. They'll have to put the bag on him pretty soon, one way or the other."

I hung up and went back to work. Skinner was too dumb to cure and too smart to worry about, and his work was none of my business.

The news out of Tripoli is still slow, but the pace will pick up soon enough. Even maniacs need time to reload, but it is a rare quirk in history when they all run out at the same time, and anybody who has spent any time around wars will tell you that a sudden calm, for no reason, is almost always a time to get braced. Strange and ugly things are about to happen.

January 20, 1986

Meat Sickness

Super Sunday was a foul gray day in Chicago. First there was snow, then freezing fog, and finally a long subzero night with icy winds off the lake and a wind-chill factor at midnight of 44 below . . . but none of this mattered to the natives: They ripped off their shirts and spit beer on women and ran wild in the streets like hyenas, to celebrate another great victory.

I had my own problems and most of them had to do with gambling. They were many and varied, but the nut of the matter had to do with the fact that I came awake on Sunday morning with the uneasy knowledge that I had taken New England and 13 points, which was beginning to feel uncomfortable. I had done it on the advice of Rev. Desmond Tutu, the Anglican bishop and Nobel Peace Prize laureate from South Africa, who made a speech in Chicago on Friday.

The problem with Tutu is his accent, or perhaps his feeling for emphasis. He had warned me, I thought, to stay away from the Bears, which disturbed my basic gambling instinct and ran counter to all my analyses. Until I spoke with Desmond I was taking the Bears and not worrying too much about points. . . .

It seemed clear that the Bears would score at will and make a mockery of the whole thing. They had shut down the best running games in the NFL, and their only loss of the season looked more like boredom or carelessness than a sign of any real weakness. My instinct was to give 20 points and not even bother to watch the game—

But when the bishop fixed me with his glittering little eyes and uttered the equivalent of "Nevermore, quoth the raven," I took it as a serious sign: Take the points.

But it made me nervous, and by midnight on Saturday my confidence was turning to wax. I raved for a while on the phones, and too many smart people snickered when I said I was switching my whole nut, on the word of some bishop from South Africa who had never even seen a football game.

It was my old friend Craig Vetter, in fact, who finally had to point out to me that there was nothing in what Desmond had said to me that could be taken as a warning to bet heavily against the Bears. It was mainly a moral admonition: Stay away from gambling—which had nothing to do with the point spread.

Had I gone mad, I wondered, to reverse a whole lifetime of sporting wisdom on the word of some mischievous quack?

Vetter laughed all night at my queasiness, and by noon on Sunday I was grabbing everything I could get on the Bears and giving up 10. Here was a chance for a two-point "middle," time honored gamblers' trick to win coming and going, to collect on both ends. If the Bears won by 11 or 12, I would be home free—and that spread was not out of the question. I also picked up a huge piece of coverage on the chance of a shutout, at seven to one, plus a three-to-one side bet that Walter Payton wouldn't gain 100 yards . . . by the time the big countdown started on Sunday I was covered in many ways, and Desmond was somewhere over the Atlantic on a 1,300-mph Concorde, en route to Paris and Cape Town.

There was no shortage of good places to watch the game on TV, but the best one for my purposes was a 40-foot-high Diamond Vision screen in downtown Daley Plaza, where a huge and essentially goofy iron statue by Pablo Picasso looks down on the jabbering crowds who have been flocking in all week, from places like Cicero and Galesburg. They pressed in on the plaza like lemmings, despite the unholy cold and winds that swept in off the lake like some nightmare freeze-out of the Cremation of Sam McGee.

There is nothing quite like the cold that you feel on a bad winter day in Chicago. It is a genuinely frightening pain that is like being plunged into ice water, or feeling your skin on fire. . . . But pain meant nothing to these people; they tore off their clothes and raced around the plaza like slam dancers, totally ignoring the game. Later that night, I heard a radio news bulletin that said they were all transvestites, giddy drifters who lived off the land and sold industrial ether for a living and whipped their own dogs at night to relieve the terrible tensions that come with the life of the bull fruit.

The game was over by halftime, with the Bears up by 23 to 3 and rapidly pulling away. About half the crowd was gone, by this time, and the ones who remained were drunk.

On our way through the plaza, we were joined by a man named Willis, who seemed vaguely familiar and claimed to be a friend of Mike Ditka. I sensed that he had a problem of some kind, which turned out to be true. . . . His wife, he explained, had left him unexpectedly and moved into a penthouse apartment on Lake Shore Drive with three Bears—two brutes from the special teams unit and one on the injured reserve list.

They had made her a sort of team mascot for most of the season, and then rudely kicked her out and banned her from the team hotel in New Orleans. . . . She didn't even make the trip, but took up with the rookie linebacker who was still on injured reserve and said he was going to marry her, once his status finally cleared up.

"The slut is driving me crazy," said Willis. "Every time I see her she's staggering around in some meat rack on Division Street, wearing Kevin Butler's jersey. It's No. 6. She wears it like a dress; I see the rotten thing in my dreams."

His hands were unsteady and his eyes were like unripe tomatoes. "I have a feeling that she's about to do something desperate," he said. "I need some advice. What would you do in a situation like this?"

I jammed my hands deep into the pockets of my thin Palm Beach dinner jacket, shuddering from the cold and The Fear. His tale was too much to deal with, and I was late for dinner with Vetter at the Pump Room.

Willis asked again for advice, and I could see that he needed an answer. "Call my friend Bishop Tutu," I told him. "He's always been a great help to me."

January 27, 1986

Last Train from Chicago

A wino approached me in the lobby of Union Station and said he was a friend of John Madden. "I was supposed to meet him here," he said. "Our train for the coast leaves at 2:30." He looked anxiously down at his watch. "Maybe he meant I should meet him on the train," he said. "You think he's already aboard?"

"Let's hope so," I said. "The damn thing leaves in 12 minutes. I'll be lucky to make it, myself."

I was hauling a huge cart of baggage, not knowing which one of the many tunnels led out to the California Zephyr. . . . and Maria had gone off in a funk with all the cash, and also our tickets.

Madden's friend was still ambling along beside me. "I see you're wearing a Raiders jacket," he said. "So I thought you might have seen Johnny."

"Not yet," I said, "and this is not a Raiders jacket. It's from the flight of Apollo 11."

He leaned closer to examine the finely embroidered lettering on the shoulder patch of my NASA-style silver jacket. "The Eagle Has Landed," he muttered. "Yessir, I sure as hell remember that one. Are you the guy that walked on the moon?"

I nodded. Maria was nowhere in sight, and our train was pulling out in nine minutes—from some gate that I didn't know and probably couldn't get through anyway, because I had no money or tickets.

I eyed Madden's friend with new interest. "I knew John in Oakland," I said. "What gate are we leaving from?"

"It's No. 22," he said. "We're late. Let me help you with these bags."

He seized the front bar of my luggage cart—a thing about the size of two bathtubs—and proceeded to haul it through the crowd at top speed, shouting: "Get out of the way! It's John Madden!"

I followed sheepishly in his wake, but convinced that he would almost certainly get us through Gate 22 and safely onto the train.

He was, after all, on his way to the Coast with Big John. There would be no misunderstanding at the gate, tickets or no tickets. . . . Our train left in seven minutes; there was no time to check character references.

"Johnny will be in the club car," said the wino. "We have a big suite in the back, but he always goes to the bar. I've traveled with him a lot."

That's good, I thought. A wild-eyed man in a red uniform was bearing down on us. "Get your hands off that cart," he shouted. "That's Red Cap property. Let's have a look at your tickets."

I smiled meaningfully at my buddy. "He has them," I said. "We're with John Madden. This is part of his luggage from the Super Bowl."

The Amtrak man laughed. "Don't mess with me," he snapped. "Do you people have tickets, or not?"

My own memory is vague, now, on the details of what happened next. It was all in a matter of seconds. My man looked wildly around him, then suddenly bent over and grabbed his stomach with both hands. "Call Johnny!" he moaned. "I'm having another attack!"

Just then Maria arrived, waving a handful of tickets, and the Amtrak man reluctantly let us through. A real-life Red Cap suddenly materialized and took control of the luggage cart.

"Let's hurry it up," he ordered. "Get a move on, folks. This train runs on time."

We rushed down the platform in a confused babble and arrived at the big cavelike door to our sleeper—the last car on the train—with 30 seconds to spare. I heard whistles from up in front, and a roar of steam vents underneath. The Zephyr was pulling out.

Many hands lifted our luggage aboard, and within moments we were rolling at speed through the dead old industrial wasteland of what was once the main business district west of Wall Street. Riding the rails out of Chicago is a quick education in the socioeconomic realities of recent American history—miles of dead factories and warehouses, abandoned brick hulks with boarded-up windows and signs like "Cemak Meats" and "Adams Pressed Metals Corp."

We were just settling into our Deluxe Bedroom Compartment on Car No. 3530—adjusting the bunks and the shower head and the typewriter table by the big picture window—when I realized that we were, in fact, not alone. There was a ratty old suitcase in the room that I didn't recognize, and also another person.

It was Madden's friend. He'd moved smoothly into the compartment and pulled the curtain closed behind him. "Jesus Christ, man," he said, as he sat down on the end of the bunk. "You sure as hell travel heavy. I thought we'd never get all this stuff aboard."

"Where's Johnny?" I asked him.

"Don't worry," he said, lighting up one of my Dunhills. "I'll find him. Just let me sit here for a minute, or at least until they take up the tickets."

I smacked him on the side of the head and he suddenly went all to pieces.

"Please," he blurted. "Don't turn me in. I have to be in California by tomorrow, or they'll revoke my parole." He slumped on the bunk and began sobbing. "I'm sorry I lied to you," he moaned. "But I had to get out of town. They were after me—and besides, you looked like a Raiders fan; I thought you would be on my side."

I shook my head sadly and reached into my Spanish leather kit bag, coming up with a small plastic tag from a long-ago conference of the National District Attorneys Association, which occurred in Las Vegas, Nev., in the time of Richard Nixon. It said, "THOMPSON HUNTER— LOS ANGELES, CA." Underneath the name was a small, five-pointed lawman's badge, with silver scales in the middle.

The wino went instantly wild when I showed it to him. "You lying bastard," he screamed. "I knew there was something wrong with you! You're a cop! You were never a friend of John Madden. He wouldn't do this to me." Then he leaped sideways off the bunk and grabbed for my bottle of Chivas.

A brief scuffle ensued, then the steward, Frank Thompson, arrived with a rope. I had no choice. We had him taken off forcibly by railroad dicks in Naperville, still cursing me for betraying what he called "the spirit of the Raiders."

He was right, in a sense, and I felt vaguely unclean as the Zephyr rolled out, once again, toward Galesburg and Monmouth and the Mississippi River—which we would cross again on schedule, around sundown.

February 3, 1986

Kill Them Before They Eat

Slow news days are a routine curse in the journalism business. These are the ones—usually Tuesdays and Wednesdays and always Saturdays—when George Jones or Angus Drew is "sitting in" for Peter Jennings on the ABC evening news, and Dan Rather leads off with a story about Chinese pandas refusing to mate in public—in full view of leering, hooting crowds—at the National Zoo in Washington.

CNN will fill 13 minutes with grim vignettes on "The Death of Sex in the '80s." Jerry Falwell will lecture on the horror of herpes and AIDS, along with the tragic epidemic of teen-age pregnancy . . . and Tom Brokaw will be seen to doze off, on camera, mumbling fitfully about lost dogs and lip cancer and constitutional flaws in Gramm-Rudman.

Days like these are not rare: They run about 50-50, even for wire editors and news junkies. . . . But every once in a while the balance will tip all at once, jamming eight or nine big ones into the hamper before people like Rather and Brokaw even get to work, and by sundown they are all getting crazier.

Last Friday was one of those days, a genuine howler with an energy all its own. My story list got faster and fatter by the hour. The original plan was for a long-delayed and deeply political screed on the planned murder—by Reagan and Gramm and Rudman—of Amtrak, our national passenger-rail system.

The pigs meant to kill it off, for reasons that would shame every greedhead since Ebenezer Scrooge. It was a good story, but only one of many. By noon I was half mad with new input, and Amtrak was beyond the back burner.

The early news feeds on the big dish had Gramm-Rudman gutted in court, for constitutional reasons; Baby Doc Duvalier had fled Haiti as mobs gnawed the bones of his father; and the presidential election in the Philippines was dissolving in fraud and violence.

Even Peter Jennings was stunned, weeping helplessly on camera in Manila as thugs ran off with the ballot boxes. Official U.S. "observer" Sen. Richard Lugar, R-Ind.—once known as "Richard Nixon's favorite mayor" when he ran Indianapolis—was so appalled by President Ferdinand Marcos' flagrant abuse of the democratic process that he angrily denounced Marcos on international TV, a move that could threaten the whole U.S. military presence in Southeast Asia if Marcos steals the election.

• • •

That would have been enough, even for a fast day in the news business—but as the hours went by, there was more:

Saturday was Bob Marley's birthday, and also James Dean's; Clint Eastwood was making an ugly run for the mayor's job in Carmel; and in Chicago, Mike Ditka was denouncing former Bears defensive coach Buddy Ryan as a show-hog who got too big for his britches.

Ryan has already hired Bears' receivers coach Ted Plumb to help him run the hapless Philadelphia Eagles next season, and rumors out of Chicago say Buddy is now dealing for the core of the Bears' defensive unit.

Starting safeties Gary Fencik and Dave Duerson are free agents, Super Bowl MVP Richard Dent is still without a contract, and all-pro middle linebacker Mike Singletary has said more than once: "If Buddy Ryan leaves, I want to go with him."

So much for dynasties. The Bears will be lucky to make the playoffs next year. Names like Dent and Fencik and Singletary are no small cogs in the vaunted "46 Defense," which humiliated that gang of half-mad neurotics from the outskirts of Boston in the Superdome. A Philadelphia sports writer, in fact, wrote that "Singletary gave the Patriots their Drug Problem—i.e., he drug them all over the field."

Raymond Berry should have had the grace to be quiet. The Patriots are a death ship now. They will not make the playoffs for another 20 years.

Many things happened on Friday. Fidel Castro swam naked with 200 blind Mexican children off a public beach in Havana; Moammar Khadafy threatened to kill any Jew who tried to cross the Mediterranean; and Nelson Mandela was allegedly freed by the Huns in South Africa. . . .

But none of these things really mattered, when the Big Shoe finally dropped. It happened late in the day, when my voice was totally gone from some kind of pox or swine flu.

It was Skinner, calling from Miami to say that he'd booked rooms at the Club Med in Haiti for the first week of Carnival.

"Port-au-Prince will be totally crazy," he said. "I have a chartered plane standing by. How soon can you get here?"

"Pretty quick," I replied. "But I have no passport. It was stolen in Spanish Wells."

"Never mind passports!" he shouted. "Nobody's going to ask. The police were all slaughtered by rioters. The government is gone. There is no law at all." He laughed harshly and I could hear him dropping ice in a glass. "I know these people," he said. "We can go wherever we want."

At that moment I was watching a news clip on TV of Baby Doc at the wheel of his own BMW, leaning on the horn as he raced through a hostile mob on his way to the airport and France. The Duvalier dictatorship, even older than Marcos' 20-year reign in Manila, was finally collapsing, and there was no law at all in Haiti.

There was also a voodoo angle, Skinner said—ominous reports from the countryside of zombies wandering aimlessly about the fields—"the undead," as they say in the trade, half-alive natives who were dug up, out of graveyards, and put to work harvesting sisal.

These tales were all formally documented, he said, by American doctors and experts. Local voodoo priests had created their own monstrous labor pool, making everything from American baseballs to fine rum and Haggar slacks.

It made no sense, but as a story it was hard to ignore. "It's all confirmed by CIA research," he assured me. "I can put you in touch with the Big Boys, the voodoo priests and the zombie masters."

Why not? I thought. It seemed like the right time to go, so I told him to hold the plane and make arrangements to pick up some cash in Miami. We would get into Port-au-Prince in time for dinner tonight.

February 10, 1986

Four Million Thugs

Nobody was smiling in Haiti last week. It was a good revolution to miss. They ran out of ice, Carnival was canceled and bloodthirsty mobs roamed the streets. The yuppie dictator had fled into exile, the nation was finally free. But somehow there was no satisfaction.

Wild celebrations attended the fall of the genuinely black trash House of Duvalier. There was dancing in Boston and Brooklyn and the north part of town in Miami. Thousands of Haitian refugees booked passsage on the first available plane to Port-au-Prince, where the airport is still listed in most travel guides as François Duvalier International.

That will not last for long. They sacked the Old Man's tomb last week—gangs of berserk young men carrying rock hammers and quarts of black rum pounded "Papa Doc's" white marble mausoleum into gravel, but they failed to turn up any bones.

Nobody knew what it meant, but the sight of the empty tomb had a bad effect on the mob. Many fell to their knees in despair.

The man was *gone.* They had sealed him up like a bee in clear Plexiglas, but somehow he had drifted away. There was no trace of the uniform he was buried in—not even his whip or his boots.

Some said the army had carried his corpse away to Some Other Place for safekeeping—but nobody really believed it. The mob understood. In a country that is 80 percent Catholic and 90 percent arcane Voodoo persuasions, the sight of an empty crypt where The Devil Himself had been safely entombed forever is not an acceptable thing.

TV films of the scene show a strange hush on the crowd at that moment, an eerie stiffness that lasted just long enough for the mean drunks among them to go crazy with rage and remorse.

The Old Man was *not* gone. He was *with* them. He was *present.* In the way that he'd said he would be. Ever present and all-powerful, as always—hovering quietly above them one moment, then zooming off through the Albizzia trees like a fruit bat.

The Old Man was *magic,* final wisdom and God of all gods . . . his son had been weak and weird, but so what? He was gone. Mr. Reagan had carried him off to France. The revolution was over. What the nation needed now was a strong leader.

We all had problems that week. I was snowed in for three days by a blizzard, Lee Iacocca was fired, and Skinner called on Wednesday to say that our pilot had been arrested on weapons charges at Opa'Locka airport, and that the man he had hired to be our personal driver in Haiti had been hacked to death in broad daylight by thugs from the Tonton Macoute. He was mixed up in voodoo, Skinner explained, and murdered for utterly mysterious reasons: black magic and primitive worship.

"We are talking about Fugu fish," he said, "the most poisonous thing in the world—500 times more deadly than cyanide—and 160,000 times more potent than cocaine, when used as an anesthetic."

"Never mind these things," I said. "We have no pilot or driver. How will we get into Haiti?"

"It will take a few days," he replied. "All my contacts over there have been murdered."

But he knew a Haitian lawyer, he said, an activist-exile who ran boats in and out of the Keys and had connections in Port-au-Prince. He could arrange for a trustworthy driver who would meet our plane at the airport and be helpful in many ways.

"We'll lay low for a while," Skinner said. "Spend some time on the boat with Mel Fisher. He's finding emeralds the size of your thumb in 40 feet of water just a few miles off Key West."

I agreed. We had run out of functional options, and Skinner was losing his grip. Three of his people were dead, and two had been crippled by torture.

It was taking a toll on his nerves. He began to drink Scotch by the pint and bash his fists on the oak doors, which left flecks of blood on his shirts. The lawyer, Maurice, said the airport in Haiti was still closed but would be reopened soon with a new name—Ronald Reagan Memorial Field. The curfew would be lifted by Friday.

"They'll be finished with the killing by then," Skinner said. "The people we need are still underground. We'd be butchered like hogs if we tried to go in there alone. They're still killing the Tonton Macoutes, beating them to death in the streets."

There was not much news out of Haiti, but the networks had some ugly film of ex-Tontons—the infamous "secret police" and plainclothes enforcers who had terrorized Haiti for three decades like a personal Gestapo for the Duvaliers—being dragged from their homes and ripped apart like chickens by vengeful mobs with machetes.

There were scenes of men being mauled and flogged in public then set on fire and stoned to death, just a few feet in front of the cameras—with a shaky voice-over saying that all those who had so far managed to escape had taken to the mountains and holed up in caves like palm rats, with all the guns they could carry. They were crazy with fear and would fight to the death like wild beasts.

It was a serious problem for the new government. The Tonton Macoute is not like your average law-enforcement agency. They are a special case, a private army of hired killers and thugs and enforcers who maintained political stability in every corner of Haiti for 28 brutal years, with a license from The President to whip and torture and kill anybody who got in their way.

On the day before Baby Doc fled, there were 15,000 Tonton Macoutes on the payroll—twice the strength of the Haitian army, navy and air force combined.

That is a lot of fear-crazed killers to have running around loose like mad dogs in the countryside. There would have been no Watergate scandal if Richard Nixon had had an army of bodyguards twice the size of the U.S. armed forces. He would either still be our president or we would have had a new kind of hell on our hands when he was finally forced out of office—a gang of 4 million heavily armed thugs with a price on their heads and hearts full of cheap speed, a hideous plague on the land.

The Hell's Angels never had more than 600 members in their best years. Four million of them would have been a very different situation.

February 17, 1986

Memo from the War Room

"The park is always crowded on Sunday."

Ferdinand Marcos said that last Sunday afternoon in Manila. He spoke in measured tones, they say, as he paced around on his balcony and shrugged now and then for the TV cameras, with the air of a man who never really liked Sundays, anyway—or parks either, for that matter.

Ferdinand was never one of those guys you saw kicking the soccer ball around in Rizal Park on Sunday afternoons. He was busy all the time, even on The Lord's Day.

Politics. Always politics. If it wasn't brunch with the man from Krupp, it was phone calls from Singapore and complaints about the latest shipment of fat young boys for the Cabinet meetings, or the price of bullets in Belgium.

Sundays were never easy for the Marcos family, but this last one had a life all its own. Rizal Park was not just *crowded* that day: It was jammed shoulder to shoulder, sidewalk to sidewalk for what looked like two or three solid blocks in every direction, maybe a half-million people—and they were all calling for Ferdinand Marcos' head.

Bad business in the Philippines. By midnight on Saturday, Marcos had lost control of the army, and rogue generals were calling mutinous news conferences . . . and by Sunday, the jig was up. Only the dealing remained, and presidential licenses for the nation's dog-racing tracks have not been renewed this year.

Ferdinand is big in the greyhound business—$2 million or $3 million a year, just for shaking hands on the portico with any sweating round-eyed fixer who would front all the dogs—and then a quick autograph on the contract, washing his hands of the details, or leaving it all with Imelda. His wife was good at business.

She will get along well with Michele Duvalier, the sleek and extravagant wife of the doomed Baby Doc, when they finally get settled into their digs on Vesco Island, where we should have put the shah.

We need a home for these people, when they go belly up and start looking around on short notice for a place where they can act like they did in the Old Days, and mingle endlessly with their own kind.

It is a hideous thought—a small and stateless island with no extradition treaties, where all the neighbors are guilty and no crime is seen as too heinous.

People like Marcos and Duvalier and Idi Amin will be there—Bebe Rebozo and D. B. Cooper—living together in some kind of monstrous Tangier-style harmony and locked away forever, with plenty of whiskey and servants, from the cares of the outside world.

Meanwhile, we are going to see some very tangible human episodes on the TV news out of Manila in the next few days. There will be examples of extreme behavior on both sides. . . . But Phil Habib has done his work well; Ferdinand will be off to Vesco Island before the next full moon.

Take my word for it—and please forward official receipts for the brown bag of expense money that I sent back, which was mainly a matter of discipline.

As for Haiti, there is no word yet from Mick Jagger and no rooms at the Great Ollufson Hotel—at least not until Mick arrives, and in the meantime I have people to see in Miami. These things will come together in due time.

Yesterday a blizzard filled The Dish with two tons of wet snow. I had to clear it by myself with a small broom.

A film crew recorded my struggle; and Nazi Jay, the tenant, came out of his house to mock me, as I staggered around in the snow-drifts.

He has no rights to the Big Eye, no possible way to wire in. It would split and diminish my signal. . . .

And *we could do that,* like The Boss used to say—but It Would Be Wrong. There is no point in scanning the skies with anything less than the finest and most sensitive equipment.

Last night I pulled in a hazy black and white signal that was not even listed. It was an old Jim Morrison concert, or maybe a pirated video. These things are never made clear.

The Bird scans 22 satellites from West to East, six or eight seconds apart—maybe 200 channels full of old movies and Jesus freaks and raw network news feeds from places like WXYZ in Detroit, along with NASA transmissions from Houston and 40-year-old stag films out of Mexico City.

There is too much lame garbage—far more than a sane man can stand. With the right kind of equipment—or even the wrong kind, and a fine hand on the knobs—you can pick up the collected speeches of Henry Kissinger, a censored version of *Deep Throat,* and 101 Famous Games of the Harlem Globetrotters. There is no end to it: all day and all night, in some kind of relentless auto-reverse that never sleeps.

But you don't get a lot of Jim Morrison. That is what we call a Special—straight black-and-white footage of Crazy Jim on stage in the old days, with a voice like Fred Neal's and eyes smarter than James Dean's and a band that could walk with the King, or anybody else. There were some nights when The Doors were the best band in the world.

Morrison understood this, and it haunted him all his life. On some nights he was noisy and lewd, and on others he just practiced—but every once in a while he would get it into his head to go out and dance with the big boys, and on a night like that he was more than special. Jim Morrison could play music with anybody.

One of these days we will get around to naming names for the *real* rock 'n' roll Hall of Fame—in that nervous *right now* realm beyond

Elvis and Chuck Berry and Little Richard—and the talk will turn to names like Bob and Mick, and to tunes like Morrison Hotel.

Play it sometime. Crank it all the way up on one of those huge obsolete wire-burning MacIntosh amps and 80 custom-built speakers. Then stand back somewhere on the mainbeams of a big log house and feel the music come up through your femurs . . . ho, ho. . . . and after that you can always say, for sure, that you once knew what it was like to hear men play rock 'n' roll music.

February 24, 1986

The Gonzo Salvage Co.

Sugarloaf Key, FL—The TV is out tonight. The set went black about halfway through "Miami Vice," just as Don Johnson dropped a KGB thug with a single 200-yard shot from his high-tech belly gun.

The storm got serious after that, and the mood in The Keys turned mean. Junk cars crashed in the mango swamps and fishheads whipped on each other with sharkhooks in all-night bars and roadhouses along Highway A1A. These people will tolerate almost anything except being cut off in the middle of "Miami Vice."

On nights like these it is better not to answer the telephone. It can only mean trouble: Some friend has been crushed on the highway by a falling power pole, or it might be the Coast Guard calling to say that your boat was stolen by dope fiends who just called on the radio to say they are sinking somewhere off Sand Key and they've given you as their local credit reference, to pay for the rescue operation.

In my case, it was a just-reported shipwreck involving total strangers. An 88-foot tramp motor-sailor called *The Tampa Bay Queen* had gone on the reef in Hawk Channel, and all hands had abandoned ship.

There were only three of them, as it turned out. They had all washed ashore on an ice chest, raving incoherently about green sharks and coral heads and their ship breaking up like a matchbox while they screamed for help on a dead radio.

"Why not?" I thought. We are, after all, in The Business—and besides, I had never covered a shipwreck, not even a small one . . . and there was also talk about "losing the cargo" and the cruel imperatives of "salvage rights."

None of this talk seemed worth going out in a storm to investigate at the time, but that is not how The Business works. I went out, and not long after midnight I found myself huddled with these people in a local motel where they'd been given shelter for the night . . . and by dawn I was so deep in the story that I'd hired a 36-foot Cigarette boat to take me and the captain out to his doomed wreck, at first light, so he could recover whatever was left of it.

"We'll have to move quick," he said, "before the cannibals get there. They'll strip her naked by noon."

The sun came up hot and bright that morning. The storm was over and the chop in the channel was down to 3 feet, which means nothing to a fast Cigarette boat. We were running 40 mph by the time we got out of the bay, and about 40 minutes later we were tying up to the wreck of *The Tampa Bay Queen*. It was lying on the bottom, tilted over at a 45-degree angle, and the sea had already broken it open.

There was no hope of saving anything except the new nylon sails and the V-8 engine and six nickel-plated brass winches, which the distraught captain said were worth $5,000 each—and maybe the 80-foot teakwood mast, which would fetch about $100 a foot in Key West, and looked like a thing of beauty.

We climbed up the steep rotted deck and the captain set about slashing down the sails with a butcher knife and ordering the first mate to take a hatchet to the winches. "Never mind a screwdriver," he shouted. "Just rip 'em out by the stumps."

The first mate was in no mood to take orders. He had not been paid in three weeks, he said, and he was wearing fancy black leather pilot's boots with elevator heels and slick leather soles, which caused him to constantly lose his footing and go sliding down the deck. We would hear him scream as he went off, and then there would be a splash. I spent most of my time pulling him back up the deck, and finally we lashed him to the mast with a steel safety cable, which allowed him to tend to his work.

By this time I had worked up a serious sweat, and the mystique of this filthy shipwreck had long since worn off. The captain was clearly a swine and the first mate was a middle-aged bellboy from New Jersey and the ship was probably stolen. . . . But here I was out on the high sea with these people, doing manual labor in the morning and bleeding from every knuckle. It was time, I felt, for a beer.

I was moving crabwise along the deck, homing in on the cooler we'd left in the Cigarette boat, when I saw the scavengers coming in. They had been circling the wreck for a while, two half-naked thugs in a small skiff, and the captain had recognized them instantly.

"God help us now," he muttered. "Here they come. These are the ones I was worried about." He looked nervously out at the two burly brutes in the cannibal boat, and he said he could see in their eyes that they were getting ready to board us and claim the whole wreck for themselves.

"It won't be much longer," he said. "These bastards are worse than pirates. We may have to fight for it."

I shrugged and moved off toward the beer cooler, at the other end of the wreck. The captain was obviously crazy, and I had lost my feel for The Story. All I wanted was a cold can of beer.

By the time I got to the Cigarette boat, however, the thugs had made their move and were tying up alongside us, grinning like wolves as they crouched between me and the cooler. I stared down at them and swore never again to answer my phone after midnight.

"Was this your boat?" one of them asked. "We heard you whimpering all night on the radio. It was a shame."

The next few minutes were tense, and by the end of that time I had two new partners and my own marine salvage business. The terms of the deal were not complex, and the spirit was deeply humane.

The captain refused to cooperate at first, screeching hoarsely from the other end of the wreck that he had silent partners in Tampa who would soon come back and kill all of us. . . .

But you hear a lot of talk like that in The Keys, so we ignored him and drank all the beer and hammered out a three-way agreement that would give the captain until sundown to take anything he wanted, and after that the wreck would be ours.

It was the Law of the Sea, they said. Civilization ends at the waterline. Beyond that, we all enter the food chain, and not always right at the top.

The captain seemed to understand, and so did I. He would be lucky to get back to shore with anything at all, and I had come close to getting my throat slit.

It was almost dark when we dropped him off on the dock, where he quickly sold out to a Cuban for $5,000 in cash. Mother ocean had prevailed once again, and I was now in the marine salvage business.

March 3, 1986

Salvage Is Not Looting

"The crew took a vote, and she lost, so we traded her for two cases of beer to the first boat we ran into, about 100 miles north of Aruba. It was a gang of shrimpers from Savannah. They were headed back to port. . . . That was four years ago, and the girl is still in a state mental hospital somewhere out West."

—Boat captain from Key West

Key West, FL—The sea is nervous tonight. Another cold front is coming in, a north wind is putting whitecaps on the waves. The Mako is tied up to a sea-grape tree just in front of my door, whipping frantically around at the end of its rope like a wild beast caught in a trap. I go out every once in a while to adjust the docking knots, but the line is still rubbing bark off the tree and my new Japanese wind sock has been ripped to shreds by the gusts.

The neighbors complain about my screaming, but their noise is like the barking of dumb dogs. It means nothing. They are not seafaring people. The only boats that concern them are the ones they might want to rent, and when a storm comes they hide in their rooms like house cats.

My own situation is different. I am now in the Marine Salvage Business, and cruel storms are the lifeblood of our profession. It is the nature of salvage to feed on doom and disaster.

My new partners moved quickly to consolidate our position. We formed a shrewd corporate umbrella and expanded at once into the reef-diving and deep-water game fishing business, in order to crank up the revenue stream while we plundered the odd wreck here and there, and searched for sunken treasure.

Capt. Elgin took charge of all fishing and diving operations, Crazy Mean Brian would handle plundering, and I was in charge of salvaging sunken treasure.

Our fortunes took an immediate turn for the worse less than 24 hours after we seized our first wreck, when the elegant teakwood mast on the doomed *Tampa Bay Queen* turned out to be split from top to bottom with a long spiral fracture filled with termites, black putty and sea worms. It was utterly worthless, and the rest of the ship was stripped overnight by what my partners called "filthy cowboys from Big Coppitt Key," a gang of seagoing Hell's Angels who have terrorized these waters for years.

"They stripped out a whole submarine one night," Capt. Elgin told me. "The Navy left it open so the local school kids could take tours through it, but a storm came up and the Navy guys went ashore for the night, and by morning it was totally looted. They even took the torpedoes."

Our only other asset was an ancient cannonball that Crazy Mean Brian had plundered from a site that he refused to disclose, because he said we would have serious problems "establishing jurisdiction."

"There are a lot more of them down there," he said, "along with at least two brass cannons, but we would have to drag them at least three miles underwater before we could file for salvage rights."

They weighed about 1,600 pounds each, and they would not be easy to sell on the open market, due to the maze of conflicting claims already filed by other thieves, looters and competing treasure salvagers.

"Nobody took this stuff seriously until Mel Fisher came along," Capt. Elgin explained, "but the way it is now you can't come in with anything older than one of those green glass Coca-Cola bottles without having the whole federal court system on your neck." He laughed bitterly. "If we try to sell this cannonball in town, Mel Fisher would have us in jail for piracy."

"Nonsense," I said. "I've known Mel for years. He'd be happy to help us out."

They both hooted at me. "We'd be better off trying to rip souvenir teeth out of living sharks," said Crazy Mean Brian. "You *have no friends* in the marine salvage business."

I called Mel Fisher at once and arranged to tour his facilities on the Navy base in downtown Key West.

I met him at the Two Friends Patio, a chic hangout on Front Street, where the whole Fisher operation goes after work because, they say, they drank there for free before the Mother Lode came in.

Fisher, of course, is wallowing these days in gold bars and emeralds. He has discovered more wrecks than the Triple A in a New York blizzard, and he appeared on "Good Morning America" the other day to trumpet his recent finds.

The wreck of the fabled *Atocha,* a Spanish galleon that went down in a storm off Key West in 1622, was located by Fisher's divers a few years ago and estimated to be worth about $400 million, mainly in gold and silver—but Mel said all that was chicken feed, now that he'd found emeralds.

"It's into the billions and billions now," he said.

Mel started out with a dive shop in the back of his parents' chicken farm in Redondo Beach in the late '50s. He'd moved from Indiana to California where his destiny was almost certainly to become heir to a poultry empire. In retrospect, and only recently so, Mel seems to have chosen the wiser path.

There are 12 boats in the harbor tonight, and four of them are ours. My 17-foot Mako is the smallest of the lot, but it is extremely fast and agile and it will go anywhere, day or night.

Crazy Mean Brian's new boat is tied up just behind mine. The local charter fishermen are not comfortable with the sight of it, because it reminds them of the "old days," when everybody was crazy. It is a 27-foot custom-built hull, with no name, mounted with twin 200-horsepower Johnsons, and it will run to Cuba and back on one load of gas.

Opposite Brian's is Capt. Elgin's 23-foot Roballo, the *Bobbi Lynn*—the reef diving boat—next to the gas pumps, shrouded in fog, and bounding around in the sea like some kind of rotted ghost out of Key Largo.

• • •

The kid came back and took the battery out of the boat again. It happened late in the afternoon, the second time in three days.

The first time he took it for money—which was dumb, but at least I understood it. The man was a fishhead, a creature without many cells. He was like one of those big lizards that never feels any pain when you rip off its tail, or one of its legs—or even its head, as they do down in Chile—because it will all grow back by dawn, and nobody will know the difference.

March 10, 1986

Dawn at the Boca Chica

Key West, FL—The Boca Chica Lounge is distinguished in many ways, but mainly it is a savage all-night biker bar where you go at your own risk and where many ugly things have occurred.

Key West is the last stop in this weird chain of islands that runs south of Miami like a national coccyx bone on the swollen spine of Florida, and the Boca Chica is the only place in town where real men are still whooping it up at 5 o'clock in the morning.

We got there around 5:03—after a failed visitation with the Halley's comet crowd on the beach in Key West—and took the only two seats at the big horseshoe-shaped bar. I ordered a Bud and a Coke, and Maria became instantly involved with a wild-eyed Cuban gentleman standing next to her, who was feeling crazed by loneliness.

"I'd like to talk to somebody someday," he said. "I'm not that bad. I'm a nice guy."

The bartender reached over and smacked the guy in the neck. "So what?" he said. "Keep your weepy bull– – – – to yourself."

The Cuban cringed, but the bartender was obviously in a mood for personal action. "You dirty little animal," he said. "Why don't you get on the floor and dance for a while?"

Across the bar, behind a chain-link hurricane fence that separated the whole place into quadrants, I could see a crowd of 20 or 30 swarthy bikers milling around the pool tables in a haze of rancid smoke. A smell of beer was heavy on the place, and the sharp click of pool balls cut through the dense thumping of the music.

The DJ in his smoked-glass booth above us was cranking the music out to a serious full disco frenzy. The terrible flashing of the strobe lights made us all seem like ghosts, and the music was like the amplified sound of a Studebaker throwing a rod.

The weepy Cuban was still refusing to dance, but the floor was filling up with other players. A tall transvestite wearing a black corset and a red garter belt was sandwiched between two boys from the Boca Chica U.S. Naval Air Station, just down the road—and a bearded man wearing short pants and flipflops had put aside the ball point pens and the fat spiral notebook he'd been laboring over all night, and suddenly gone wild on the dance floor.

He was graceful, in his own way, and he seemed to feel in his heart that at any moment he would take off and soar with wild sea birds. He flapped his arms like wings and tried to leap high off the floor.

He was wrong—but I understood the spirit of the dance, and I sensed what he was trying to say. He had been observing the action in the Boca Chica, making copious notes, for about as long as he felt he could handle it—and now he was expressing himself.

His girlfriend, a plump blonde wearing wet cutoffs and a T-shirt that said, "Drink whiskey or die," had been admiring his antics with starry-eyed affection for a while, but when he appeared to be getting away from himself she jumped out on the dance floor and seized him from behind in a spoon grip.

Maria was weeping from the pain in her legs and dawn was coming up outside. I turned to the man sitting next to me—who looked like Sting, the rock singer—and asked him if Tennessee Williams was buried anywhere nearby.

He quickly palmed the small bottle of RUSH he'd been snorting from and eyed me nervously. "I don't think so," he said. "Why do you ask?"

"I thought I just saw his name on TV," I replied. "And I drove past the graveyard tonight while we were looking for Halley's comet." I offered him a Salem from a pack I'd found on the sidewalk outside. "I had a terrible experience today," I said. "My boat went up on the rocks and I had to swim ashore naked with an oar."

He shrugged. "Mister Williams is not buried here," he muttered. "The highest point on the island is only two feet above sea level. You can't dig down more than two feet without hitting water."

"So what?" I said. "You go down three feet and you hit rocks. I destroyed my whole lower unit today, and they mocked me when I climbed up on shore. I had to carry my clothes and my cigarettes above my head in a plastic bag wrapped with duct tape."

I offered him a Budweiser, but he said he was drinking gin and was going home soon. "This place never closes," he said. "But it gets pretty dull after sunrise."

We left shortly after that, and I taped a note on the gate at Boog Powell's marina, saying my boat had run into a storm and would be needing serious repairs. The windshield was shattered and the battery had jumped out of its moorings, filling the hull with sulfuric acid and paralyzing the solenoid. Many wires shorted out and the power tilt jammed at low tide while I drifted onto the rocks in Niles Channel.

My bullhorn was broken, my flares were all wet, and my VHF marine radio blew a fuse every time I squeezed on the talk button. . . . But luckily we had gone aground at the mouth of a sleazy canal that led down to Capt. Elgin's dock, just beyond the Summerland Key Marina.

That was when I came to grips with the humiliation of having to strip naked, abandon ship and wallow ashore in full view of the local lobster-fishing community, which was a sad and crazy experience.

I left Maria on board, badly crippled from the storm, with a bottle of gin and a new Buffet tape and the big Mercury engine rumbling helplessly in neutral to maintain the electrical flow.

Capt. Elgin was sick with swine flu, but his neighbors were keeping him company and they had a good laugh when I showed up at sundown with my clothes in a bag and a broken oar in my hand. One of them, who wore the many gold chains and sharks' teeth of a successful free-lance boater, had just been told that his landlord was arrested last night on the Pennsylvania Turnpike with 16 pounds of cocaine, and that life as he had known it was coming to a fork in the road.

But I had my own problems. The sun was going down and my boat was still out on the rocks, and no rising tide until midnight.

"Never mind," shouted the captain. "The boys will go out and get her. We've never lost one yet."

Which was true. We got back at the dock in time for the evening news. I cashed a huge check and flew out to Miami the next day. When I got to Denver I made a few calls and ended up selling my boat to Gary Hart for use in the '88 Florida primary.

March 17, 1986

Let the Cheap Dogs Eat

Nine dogs bred for professional fighting were under treatment here yesterday for wounds suffered in an animal-fight arena in Sierra foothills near Porterville.

Sixty-six persons were arrested Sunday when three carloads of sheriff's deputies raided a fight in a remote area near Fountain Springs. The animals were pit bulldogs bred and trained for fighting. "It was one of the most gruesome things I ever saw," one deputy said. "The fight ring was splotched with blood and two dogs were found with their jaws locked together. Their jaws had to be pried loose with wooden rods."

—*San Francisco Chronicle*, May 9, 1969

When we got off the plane in Denver I bought a newspaper and read a story on Page 1 about the Dogfighting Business, which apparently is booming these days. It is like the stock market and pro wrestling and the new breed of law students who want to dress like Ed Meese.

We live in queasy times. The space program has exploded in front of our eyes, *Rolling Stone* has turned against marijuana, and now our aged Black Irish president tells us that in his heart he has always been a Nicaraguan revolutionary.

No longer do we see through the rose-colored glass. Times have changed; the pigs have come out of the tunnel. Pat Buchanan roams free in the White House and the new Democratic candidate for the lieutenant governorship of Illinois says the queen of England runs the international drug trade, with tentacles into Harlem and even the South Side of Chicago.

Well . . . maybe so: All things are possible in this generation of swine. But the idea that Buckingham Palace is a warehouse for the dumb-dust market in Candlestick Park and McDonald's and Madison Square Garden is going to be a hard one to sell to anybody except Ed Meese and Jann Wenner.

There *are* limits to this blathering Roundhead madness where sooner or later we will all have to urinate in a used plastic bottle every time we get on a bus. Not even Pat Buchanan will say with a straight face that every American dilemma from the Challenger explosion to Ferdinand Marcos and Baby Doc's stinking footprints in Haiti can be traced back to "drug problems."

Nobody in the dogfighting business has ever been accused of drug abuse. They don't have time for it. "You want to be on your toes when your dog is getting his eyeball chewed out," said one ex-handler. "This is a very serious business."

The headline in the POST said: "Warning: Your Pups May Be Dogfight Bait." It was a story about a woman who lost her own puppies to the dog-fighting bund, and who now "spends part of each day calling people who are offering to give away free pets to good homes."

Don't do it, she says. They will be slaughtered—fed like raw meat, for practice, to huge pit bulls who need the taste of fresh blood to get them cranked up for summer fighting season.

"Pet snatching often increases in early spring," according to special agent Walt Chin of the Colorado Bureau of Investigation, "because that's when the training sessions start for fighting dogs."

Every year about this time a low-paid network of human scum fans out across the West and buys up every available young animal on the market. A top dog in his prime is worth maybe $20,000 a night to his people, and a proven killer attracts huge stud fees.

There is also the gambling action—which is not widespread, but it is extremely intense and expensive for those who take it seriously. These people are the high-rollers of the dogfighting world, and they will feed their beasts whatever they feel is necessary. Which usually means two or three fresh kills a day.

"Trainers, or their agents, will take any kind of dog, and even a cat," says agent Chin, "to give their fighting dogs—usually pit bulls—a blood lust and prepare them to fight for money."

By the time one of these low-slung, slit-eyed brutes has ripped and killed half the stray dogs, cats, rabbits and homeless puppies in Denver, it will be in keen shape to deal with one of its own kind—and it will attract many totally committed backers.

Other peoples' puppies are nothing but fodder when it comes to honing up a dog that can win you the price of a new Cadillac Eldorado three nights a week all summer.

Big-money dogfighting is enjoying a new surge of popularity, despite its traditional onus of subhuman cruelty. On the scale of social acceptability it is far below cock-fighting. Most people would rather fail a public drug test for opium than be photographed yelling and stomping in the front row of an illegal dog fight.

The animals fight to the death—or until the loser is so ripped to shreds that he has to be dragged away by his handlers—and only the winner gets fed. There is no Home for Retired Pit Bulls.

Dogs were big in the news last week. The chief medical examiner for the state of Connecticut was fired from her $78,000-a-year-job—according to the *Denver Post*—"after she admitted that she allowed her pet dogs in autopsy rooms during examinations."

The beasts were not described as to size or breed, but it didn't really matter. A special commission investigating charges against Dr. Catherine Galvin—a Gloria Steinem type—reported that her dogs "sampled human tissue in the autopsy lab."

Not even her friend said she should go public and fight the charges. . . . And in San Francisco, a man named Gordon MacVernie, described in *Examiner* reports as a "transient dog owner who has a Concord address (please!) was sentenced to a year in jail for "hacksawing a leg off his German shepherd puppy."

The dog had some kind of distemper, he said, so he rammed tubes up its nose and held it over a fire to burn out the disease.

. . . and finally, on Friday night in Kansas City, a gang of huge lapdogs from the University of Kansas—ranked No. 2 in the nation—took a tip from Ferdinand Marcos and cheated Scott Skiles and his Michigan State teammates out of what would have been one of the great underdog victories of the NCAA tournament.

Alphonse Karr was right.

March 24, 1986

Ox Butchered in Tripoli

"The need for travel [to the Middle East] at this time should be carefully evaluated."

—State Department advisory, March 29, 1986

There was madness in the news last week. Not even Paul Harvey could handle it. Volcanoes belched ash in Alaska and the Berkeley Hills slipped another foot toward China. Yasser Arafat became chic, there were orgies in the streets of Palm Springs, and young Nazis destroyed the Democratic Party in Chicago.

On Monday the United States got involved in two wars on the same day, and the rest of the week on TV was like Grenada all over again. The big dog had decided to eat, but not everybody liked it.

On the night before Easter there were eerie reports out of Tripoli saying that Moammar Khadafy had publicly butchered an ox "with the name 'Reagan' painted on the side of it."

Nobody denied these things—not even Khadafy—and by the time all the rocks had been rolled away on Sunday night there were millions of people all over America who assumed it was probably all true.

Why not? It happened in *Apocalypse Now,* and CNN had raw film of a freshly slaughtered ox with a crowd of wild Libyans whooping all around it, waving fists dipped in blood and screaming, "Down with the U.S.A."

Whether or not the Colonel had actually slain the beast was no longer relevant. He was certainly *capable* of it. We all understood that from the things we'd seen him do on TV. . . . And in any case a full-grown ox named "Reagan" had been hacked to death in a public square in Tripoli, by the people who were not on our side. A bulletin on "Headline News" said, "They danced in the animal's blood."

We are getting used to these scenes. All over the world Our People seem to be on the run, from Baby Doc and Marcos, to Chun Doo Hwan in South Korea. . . . And the ones who are still stable, like the Germans and Japanese, may not be entirely reliable.

Not even the Italians are with us. On Friday in Rome a court freed all but one of the Turks and Bulgarians on trial for shooting the pope— and the public was apparently satisfied.

Nobody called it a fix, or a communist plot. The only demonstrations in Italy last week were a few rallies against the "warlike behavior" of the U.S. 6th Fleet off the coast of Libya.

Not even the White House denied that one. It was self-defense, they said. That maniac shot at us. He tried to destroy the Yorktown.

Which may have been true, although it made no sense at all . . . which is getting more and more to be par for the course these days, but who cares?

CNN, for instance, just moved an item out of French Guyana, down on the equator, about a French space rocket launched successfully last night, which "contained an American satellite."

Who knows what this means? The blast-off looked much like the Challenger, except that it appeared to take place at night and there was no subsequent explosion.

It was a week of senseless violence all over the world. People lined up to be crucified in the Philippines, and a man in Albuquerque was slain by police after taking four hostages in a Pizza Hut, for no apparent reason.

Some people said it was the full moon and others blamed the ides of March, but in truth there was no pattern at all except random angst and conflict. Many fishermen in the Florida Keys were stricken with a disfiguring skin disease called pityriasis rosea, with symptoms often mistaken for syphilis and no known cause except possibly the "wearing of new underwear."

My own personal physician, a man nationally known in his field, called it an utterly mysterious virus of some kind, with no hint of a cure and no long-term effects beyond a sense of shame and personal repugnance. "I had it myself, one time," he said. "It happens to a lot of people, and let me tell you it's a very ugly thing."

So what? I thought. We live in ugly times. A flatworm can crawl into your body and grow to be 50 feet long in a matter of five or six weeks. Or bloodsucking hookworms can come up through the soles of your feet and into your liver and finally into your brain, and there is nothing anybody can do about it—not even at Johns Hopkins or the Houston Medical Center.

One of my earliest memories of Easter is my grandmother telling me on Saturday night that, when she woke me up the next morning and said, "He has risen," that I should sit up in bed and reply, "He has risen indeed."

I never understood, but we did it year after year, and even now it makes no sense to me.

I have understood almost everything since then except the nature of women, pityriasis rosea and the meaning of last week's news.

But I understand politics and I know Pat Buchanan. And when the hardball comes by, I can hear it.

We all know Patrick, in a sense. He is the Director of Communications in the White House, a position of uncommon power—which he almost lost, last week, when The Boss came up 12 votes short in the House of Representatives on the question of sending another $100 million worth of bombs and guns and missiles to the "contras" in Nicaragua, or maybe Tegucigalpa.

Buchanan took the loss personally and swore that it would soon be avenged. The Senate would vote a week later, and things might change before then.

Which was true. All manner of big-bore hell broke loose in the next few days—from the Line of Death in the Gulf of Sidra to rumors of a whole new war in Honduras (only a two-day drive from Harlingen, Texas, according to Reagan's calculations) and nobody was surprised on Thursday afternoon when the Senate voted 53-47 to give the president whatever he wanted for the war in Nicaragua, and also to save Buchanan's job.

Even Bill Bradley, the ex-basketball star from New Jersey, was swept away in the finely orchestrated frenzy. He voted with Stennis and Thurmond and Goldwater, and never mind the confusion.

We have a long history of these things, and most of it has been eminently profitable. Those lines in the Marine Corps hymn that say ". . . from the halls of Montezuma, to the shores of Tripoli" are not there by accident.

March 31, 1986

Never Get Off the Boat

"We want females, as a rule. If it's a male, we just castrate it and sell it for steak in Chicago."

—George Stranahan, Colorado beef rancher

My neighbors are calfing tonight. The cowboys are working overtime and the barns are lit up with flood lamps and portable heaters. A freak snowstorm in the Rockies has made the cows nervous and they are all giving birth at the same time.

When I drove down to the Tavern around midnight, I noticed a strange glow on the horizon—which is never a good thing to see, in the country—but when I came around the bend where the road crosses over the creek, I saw that it was only Wayne's barn, lit up like a football stadium and surrounded by pickup trucks. There were sounds of cows bellowing, and men with blood up to their elbows were running back and forth in the shadows.

These people are businessmen. They are ranchers who raise beef cattle for money. Every calf born tonight will weigh a ton in two years and sell for 58 cents a pound at the Mercantile Exchange in Chicago.

I honked my horn twice and kept going. The night was cold, and wet snow on the powerlines had already knocked out my electricity for two hours. I am a good neighbor on most nights, but not in the calfing season. Writing is a hard dollar, but it is a lot better than reaching up inside a maddened cow and grabbing a breeched calf by the legs.

"Sometimes we have to drag them out with a rope," said one of the boys at the Tavern. "The things will get their hooves tangled up inside and you have to reach in and put a noose around the head. The first time I did it was for my 4-H project," he said. "After that, I quit farming and went to Scottsdale and got a job on a tennis ranch, just to get away from cows."

His life had turned hazy in those years. He went to dealers' school in Vegas, but he had the wrong temper for dealing. After that, he drifted north and found work packing snow on the ski mountains. There was no real future in it, he said, but it gave him free lift tickets and time to work on his style for the speed-racing.

"We pack it down like ice," he said. "I was clocked at 81 miles an hour today, just to get the feel of the course. At that speed, you can't even breathe."

"So what?" I said. "The record is 130."

"One twenty-nine point five," he said quickly. "But one guy did 166 on top of a car at the Bonneville salt flats. He went into a tuck and passed out at 150, but the driver said he felt no resistance and decided to go for the record." He nodded and smiled wistfully. "They made it," he said. "It must have been a bitch. By the time they unstrapped him, the wind had blown two layers of skin off his face. He never put on a pair of skis after that."

We drank for a while, and then he went home to his trailer, where he lived with a woman who had once worked for Ferdinand Marcos. He would be getting up early, he said, for a final check on the mountain before the speed-racing started at eight. A man named McKinney was going for a new record, to break the 130 mark.

We left shortly afterward. I had my own problems that night, and sleep was out of the question. The same storm that made a hellbroth of the speed-race and the calving operation had gone east across the Continental Divide, dumping two feet of snow on Denver and closing the schools and the airport.

"Hotels and motels were booked by airlines for stranded passengers," according to an AP story out of Denver. The official spokesman for Stapleton International said all flights were canceled on Thursday because of deep snow, high winds and zero visibility.

"We'll probably have some people here overnight," he said, "but we'll take care of them."

No violence was reported and wire-service reports said, "A group of tourists from Fiji entertained stranded passengers with guitar music and folk dances, while other travelers flocked to airport restaurants to await word on their flights."

Ho ho. The check is in the mail. . . . The Denver airport is getting famous for this kind of madness. It was once just a crossroads for rich skiers and cowboys, but now it is the fifth-busiest hub in the nation, and a living nightmare for anybody who takes air travel more seriously than a chance to sleep on a tile floor in public all night, while listening to folk dancers from Fiji.

"The Mile High chapter of the Red Cross also sent representatives to the airport," the report said, "to hand out things people need when they're stuck for a while, such as diapers and toilet articles."

• • •

It was a hard night in Denver, they said. Not everybody was satisfied with diapers and toilet articles. The bars closed at midnight and the restaurants ran out of food around sundown. Only three planes took off all day long, and the airport was still closed on Friday.

Many thousands were stranded, but only a few lost their grip and got into serious trouble. Some were broken in spirit, and others filed massive lawsuits.

Some things are understandable—like a sudden rash of cow births in a snowstorm on the Western Slope, or a speed-freak strapping himself on top of a bored-out Shelby-Ford prototype and running 166 mph into the wind on the Bonneville salt flats—but getting stuck in the Denver airport is a wrong way to spend *any* night.

I was brooding on this while I drove back in the snow from the Tavern. It was good to be home—but when I got there, the phone was ringing. It was George, my neighbor from the Flying Dog Ranch, about five miles up the hill. He was having trouble delivering his calves, he said, and he needed an extra hand.

My heart filled with hate, but it was clear that I had no choice.

"Should I bring rope?" I asked.

"No," he replied. "We'll use a chain—just slide it over the fetlocks and pull."

It seemed weird, but George knows cattle, and I am, after all, a farmer. I picked up my floodlight and got in the jeep and drove slowly up the road.

April 7, 1986

They Called Him Deep Throat

"You don't go out and kick a mad dog. If you have a mad dog with rabies, you take a gun and shoot him."

—Pat Robertson, TV evangelist

The market kept rising last week. Even preachers felt bullish, and there was talk on The Street about the shooting and butchering of animals. Beef prices plunged, insurance rates soared, and Pat Ro' ertson went on national TV to make a personal appeal for the head of Moammar Khadafy.

It was another bad week for the Colonel. He had already been hit once, very hard, by the high-tech flyboys from the U.S. 6th Fleet—and now he was going to be hit *again,* with big rockets and many deaths in the ranks of his own people . . . and he was being shown on American TV as a cheap Mussolini clone, wearing old Nazi headgear and a ragged pink babushka. The White House was beating him like a mule, he said, for the sins of the whole Arab world.

Which was probably true, for a cruel mix of *Realpolitik* reasons—but the Colonel was not calm in his efforts to explain his position. A loosely phrased AP dispatch out of Tripoli quoted him to the effect that his finely honed "Libyan counterattack plan" would soon destroy "the whole of southern Europe, without any discrimination," and that "Libya rejects unjust and insolent military threats which do not scare [us] at all."

He also said Libya would call on "Warsaw Pact forces to help defend [his country] against a U.S. attack." But nobody believed him, and a man named Georgi Arbatov from the Soviet Central Committee in Moscow denounced the whole thing as a pile of bad noise, and said Russia wanted no part of any haggling between Tripoli and Washington.

Pat Robertson is the genial host of a massively popular cable-TV show called "The 700 Club," the flagship production of the Christian Broadcasting Network. It is a folksy news/talk show with a distinctly religious bent. The people at CBN say it reaches 50 states every night of the week. Robertson is very hot property. "The 700 Club" reaches more people than Jimmy Swaggart and Jerry Falwell combined. In some places he is more popular than Johnny Carson.

He works out of Roanoke, not far from Lyndon LaRouche—but

nobody knows where he lives. He is a loose and friendly man, like Andy Rooney.

People *like* Pat Robertson. He is running for president this year—along with almost everybody else in politics except Ronald Reagan—and he is taking himself very seriously.

At midnight on Friday the *USS Coral Sea* was still 400 miles off Tripoli and the White House was still laying low on the "Libya question" when Robertson jumped all the other candidates by going on his own TV show to warn against the folly of taking any wimpish halfway position vis-à-vis Khadafy.

"There is an old, old saying," he said, "that you don't strike the King unless you kill him." It was Pat's way of saying that he was tired of the Old Ways, and *it was time to croak the Colonel.*

Indeed. There is an old adage in the veterinary world that says there are only two ways to deal with a rabid animal—either capture it and cut off its head, or drag it out behind the garage and put the muzzle against its medulla.

Robertson's jump was not lost on the White House, where the only response was "no comment." Donald Regan said nothing, and even Patrick Buchanan was mute. It was one of those days in the West Wing when some people yearned for the good old days—when a thing like this could be easily solved by a quick call to Gordon Liddy, in his office across the Avenue.

But that was another time. Gordon is gone now—he went off to prison and pumped iron for three years and gave them nothing but his name and his Social Security number. All the others confessed, or went belly-up from the pressure. Many were called, and in the end they were all chosen.

Except Gordon. He is still the only real Missing Link in the Watergate Story, the late-night underground voice that Bob Woodward and Carl Bernstein called "Deep Throat."

Hal Holbrook played the role in the movie, and it made perfect sense at the time. He talked like John Dean and looked like Leonard Garment, Nixon's long-time personal counsel.

Nobody doubted that Carl and Bob had tapped a main source. Deep Throat was the tap-root, the man with the final credentials. His motives were never made clear, except in some giddy gray realm of "morality," and the rape of his personal ethics.

In the legend he is a figure like Socrates, a man of long reach and wisdom, too smart for his work and obviously Not Like The Others.

He works for the President, but his hero is William Burroughs and his knuckles have grown together like crushed roots. When he comes down to Washington—from New York, where he lives—he has his own room in the south wing of the White House, with a fireplace and a Smith & Barnes piano.

He walks tall at Duke Ziebert's—and also at 14th and "U," where he is loved by the whores and the street people.

They called him Gordon, but the name on the Federal Firearms License that he carried in his black pigskin wallet was G. Liddy . . . and his name down at 15th and "L" in the newsroom was "Deep Throat."

Some people knew, but not many. Scott Armstrong knew, along with Oscar Acosta and a senior stewardess for one of the airlines. We even kept it from Frank Mankiewicz, who knew almost everything else.

It was one of those things that seemed better, at the time, not to talk about.

April 14, 1986

The Pro-Flogging View

NOTE: The following is Dr. Thompson's response to a desperate letter from his friend Ralph Steadman in England, on the subject of raising children.

Dear Ralph,

I received your tragic letter about your savage, glue-sniffing son and read it while eating breakfast at 4:30 A.M. in a Waffle House on the edge of Mobile Bay . . . and I made some notes on your problem, at the time, but they are not the kind of notes that any decent man would want to send to a friend. . . . So I put them away until I could bring a little more concentration to bear on the matter. . . .

And I have come to this conclusion:

Send the crazy little bugger to Australia. We can get him a job herding sheep somewhere deep in the outback, and that will straighten him out for sure; or at least it will keep him busy.

England is the wrong place for a boy who wants to smash windows. Because he's right, of course. He *should* smash windows. Anybody growing up in England today without a serious urge to smash windows is probably too dumb for help.

You are reaping the whirlwind, Ralph. Where in the name of art or anything else did you ever see anything that said you could draw queer pictures of the prime minister and call her worse than a denatured pig— but your own son shouldn't want to smash windows?

We are not privy to that level of logic, Ralph. They don't even teach it at Oxford.

My own son, thank God, is a calm and rational boy who is even now filling out his applications to Yale and Tufts and Bennington and various other Eastern, elitist schools . . . and all he's cost me so far is a hellish drain of something like $10,000 a year just to keep him off the streets and *away* from the goddamn windows. . . .

What do windows *cost,* Ralph? They were about $55 apiece when I used to smash them—even the big plate-glass kind—but now they probably cost about $300. Which is *cheap,* when you think on it. A wild boy with a good arm could smash about 30 plate-glass windows a year and *still* cost you less than $10,000 per annum.

Is that right? Are my figures correct?

Yeah. They are. If Juan smashed 30 big windows a year, I would still save $1,000.

So send the boy to me, Ralph—along with a certified cheque for $10,000— and I'll turn him into a walking profit machine.

Indeed. Send me all those angry little limey bastards you can round up. We can do business on this score. Just whip them over here on the Airbus with a $10k cheque for each one, and after that you can go about your filthy, destructive business with a clear conscience.

The prime minister *is* a denatured pig, Ralph, and you *should* beat her like a gong. Draw *horrible* cartoons of the bitch, and sell them for many dollars to *The Times* and *Private Eye* . . . but don't come weeping to me when your own son takes it into his head to smash a few windows.

Have you ever put a brick through a big plate-glass window, Ralph? It makes a wonderful goddamn noise, and the people inside run around like rats in a firestorm. It's *fun,* Ralph, and a bargain at any price.

What do you think we've been doing all these years? Do you think you were getting paid for your goddamn silly *art?*

No, Ralph. You were getting paid to smash windows. And that is an art in itself. The trick is getting *paid* for it.

What? Hello? Are you still *there,* Ralph?

You sniveling, hypocritical bastard. If your son had *your* instincts, he'd be *shooting* at the prime minister, instead of just smashing windows.

Are you ready for that? How are you going to feel when you wake up one of these mornings and flip on the telly at Old Loose Court just in time to catch a news bulletin about the prime minister being shot through the gizzard in Piccadilly Circus .... and then some BBC hot rod comes up with exclusive pictures of the dirty freak who *did it,* and he turns out to be your own son?

Think about that, Ralph; and don't bother me anymore with your minor problems. . . . Just send the boy over to me; I'll soften him up with trench work until his green card runs out, then we'll move him on to Australia. And five years from now, you'll get an invitation to a wedding at a sheep ranch in Perth. . . .

And so much for that, Ralph. We have our own problems to deal with. Children are like TV sets. When they start acting weird, whack them across the eyes with a big rubber basketball shoe.

How's that for wisdom?

Something wrong with it?

No. I don't think so. Today's plate-glass window is tomorrow's BBC story. Keep that in mind and you won't go wrong. Just send me the boys and the cheques. . . .

I think you know what I mean. It's what happens when the son of a famous English artist shows up on the telly with a burp gun in his hand and the still-twitching body of the prime minister at his feet. . . .

You can't even run from that one, Ralph—much less hide, so if you think it's a real possibility all I can advise you to do is *stock up on whiskey and codeine.* That will keep you dumb enough to handle the shock when that ratchet-head, glue-crazy little freak finally does the deed. . . .

The subsequent publicity will be a nightmare. But don't worry—your friends will stand behind you. I'll catch one of those Polar-Route flights out of Denver and be there eight hours after it happens. We'll have a monster news conference in the . . . lobby of Brown's Hotel.

Say nothing until I get there. Don't even claim bloodlines with the boy. Say *nothing*. I'll talk to the press—which is, after all, my business.

Your buddy,
HST

P.S.: Jesus, Ralph, I think I might have misspoke myself when I said ten thousand would cover it for the murderous little bastard. No. Let's talk about *thirty*, Ralph. You've got a real monster on your hands. I wouldn't touch him for less than thirty.

April 21, 1986

Just Another Terrorist

"My adversaries . . . applied the one means that wins the easiest victory over reason: terror and force."

—Adolf Hitler, *Mein Kampf,* Vol. I, Ch. 2

There was action all over the globe last week. Ed Meese went to Holland, volcanoes menaced Alaska—and almost everywhere else in the world, except Hawaii, American tourists were being chased down and shot like wild animals by international terrorists.

President Reagan, meanwhile, flew to Hawaii to rest up for his visit to Bali and also to chat with his old friend Ferdinand Marcos, from the Philippines. The Man from Manila was still hunkered down in his cut-rate beach house near Diamond Head, cursing the kinks in his revenue stream and blowing most of his pocket money on new pairs of shoes for his wife.

The woman is insatiable. She *must* have new shoes. Even now—after leaving 3,000 pairs in Manila—she needs a delivery every day. It is a jones worse than China White. She will take black spikes or Capezios or even foam-rubber flip-flops—just as long as they're the right size, and new.

The whole world laughed, but Marcos was not amused. He was, after all, The President—and if his wife had a shoe fetish, so what? Shoes are cheap, and those who complained were probably communists anyway. They would be turned into pillars of salt when the sun came up in the morning. And in the meantime he would stomp them and burn all their ballots. It was clearly the right thing to do.

Or at least it seemed that way, at the time—but in fact it was just another dumb bare-knuckle type of terrorism that looked on TV about as bad as anything normally blamed on Khadafy or Arafat or Abu Nidal in Syria.

Innocent people were beaten and shot at the polling places. Whole towns were terrorized by thugs in the pay of the president, who wrote his checks on the national treasury.

It was arrogance on a level that shocked even his own generals. The discovery of 3,000 pairs of shoes in Imelda's closet was viewed with an almost universal repugnance in the English-speaking world.

Not even Ted Koppel could tolerate it. When he interviewed Marcos on "Nightline" he saved The Shoe Question for last—but Ferdinand just shrugged and dismissed the whole thing as a red herring. "Why all this talk about shoes?" he muttered. "We *all* wear shoes."

And he was right, in a way. What is the *cost* of new shoes? Maybe $100 apiece? Or even $500?

So what?

We are talking, here, about a man who ran the whole Philippine islands for 26 years like it was some kind of personal dog kennel. He used silk handkerchiefs like Kleenex and routinely stole 10,000 full-grown mahogany trees with a single telephone call.

Manila was no place for amateurs in those days. Not even Bob Arum could handle it. At one point, a few years ago, he talked to Imelda and thought he had a lock on the national dog-racing concession. . . . But when he finally went down to The Palace she stiffed him and demanded more front money than even Don King would call reasonable.

Arum left in a funk and never went back. The dog-racing license was pieced off to a combine from Singapore, which prospered briefly and then went up in smoke when Marcos bit the bullet.

Many investments went sour that day. Even smart people panicked and went out to find palm-readers on Pilar Street. Men stared at each other in the aisles of the Metal Exchange in Hong Kong, and the Landlords' Club in Luzon closed its doors because all the help disappeared. Bob Arum smiled and had a methuselah of Dom Perignon sent up to his office on Park Avenue.

These things happen. One day you run everything, and the next day you run like a dog. When they took Ferdinand out of the palace he thought he was just going on a short flight up the coast to his home province of Ilocos Norte.

But when he woke up he was in Guam, being shuffled around like a prisoner by a convoy of U.S. Secret Service agents—and after that he was taken to Honolulu, where all his luggage was officially seized and impounded.

There were trunks full of jewels and stacks of Swiss bonds and two crates filled with $26 million of freshly printed Philippine pesos—so new that the ink was still wet.

It was all seized—along with two crates of pesos belonging to Gen. Fabian Ver, his traveling companion and former chief of the army, who is no longer mentioned in news stories out of Hawaii.

Gen. Ver is gone now, along with $20 billion that Marcos was originally accused of stealing and embezzling for his own gain. Nobody knows where it went. The records are missing and the bank books are not reliable. Only Imelda knows for sure, but every time she gets on the telephone she hears a click that tells her the Secret Service is listening.

Why not? They are paying the phone bill, and the game is for very high stakes. Twenty billion dollars is half of the Philippines' gross national product for 1984.

It is enough money to buy half of Kowloon—or a whole new air force of Soviet-built MiG-23 Floggers for Moammar Khadafy in Libya, who currently has only 584 combat planes—according to Soldier of Fortune's official spring listing for 1986.

If the colonel had that many more hot rod jet fighters we would all be in serious trouble. . . . And if Ferdinand Marcos could get his hands on that $20 billion he allegedly skimmed out of Manila while he was president, he could buy a nice ranch in Tripoli and live once again like a king.

Libya is a big country. There is plenty of room for rich exiles who can't go home again. There are millions of acres out there in the desert where swine like Marcos and Duvalier can live on huge estates with gold walls, and be at peace with their neighbors. They will grow old and fat like gibbed cats, with plump little fingers and soft hair on the backs of their necks . . . and they will not be inclined to adventures in international terrorism.

April 28, 1986

The Woman from Kiev

"I get the feeling that the American press is not happy there are so few victims."

—Vladimir B. Lomeiko
Press Department Chief, Soviet Foreign Ministry

Most weeks are slow in the news business. Wild things happen to some people, but not many. Jack London fought wolves, and Ed Murrow worked routinely in a nightmare of bombs and rockets and screaming air-raid sirens that shattered the best microphones CBS could build for him. . . .

But those things are not the norm. The daily diet is lean for the infantry. The bellowing of Sam Donaldson and the simpering of Robin Leach are not music to the ears of some hot rod from Columbia or Northwestern who spent the best five years of his life studying academic journalism, and the next 10 covering city hall in St. Louis, or price wars between Safeway and Albertson's.

It is like joining the Navy and expecting to fly gold-plated jets off the deck of a new aircraft carrier that costs more than Egypt and shoot Tomahawk missiles that cost $2 million apiece at crazed communist Arabs in places like Beirut and Tripoli.

There is all the action you want, from time to time—but in the main it is a dull and dreary life, like journalism.

I have tried to quit more than once, and my reasons have always been righteous. A smart boy with good teeth can make more money as a gigolo in Forth Worth than most of the sportswriters in Dallas, or even a national news editor.

But some, like Pat Buchanan, have chosen the less-traveled road— the Other Fork, as it were—and hired themselves out to whatever team was winning, at the time. Patrick went straight into the belly of the beast, once again, by signing on as the official communications director for the White House.

His appointment did not go unnoticed in the trade. Strong men wept openly, and others called it a mockery, like a bad joke out of *Caligula*.

My own foul down link with the news business has never been so lucrative or respectable. It has been more like a loose cannon, in the style of Frank Mankiewicz, who once ran campaigns for the Kennedys and now works as a big-time fixer at Grey and Co., one of the most serious and powerful lobbyist connections in Washington.

Frank is known as a heavy hitter, one of the best and brightest of the smart boys, which may or may not be true—in the same sense that Frank Terpil may or may not have worked for the CIA—but he is an old friend, and when I have trouble understanding some odd kink or bolix on the dark side of politics, I call Frank.

Last week, when I was baffled by a massive disparity in the body count from the nuclear disaster in the Soviet Union—a difference between two dead, or 2,000—I dialed The Powerhouse in Georgetown.

"Who in the hell was it who said there were 2,000 killed at Chernobyl?"

"That's a UPI report from somebody in Kiev. A woman in Kiev."

"Some woman in Kiev?"

"Yeah, she said it to the UPI on the phone."

"Come on, Frank. We all know that *some* woman in Kiev."

"We all know the woman in Kiev and we all know the UPI, right?"

"Well, I'm not sure. Didn't the Mexicans buy it?"

"Huh?"

"Wasn't it bought by a Mexican of some kind?"

"Yeah, that's right, they were."

"So we're dealing with a Mexican news service, and it's claiming 2,000 people were killed in Kiev? With no source except a mysterious woman with no telephone?"

"It's interesting that the CIA keeps telling us they can tell when the goddamn Russians cut the lawn in their back yards. They got these great

cameras, right? *They can tell what kind of cigarettes they smoke in Kiev . . . but can't tell whether the goddamn city's on fire or not."*

"You must be slipping, Frank. I thought you would be the one person who would know about the 2,000 figure."

"I do know. I just don't know her name."

"Do you believe there was a report that said 2,000? Was it true?"

"I believe somebody said it, for God's sake—but I don't believe it's true. Maybe there'll be a hundred thousand 10 years from now."

"What? Come on, Frank. Let's not get too careless with our facts here. Two thousand dead means 2,000 dead yesterday—not 10 years from now. I thought you guys were smart."

"Well, the CIA liked the report, so they ran with it."

"You can't beat that. The last report I got, there was a huge yellowish gray cloud floating over Europe and heading over the polar cap."

"Scandinavia."

"And then into Seattle and Vancouver."

"Residents fled in their nightclothes."

"According to the latest CNN weather report, it's definitely going to hit Seattle."

"Police did not rule out the possibility of arson."

"Indeed. Round up the usual suspects."

"It's that old fire story—a fire of undetermined origin."

"This is just a wrist-wrestling UPI trip?"

"Yeah. Call them up. They'll tell you."

Which was true. I called Andy Tully, night editor at UPI in Washington, who took a very queasy position with regard to the Woman in Kiev— the original source for the report of 2,000 dead in the Ukraine, when the reactor melted down.

There was a long pause on the other end of the line when I asked about the woman. "Nobody knows," he said finally. "We can't find her. She was always a reliable source for us, but now she's gone—disappeared in the chaos.

"It was an *unconfirmed report,*" he explained. "It came out of U.S. intelligence. They said she was a Gray Lady of some kind, a volunteer at the hospital. She claimed she saw thousands of corpses."

"Thanks," I said. "I understand now."

May 5, 1986

Two More Years

"On balance, he's still doing fine," says a White House counselor, "and his problems are all fixable because it's still early."

—*Newsweek* memo on George Bush, April 31, 1986

Jimmy Carter was on TV last week, promoting his new book on the "Larry King Show" and having a bit of sport with the working people in Washington. David Stockman had already put blood in the water, and the scent was irresistible. Jimmy was in a good mood, very wise and relaxed—but if there was trouble in the Big House, he definitely wanted a piece of it.

There was not a lot of talk about his book. He was hooked up with King on a remote-feed from somewhere in Alabama, a safe distance from Washington, and as he talked you could almost hear the mind of the long-distance sniper at work.

He felt sorry for The President, he said. Reagan was not only wrong and dumb, but now his advisers had betrayed him and the rest of the world was treating him like a stuffed owl because they know he'll be gone in two years.

Carter leaned heavily on this last point. It was nothing personal, he said, and not even partisan politics. But somebody had to say it: The president of the United States no longer has credibility anywhere in the civilized world except Santa Barbara.

All world leaders understand this, Jimmy explained. They know Mikhail Gorbachev is going to be around for a while, and they know Reagan won't. So of course they'll do business with the Soviets. They might humor Reagan, like they did at the summit meeting in Tokyo, but they will pay attention to Gorbachev because they know in their hearts they will probably have to talk to him again.

It was ominous wisdom, but nothing special. Any Southern politician can tell you about the hazards of making deals with a lame-duck governor, and Carter understands this as well as anybody. He did not get to the White House by misunderstanding politics. He was good at it, like Nixon, and they will both be worth watching for a while.

We are in for some serious politics in the next two years. The most powerful job in the world is going up for grabs, and George Bush is the only one standing in line for it. He is the heir apparent and has no choice but to run.

This has created what they call "an interesting situation" in the political community, where the current betting on George has taken a turn for the worse.

After years of dutiful hibernation as vice president, he has suddenly come out of the closet and taken a serious flogging every time he opened his mouth. People called him a fool and a wimp, and his chances of winning were openly mocked in Washington. He was like the mechanical rabbit in a greyhound race, they said—just a creature for setting the pace. Many others would soon be in line with him, and the odds were not on his side. Only one sitting vice president since Thomas Jefferson has ever been elected president. That was Martin Van Buren in 1836, a Democrat, who won more or less by default. The once-powerful Whigs were so far gone at that point that they couldn't even decide on a candidate.

George Bush will not be that lucky. Nobody is going to default in 1988: The stakes are too high and preachers will not make the nut. The starting line, this time, is going to look like the front row at the Honolulu Marathon. There will be many candidates, but most of them are still trying to lie low.

Not even Pat Robertson has declared, despite Carter's observation that he is "drawing huge crowds" every time he appears in Iowa. Jimmy smiled the old smile when he said this. Pat Robertson is not going to win anything in 1988, and neither is George Bush. These are fast times in politics, and front-runners are swiftly discredited. Lyndon LaRouche has come and gone in the quick space of two months, and George Bush will not last much longer.

He will be gone by June, according to oil industry analysts, when the price of gasoline is up by 15 cents a gallon over May, and people are full of hate.

That will not be a good time for any front-runner to be publicly identified as The Man Who Killed Cheap Gas in America—but Bush is going to be stuck with it.

The electorate will tolerate almost anything except a sudden unexplained jump of 15 cents a gallon at the pump, in a time of world glut on the oil market.

That will not be politically acceptable in a year when Americans are suddenly afraid to travel anywhere in the world except in their own country. Between the menace of terrorism and the promise of cheap gas on the highways, a lot of people figured it was better to drive to Vancouver, or even St. Louis, instead of flying off to someplace like Cairo or Greece and risk getting blown sideways out of a TWA jet at 30,000 feet above the Sea of Sardinia.

It was humiliating, but it was not a bad deal at the price. There were rumors that it might fall below 50 cents a gallon by midsummer, if the Arabs kept flooding the market.

It was at that point that George Bush bit the bullet, on behalf of his neighbors in Houston. It was not what he wanted, but it was a thing that had to be done, for political reasons . . . he took a night flight to Jidda and leaned publicly on King Fahd of Saudi Arabia to go along with an emergency price-fixing scam that would stop the slide and "stabilize the price of oil."

It had fallen to $9.70 a barrel on April 1, and at that point the joke was over. Texas was going bankrupt and his people were on the line. They had not sent him to Washington all this time for nothing. . . .

And George understood, like a champion. By the time he got back from Jidda, the price of oil was rising sharply. It was up another 53 cents a barrel on Thursday, and the chairman of Mobil Corp. said it could stabilize at $20 very soon, "if OPEC finally agrees to a new production policy this year."

King Fahd shrugged it off, but he let George get out of the country before he denounced him as a dumb brute . . . and by the time Bush got back to the White House he was looking at a personal tragedy. Texas was saved, but he was not. At 15 cents a gallon, he was doomed to a fate like the Ancient Mariner. The albatross was on him, and he will be better off out of the race. Others will come and go before he dies in a fog like George Romney. We will march on a road of bones, he said, and then he disappeared.

May 12, 1986

They All Drowned

The news was not funny last week. The pace was fast and the stories were cruel, but there was not a lot of humor in it. The headlines were dominated by stories of failure, madness and treachery. . . . The weather was foul almost everywhere in the country except Long Island Sound, where local vigilantes killed a white Beluga whale. It washed up on the beach with at least two .22-caliber bullet holes in its head, slain for no apparent reason.

The death of the whale was quickly made the subject of a federal investigation—along with Michael Deaver, Jackie Presser and Kurt Waldheim.

A sudden blizzard in Oregon killed nine people on Mount Hood, and berserk rural terrorists bombed an elementary school in a hamlet called Cokeville, in Wyoming. . . . Teddy White died in New York, the Teamsters rallied in Las Vegas, Ronald Reagan canceled the SALT II treaty with Russia, and Attorney General Ed Meese declared war on Sex and Violence.

It was one of those weeks when nothing seemed to work. The U.S. "space program" went belly-up when NASA collapsed; Commander Zero quit the war in Nicaragua and turned himself in to the Red Cross; two Chamber of Commerce officials in Texas were locked up for sodomy and cannibalism; and Richard Nixon appeared on the cover of Newsweek.

In the midst of all this my friend Skinner arrived in Colorado for what he called "a long rest and some serious fishing."

He had been on the road for six or eight weeks in places like Tripoli, Tunis and Cairo, and the experience had made him bitter. "The Arabs are different from us," he said. "They are evil."

He spent a week in our guest room and went fishing every morning with a 12-gauge shotgun and a green plastic net. He would prowl the banks of the creek, from one trout-pond to another, and whenever he saw a big fish near the surface he would blast it with the shotgun and then scoop it up with the net, before the shock wore off. On some mornings he would bring back five or six big trout for breakfast—and there was rarely any problem with the bones, which had been turned into mush by the blast. We ate them like eggs, with black pepper and jalapeño sauce. But it made the neighbors uneasy, and we were happy to see him go.

He was on his way to Michigan, for the Second World Conference on Large Lakes, which began last Sunday in Lansing. Skinner is not big on hobbies and he has few personal interests beyond weapons and power and politics, but he is deeply involved in things like environmental fraud, acid rain and toxic pollution of Fresh Water Reservoirs.

"We are all slaves to the water," he told me. "It's the last pure thing in the world."

One of his major concerns—almost to the point of obsession—was the relentless and logarithmic rise in the level of the Great Salt Lake, in Utah, which is now the fastest-growing body of water in the world.

Utah will be under water by the year 2000, he said. The lake has been doubling its own depth and volume every four years, despite all efforts to manage it.

In 1975, according to the New Columbia Encyclopedia, the Great Salt Lake was "a shallow body of salt water covering 1,000 square miles, with an average depth of 13 feet, or 4 meters."

Ten years later the average depth was 24 feet, and still rising. The waters have already caused $175 million in damage to farms, highways and railroad tracks.

Last week the Utah Legislature approved a $72 million emergency plan to lower the lake by pumping millions of gallons of salt water into the desert to the west—creating what Gov. Norman Bangerter calls a "temporary sister lake," about one-third the size of the 30 million acre-feet of the Great Salt.

It is a weird plan, rife with madness and a sort of low-tech desperation that nobody in Utah is proud of. . . . But it is necessary, they say, and it will not be the first time that white men in the Western Hemisphere have gotten involved in a tragic lake-draining project.

One of the ugliest of these is the saga of the draining of the Lago de Amor, a remote inland lagoon in the highlands of Colombia where the legendary Treasure of El Dorado still rests in the foul black mud.

This nightmare is described in a book called *The Fruit Palace,* by a Britisher named Charles Nicholl, who came on the place while chasing a cocaine dream.

"Eldorado was not originally a place," Nicholl says, "but a person— *el dorado,* the gilded man." He was the main figure in a coronation ceremony held for a new territorial chieftain *(cacique)* in the *Chibcha* empire.

"At the shores of the lagoon he was stripped naked, anointed with sticky resin, and sprayed with gold dust. A raft of reeds was prepared, with braziers of *moque* incense and piles of gold and jewels on it."

He and four other *caciques* floated to the middle of the lake, where he then dove into the lake, washing off the gold. The ceremony concluded with all the gold and jewels being thrown into the lake.

When the Spanish learned of the ceremony, they began many attempts to drain the lake, starting with Hernan Pérez de Quesada in 1545.

"Using a bucket chain of Indian laborers with gourd jars, he succeeded in lowering the level of the water by some ten feet, enough to recover about 3,000 pesos of gold." They managed about three feet a month, but rain refilled the lagoon almost as quickly. Antonio de Sepulveda and a crew of 8,000 Indians lowered the level by 60 feet about 40 years later. He recovered some gold and gems "including an emerald the size of a hen's egg." He failed to get financing for subsequent efforts and died "poor and tired."

A French scientist estimated in 1825 the value of the unrecovered treasure at 1,120,000 pounds.

The lake was completely drained after a British joint-stock company, Contractors, Ltd., bought the rights "to exploit the lagoon" in 1899.

"They drilled a tunnel right under the lake and up into the centre, and the water was sluiced away down this giant plughole, with mercury screens to trap any precious objects."

The lakebed, however, proved intractable, impossible to walk on because of layers of mud and slime, which became concrete with the sun's heat. Not even drilling equipment could free the mud-clogged sluices and tunnel, and eventually the lake refilled.

May 19, 1986

Four More Games

Last week was a fast one for news. There was a feeling of speed in the headlines, a sense of things cranking up. . . . Nazis marched in South Africa, more bombs ripped Beirut, a typhoon hit the Solomon Islands, and U.S. scientists in Nevada detonated another nuclear device.

The Houston Rockets flogged the Lakers by 10 points on Sunday, then finished them off Wednesday night on a crazy last-second shot by Ralph Sampson.

The Lakers played hard, but in the end they died like rats in a tunnel and rolled over. . . . The Rockets flew back to Texas, and got ready for a serious beating at the hands of the Boston Celtics.

That will start happening today. The spread is nine for game one, but the Celtics will probably win by 14 or 15, and game two will go the same way. Boston is 7-1 to win the series, and at least twice that to do it in 4 straight. That seems about right, or maybe even a little bit generous. . . . The Pacific Basin Desk might go as low as 10, with a little grease on the side and serious cash held in escrow.

Not everybody in the gambling community feels this way. There are people who think Houston might even win the series, because man-for-man they are bigger and better athletes. Sampson and Akeem Olajuwon might terrorize the Celtic's front line, like they did Kareem at the Forum.

Even Jack Nicholson was stunned, they said. Ushers led him away through a side exit, where he was greeted with jeers by a surly mob in the parking lot.

Meanwhile, back in Washington, CIA Chief William J. Casey was filing charges of treason against NBC News, and Ronald Reagan himself put the whack on the *Washington Post*. . . . When Casey was unable to prevent the *Post* from publishing a massive Bob Woodward article on current CIA operations, good old Dutch just smiled and said shucks—and then he picked up the phone and spoke personally with *Post* publisher Katharine Graham, who called the story back for major cuts and re-editing.

Woodward bristled and bitched, but the lawyers called him paranoid and his piece was eventually gutted, for reasons of national security. It was such a clear case of censorship and journalistic nut-cracking by the White House that even *USA Today* called it shameful. "The *Post* gave in," said columnist Michael J. Gartner, "and published a censored article that was five feet nine inches long and that was as bland as it was lengthy."

The collapse of the *Post* sent a rumble of fear and confusion through the whole journalistic community. It was like spreading rumors in Boston about Larry Bird shaving points, or priests selling fat young boys out of vans behind Fenway Park.

Nobody wants to hear these things. If the *Post* can be intimidated, who else can feel safe? NBC was still holding, but Casey was pushing for serious criminal penalties and a final decision by Attorney General Ed Meese, who is currently tied up in his own campaign against pornography, and will soon be publishing the findings of his controversial commission's investigation.

I have not seen the MEESE REPORT yet. It is not officially due for another few weeks—but it is already much in the news and we are going to have to deal with the fallout for longer than even lawyers will enjoy. They will have all the work they need before this thing is over.

In the meantime everybody even vaguely connected to the sex business is going to be publicly flogged on both coasts for about the next six months—while Meese tries to make a case for the link between Sex and Violence. That seems to be the crux of his long-awaited Report, and we are all stuck with it. He has cranked up so much volume of federal machinery behind the report that it would take two years for them even to dismantle it and back off. . . .

Which is not likely to happen in any case. There is too much ordnance already committed. The feds can't afford to back off now, without at least a few trophies and scalps. Hundreds of junior prosecutors and assistant D.A.'s all over the country have already made career decisions on the basis of their professional involvement in Big Ed's War on Pornography.

The whole Frankenstein monster of federal government machinery seemed involved in one way or another last week in the business of crime and punishment. Meese was handling the sex fiends, Casey had the press, and George Shultz was de facto responsible for almost everything else except Miami and Saudi Arabia, where George Bush is still in control.

These boys run a very tight ship, for an old-timey laissez-faire government, and there are not many seams in the defense. The only good news out of Washington last week was The Saga of Captain Midnight—the mysterious Video Terrorist who became an instant legend by jamming a prime-time movie on the HBO channel and cutting in with his own 30-second commercial, in four colors, protesting the network's new policy of full-time scrambling and a whole new schedule of taxes and fees and mandatory high-tech deciphering machinery for millions of satellite dish owners.

Captain Midnight is still on the loose, despite the best efforts of the FBI, the FCC and a handful of spooks from places like Rotterdam and Lockheed and Mossad, the Israeli secret intelligence unit.

People like Meese and Casey and Webster have sent FCC officials off to Congress to draft a bill that would raise the penalty for satellite interference from a $10,000 fine and/or a year in jail to a $100,000 fine and/or 10 years in jail.

The problem with Captain Midnight is not so much what he actually did, but the fact that he was able to do it. The best brains in the SatCom business had told the HBO brass that it was not possible for any pirate to cut into the main movie signal—but nobody had ever even thought about the possibility of some freak boring into the transponder with a massive 2,000-watt signal.

HBO was transmitting at 125 watts that night, and Captain Midnight's odd signal was not taken seriously at first. It happened at 12:32 A.M. in New York and engineers on duty at the main HBO transmitter on Long Island at first tried to keep up with the unholy power surge generated by Captain Midnight's huge transmitter—but when the illegal hit 2,000 watts the HBO boys backed off and called the FBI.

May 26, 1986

Last Dance in Dumb Town

I was sitting at the bar in the Woody Creek Tavern last week, sipping my normal huge flagon of whiskey and getting cranked up to the right level of alcoholic frenzy for an afternoon of fast driving on the local highways, back roads and maybe even a few residential districts, when a man from Miami came in and said he had a fast motorcycle to sell, for $5,000 cash.

It was a cafe racer, he said—a fancy little hot rod with a silver engine the size of a football and hand-tooled Italian leather seats. . . . And he had it just outside in the parking lot, strapped down with pink bungee cords on the back of what looked like a flatbed Peterbilt truck.

Nobody paid any attention to him. There was a film on TV about a team of French scientists trying to load a polar bear onto the fantail of what looked like a Caribbean tourist yacht. The beast was howling and thrashing, but they had it wrapped up in a steel mesh-net—and then a woman wearing a topless bikini came out and shot it in the back with a tranquilizer gun.

It was the middle of a slow afternoon on a cold day in the Rockies, and there were only a few paying customers at the bar, all of them deeply engrossed in their own business. . . . They were locals, cowboys and gamblers, and the last thing any one of them needed was a high-speed Italian motorcycle.

The stranger took a long look at the place, then he slumped on a bench near the window and ordered a sloe gin sling. "Who gives a damn about polar bears?" he muttered. "They're dumber than dogs and they'll turn on you for no reason at all."

I saw Cromwell shudder on his stool at the far end of the bar, where he had been nursing a Moosehead all morning and brooding helplessly on the 9-point spread for the Celtics-Rockets game that was coming up on TV around sundown. . . . He had bet heavily on the Rockets and given 16-1 against four straight, and now he was feeling deep in the hole.

The day was already queasy. The morning had bloomed warm and bright, but by noon it was raining fitfully and the sky was turning black. By 2:30 we were getting thunder and lightning, the first spring storm of the season.

The polar bear film was still rolling. The brutes were being taken off to some zoo on the outskirts of Paris, where they would be loaded with electrical implants in the softer parts of their bodies and then turned loose on the slopes of Mount Ararat.

The reasons would never be explained. It was one of those top-secret international security gigs that only the French can do prop-erly. . . . And meanwhile, on the other side of the world in a pure behavioral sink 8,000 feet up in the Rockies in a roadhouse on a two-lane blacktop on the low-rent side of the river, some nervous little fruitbag from Miami was trying to peddle a slick Italian motorcycle.

Cromwell eyed him balefully for a moment, then he stood up and pulled a pair of ribbed leather gloves out of his hip pocket. "OK," he said. "You've come to the right place. Let's have a look at the bugger."

"What?" said the stranger. "You want to buy it?"

"Not yet," said Cromwell. "But I *will,* if it's fast. I just got back from Vegas and I have a lot of money."

There was a hoot of dumb laughter from somewhere back in the kitchen, but I kept a straight face.

The price was $10,000, said the stranger, but he was new in the neighborhood, so he would let it go for five. . . . The only other one of these things ever built, he said, was sold to Steve McQueen for something like $40,000.

"Which one of us should ride it?" Cromwell said. "I want to run it against my Jeep for about a mile down the road—to the gravel pit."

We went outside in the rain and unloaded the slick little speedster down off the flatbed truck.

Cromwell pulled on his motocross gloves. "If it's faster than my Jeep," he said, "I'll give you ten grand—but if it's not, you give it to me for *nothing.*"

The stranger stared at him, and nobody else said a word. "Are you nuts?" he said finally. "You want me to race my Ducati against a goddamn Jeep? For $10,000?"

"Why not?" said Cromwell. "Let's go do it before the storm hits."

We all agreed. It was winner-take-all. Cromwell backed his rotten-looking, mud-covered Jeep out of a corner of the parking lot and aimed it down the road, while the man from Miami got his bike tuned up. . . . I drifted around behind Cromwell's machine and pulled a Parnelli Jones-Baja bumper sticker off the rear end; the thing was a monster, so fast and strong that he was afraid to even drive it on the roads in Colorado. The engine was a 600-hp, turbo-powered Ford-Cosworth.

Money changed hands. There was serious talk about "honest dollars" and escrow. A man called Tex stepped forward and agreed to hold the cash without prejudice.

We were all involved in this thing, more or less, but nobody really cared . . . and it was just about then that the whole world exploded with a boom and a flash that blew us all sideways. Cromwell's Jeep turned blue like a gas bomb, and then fell on top of the motorcycle, sending up a cloud of nasty electrical smoke.

We were all knocked stupid. The next sound I remember hearing was a woman screeching, "Please, Tex—don't die." And then I felt myself being dragged across the road by people I didn't recognize. There was a smell of burning hair all around us, and I heard voices talking about "oxygen" and "heart failure" and "burned like a human cinder."

No money changed hands that day, and we never saw the man from Miami again. Several days later I went back to the tavern and heard more or less what happened. We were whacked by a huge blue ball of lightning that bounced once in the parking lot and then rolled down the road about 200 feet before it exploded in the creek.

Tex lived, but his heart was like a small lump of charcoal and his face shriveled up like a raisin. A doctor in Phoenix said his body was about 400 years old, and if he ever bumped up against anything solid he would probably break like cheap glass.

I never saw him again. His family put him in a rural hotel somewhere in Arizona, where he remained helpless for whatever was left of his life.

There is still a big crater in the parking lot across the road from the Woody Creek Tavern, with a crust of black ash on its edges and a pool of stagnant water at the bottom. . . . I have not been back there since I quit work and moved north, for professional reasons.

June 2, 1986

Rise of the TV Preachers

"Beware of false prophets, which come to you in sheep's clothing, but inwardly they are ravening wolves."

—Matthew 7:15

There was a whole new mood in the evangelical community last week, a feeling of joy and adventure. They are moving into national politics with an energy not seen since the days of William Jennings Bryan, and they are filled with a sense of adventure.

The business of saving souls at high speed has never been dull—but there has nonetheless been a feeling of angst and unfulfilled dreams in recent years, among even the most serious Jesus People, as more and more of them have come to suspect that God's all-powerful will might be better dispensed—and be made even *more* powerful, for that matter—if his servants lived in the White House, instead of some dingy church in Moline.

They have had these feelings before—usually to no good end—but that kind of temptation never really goes away. It is like lust or malaria, and once you've seen one of your own kind standing next to the president on a balcony in the White House and waving down on a cheering mob, life will never be the same.

That is what happened last year, in the mind of a big-volume standard-brand TV preacher from Virginia Beach named Pat Robertson, when he turned on his set one morning and saw the Rev. Jerry Falwell—an evangelical warrior not unlike himself, and with a far smaller mailing list—lounging around in the Oval Office and swapping jokes with Ronald Reagan.

It was a haunting vision, for Robertson, and not long after that he heard the voice of the Lord, telling him to run for president of the United States on the Republican ticket in 1988. The message made him nervous, at first, he said. It was not what he wanted to hear—but the Lord was seldom wrong in these matters, and Pat saw that he had no choice. . . .

And especially not now, at this crucial juncture in history when his old nemesis, Falwell, had already seen the new light and seized the political high ground. There was no longer anything magical in the notion of some hard-edged Pentecostal evangelist getting the ear of the president and becoming a power in national politics.

Falwell had already managed that. He had somehow crept into the White House inner circle, and now he was fighting shoulder-to-shoulder against pornography with Attorney General Ed Meese and writing campaign speeches for Vice President Bush; his voice was officially large, and the guards at the gate of the White House called him Jerry.

Pat Robertson noticed these things, and made his own plans accordingly. He was, after all, the biggest voice in TV evangelism—with a mailing list bigger than Falwell's and his own TV network that reached into 28 million homes every day of the week.

Pat waffled for a while, but the temptation was irresistible. He soon formed a tax-exempt board of advisers called The Freedom Council, and got seriously into politics.

Some people snickered at the time—but not Falwell, who understands numbers in a way that George Bush never will. Or at least well enough to see a nasty black cloud on his own political future, last week, when the Rev. Robertson trounced both Bush and Jack Kemp, the young conservative favorite, in an obscure state-level election in Michigan that was supposed to mean nothing at all to anybody—except maybe to some guaranteed front-runner like Bush, if he somehow managed to lose.

Which he did, for reasons that are still not explained, and the net result was a huge boost for Robertson—although he is still running far behind Bush in the polls and is not a good bet to gain real ground on anybody except possibly Lyndon LaRouche.

The results out of Michigan were called "freakish" by political pros, but not all of them really believed it. . . . Pat Robertson may have ambushed the front-runners when they weren't looking, but there was nothing freakish in the humiliating failure of both the sitting vice president and the main champion of Reaganomics in Congress to beat back the uppity challenge of some dark-horse quack preacher from a tidewater church in Virginia.

There is no smart consensus about what all this might eventually mean, down in the stretch when the heavy hitters get rolling . . . but there are men wearing red ties and blue suits at the bar in Duke Ziebert's tonight who get paid to be smart about politics, and they are not advising their friends to bet money on either George Bush or Jack Kemp when the crunch comes.

They are not betting heavily on Pat Robertson, either, for that matter. He is, after all, just another one of those millionaire high-rolling preachers who have come to see big-time politics as just a new way of passing the collection plate. He looks like Johnny Carson and he talks like everybody's favorite rich uncle. But if George Bush is a doomed wimp and Jack Kemp is a giddy windbag, Rev. Pat looks pretty good right now—or at least like a genuine spoiler, until something better comes along. He may not ever be president, but he thinks he has God on his side and he will not be easy to beat in places like Texas and Florida.

He is a likable man, and that counts for a lot in politics. Richard Nixon won many great victories, but he was not a likable man, and in the end he was chased out of Washington like some kind of poison troll. He was lucky to get out alive. . . .

Pat Robertson will not go that way. He is a healer, he says, a genuine prophet of God. He has said these things more than once, and he seems to believe them.

There's a famous story about the time he saved a human being on TV whose lungs were "deteriorating with cancer."

"There are actually chunks of lung itself being coughed up," Robertson said. "I don't understand exactly what it is, but God has healed you right now. Amen."

June 9, 1986

Dealing with Pigs

"The life of the people must be freed from the asphyxiating perfume of our modern eroticism, as it must be from unmanly and prudish refusal to face facts. . . . The right to personal freedom comes second in importance to the duty of sustaining the race."

—Adolf Hitler, *Mein Kampf*, 1924

The Meese report went to press last week, but nobody seemed to know what it said. The whole question of "pornography" was lost, once again, in a maze of blind dumbness and bitterly conflicting rumors that meant nothing at all and was put together on a budget about half the size of what the Mitchell Brothers spent for postage stamps last year.

The 11-member commission, a sleazy mix of priests, lawyers, moralists and professional punishment freaks, had spent the past 12 months roaming around the country checking out rumors of alleged sex crimes in places like Houston and Newark and the slums of East St. Louis.

The idea was to establish a pattern of some kind between sex and violence and child molesting—but there was no real agreement on anything except the high price of filthy video tapes.

There is little written or even spoken evidence of what conclusions were drawn, but two women on the panel issued a statement suggesting the other nine were fundamentalist zealots worse than Frank Kush or Hermann Goering and had spent most of their investigative efforts hanging around public urinals and grade-school locker rooms.

Other mutterings and unfounded paranoid whining came from pimps, preachers, crooked cops and smut merchants. Men with body lice and open sores on their necks shook their fists at old women and ripped antennas off parked cars. There was a feeling of helpless ignorance and anger among sex professionals.

The New York Times news service sent out a Page 1 analysis that ranked with some of the worst and most baffling outbursts of utterly meaningless gibberish in English-language journalism since the days of Yellowboy Willis.

The final report by the Meese people will apparently be a voluminous guide to everything ever written or photographed in all aspects of the sex business—hundreds of color photos, thousands of films and massive lists, discussions and descriptions of every kink, crime and subhuman perversion since Nero and prehistoric Japan. The book, due out sometime in July, is already a guaranteed best-seller.

"It will sell more copies than *The Joy of Cooking*," said one editor in the high end of the publishing business. "If I had a fat young daughter, I would lock her down in the basement and shave her head and bend her fingers down like pretzels, so she could never drive a car. The last time one of these things came out was in 1970 when Nixon was still the boss, and it cost my dignity and made a really dirty little animal out of my first wife. She disappeared with a farmer down in Yuma, and then he had her locked up for dealing with pigs."

There is also widespread betting that the new sex manual will cause Ed Meese to be appointed to a seat on the U.S. Supreme Court—even if no deaths occur before then among the current aged justices. There are persistent rumors in Washington about "a deal" that has already been struck between the White House and Chief Justice Burger, who is known to be suffering from serious nervous disorders.

Other reactions to the Meese report were less intelligent and potentially more violent than those that swept the marketplace and the vast underground sex industry. Many pornographic filmmakers expect to be put in prison before Meese ends his term and moves to the high court.

A woman in San Francisco who has worked as a stripper in most of the live sex shows all over the West, including loop joints and brothels in Nevada, insists that no connection exists between sex and violence, except among "some of the working professionals" and a few unstable policemen.

"I've only had one guy who was really wild. He was very religious. He started writing me letters two or three times a week. He talked to God through his radio, and he talked to me telepathically," she said.

"He frightened me, so I wrote to his psychiatrist. She wasn't much help so I called a friend of mine who's a cop that deals with psychiatric cases. He looked him up, and this guy never had so much as a speeding ticket.

"The only other problem I've had was this man who was about 40 and talked about fooling around with his grandma," she explained. "But that was about 30 years ago. I thought it was a little weird.

"But I am selling sexual fantasies, and there are certain pressures that are a little different." She paused. "A lot of the men don't relate well to women.

"But I've never been followed as I've left the building, and as far as I know, none of the girls I've worked with have ever been raped or molested.

"I don't see the customers as people who go out and commit rape. Sometimes computer programmers from San Jose might try to grab you when you walk through the aisle," she said, "but after sitting on laps for years, you can almost anticipate their moves."

June 16, 1986

Deported to Malaysia

There was heavy fog on the Avenues when I drove out to the beach to meet my attorney yesterday morning. Sunrise was officially at 5:47, but that was only for the downtown people. Out around 44th Avenue there was no sunshine at all until 9:30 or 10, and on some stretches of the Great Highway it never came up at all.

The lawyer had called me just before dawn from the Boathouse Lounge to say that he had a tragedy on his hands and he needed physical help—an elderly Chinese gentleman, one of his wealthiest and most influential clients, had spent most of the night trying to commit suicide in the woods around Lake Merced.

The attorney had caught up with the old man just as he was about to row out in the fog on the foulest day of the year in a tin boat with a bar of pig-iron chained around his neck. A struggle ensued, but he eventually calmed down and agreed to go inside and have at least one final cup of hot coffee.

I said I would be there immediately. "You're just down the road from the golf course. I'll bring my clubs."

"Are you crazy?" he shouted. "I have this terrible tragedy on my hands, and you want to play golf? That's madness. The fog is so thick out here that you can't even see the lake."

"That's just about right," I said. "I have a new one-iron and I want to try it a few times before I risk hitting the bugger in public."

"A one-iron?" he said. "Jesus! Get rid of it. Not even God can hit a one-iron."

He told me the man had been suicidal for months—ever since the Immigration and Naturalization Service had filed papers to have him deported, back to Malaysia, where he came from about 30 years ago.

He had been arrested for fishing without a license, in a public lake, while teaching two of his grandsons to cast with a rod and reel. It was a minor offense worth about a $9 fine in most jurisdictions, but when the game warden sent his name into the big computer, word came back that he was an illegal alien.

He had no citizenship papers, and now they were giving him 13 days to get out of the country—despite the pleas and protests of the whole Asian community. The man was well-loved, the owner of many flower shops and the scion of a very extended Chinese family. He had nine children of his own, and 12 grandchildren. The family had been powerful in Chinatown since 1933.

When I got to the Boathouse Lounge I found them hunkered down in a dark corner of the room, staring off across the lake at the firing range and drinking straight gin out of jiggers. The place was not open yet, but the old man had connections with the Taiwanese family that owned the lease, and he'd been hiding out there for three weeks, ever since he'd jumped his bail and become an official fugitive.

The feds were actively chasing him now. He would be deported just as soon as they got their hands on him. It was an agonizing situation, and my attorney had been trying desperately to cure it—but he said there was not much hope.

The old man whacked on the table and cried out: "Why Malaysia? They will kill me if I go there! My mother's whole family was executed for collaborating with the Japanese."

I put an arm on his shoulder. "I know," I said. "It's horrible. Malaysia has turned into one of the most brutal societies in the world. I talked to a man from Hong Kong the other day and he said two of his good friends from Australia were about to be hanged in Malaysia for a minor drug violation."

"Hanged?" he said. "You mean the gallows?"

"They hang a lot of people in Kuala Lumpur," I said. "The place has changed. You won't stand a chance. People with black hoods on their heads will grab you the minute you get off the airplane."

"Oh God!" he screamed. "It's true. They'll kill me in public like a sick animal." He jumped up and grabbed a jagged metal spear off the wall behind the bar, but my attorney grabbed him around the shoulders before he could use it on himself. "Don't do it, Benjy!" he snapped. "It can't be that bad. There's still a chance that we can get you into Hong Kong."

At this point a wild-eyed Asian woman rushed into the room and threw her arms around the old man, weeping loudly and clinging to his neck. "Don't let them kill you, Papa," she screamed. "Don't let them hang you."

He tried to comfort the woman, who seemed to be his daughter, but he appeared to be deeply depressed. "Get away from me," he snarled. "It's all over now. We're all going to be killed, one by one. They will get the whole family, every one of you whimpering dogs."

He laughed wildly and grabbed again for the spear, but the woman quickly ran off. We grappled with him for a moment, then he collapsed on the floor and began jabbering in Chinese. It was an ugly thing to see—especially at that early hour of the morning in the thick fog—and I frankly wanted no part of it.

"Let's get out of here," I said. "We can get some good blood sausage up the hill at the golf course."

The lawyer stared up at the high wooden ceiling for a long moment, then he nodded slowly and said, "Of course. We can have a spot of breakfast and then hit some balls with your new one-iron."

"Why not?" I said. "These criminal foreigners have caused us enough trouble. From now on they should be dealt with by their own people."

My attorney stood up quickly and went off down a hallway toward a pay phone. The old man was weeping softly. He was guilty, and the reasons were none of our business. It had something to do with fish. He had not taken care of his paper work.

On our way out to the parking lot my attorney paused and exchanged a few whispered words with the woman who claimed to be his daughter. She smiled and said it was no problem. She would see us later.

As we drove out to the road I saw a black van pull up to the front door of the Boathouse Lounge, and four men wearing green jump suits leaped out and crashed through the front door.

"Who was that?" I asked.

"La Migra," said the lawyer. "I had no choice." He shook his head grimly. "Don't worry," he muttered. "They'll take care of that swine. We won't have to worry about him any more."

We drove up the road to the golf course. The last of the fog was burning off and the sun was out. We were golfers now. It was Sunday morning in the park.

June 23, 1986

A Clean, Ill-Lighted Place

The eyes of the American sex business were focused on Hollywood last week, as industry moguls gathered in the plush gardens and ball-rooms of a glass hotel on a hillside overlooking Universal Studios for the 10th annual Erotic Film Awards. They came from both coasts, in stretch limos and gold lamé gowns, to honor the best and brightest of their own people.

The guests arrived discreetly, checking into penthouse-style suites on the highest floors of the slick Sheraton-Premier Hotel, with their wives and even their children. Many registered under different names, or a mix of corporate blinds: A casual observer would have taken them for a convention of Chrysler Corp. stockholders. The men wore dinner jackets and the women were dressed in silk.

No searchlights probed the sky above the hotel, and Robin Leach was not invited.

This was a mainly private affair. It was part of the 18th annual convention of the Adult Film Association of America, an old-line consortium of pornographic theater owners, a profoundly endangered breed.

These are the people who have long provided the clean, ill-lighted places for people like Ricardo Ramirez from Los Angeles, the much-despised "Night Stalker" suspect, and Albert DiSalvo from Boston.

These are the nation's X-rated theaters, where filthy old men in cheap black raincoats have traditionally hung out—often for weeks at a time—between bouts of roaming the streets and preying on little children.

The guest list was so exclusive that even Sean Daniel, president of production at Universal, was turned away. . . . But Larry Flynt was there, and so was Al Goldstein, the editor of SCREW, from New York. There was also Russ Hampshire, president of powerful VCA Studios in Hollywood, and the Mitchell Brothers.

We arrived around noon at the Burbank airport and were whisked off in a white Lincoln by a man who spoke no English. On the way to the hotel he brushed heavily with a gray BMW, rear-ending it at a stoplight on Victory Boulevard in front of the Pierce Brothers Mortuary—but he stomped on the gas and sped away, appearing not to notice it. My neck was bashed sideways like the top joint of a rubber chicken, causing a whip-lash injury that plagued me for the rest of the conference. The hotel provided a masseuse and a traction bed, but the pain never entirely went away.

This was no small event. It was like the legendary Appalachian conference, except that nobody got seized or busted. There was no public sex, and the only violence was a deranged outburst by rookie sex starlet Missy Manners, who wore a body stocking all night and screeched relentlessly at her patron, Artie Mitchell. She was quickly subdued by security specialists.

A man named Grissim tried to jump off a fifth-floor balcony with a bottle of gin, but he was restrained by police, then forced under a cold shower in the hospitality lounge. His friends and associates laughed as he was taken away in a neck hold.

The big winner was filmmaker Henri Pachard, who won the "Best Picture of the Year" award with his omnibus *Taboo American Style*, a heavy favorite in the betting.

It won easily, garnering almost as many awards as *New Wave Hookers*, a cruel and trendy piece of atavistic film that featured addicts, hard rockers and other doomed scum from places like Newark and the abandoned piers of Long Beach. It had something to do with "New Wave Music" and young pimps, but in the end it was more like "Knott's Landing" or some wretched Portuguese poolroom in New Bedford, Mass.

Taboo was not much better. It featured incest, treachery, ruined lives and child abuse in a four-part "Dallas"-style miniseries that ran for six hours.

These were the big winners for 1985, which was not a good year for sex films. The pendulum has apparently swung back, or at least into some kind of lame gray area, from the years in the early Seventies that were known as "The Golden Age of Porn."

That was the time of such breakaway classics as *Deep Throat* and *The Story of O*.

Since then, budgets have shrunk and cinematic concepts have withered to the point where *Thunderthighs, Backdoor Housewives* and *Swedish Children with Animals* have become the bellwethers of the industry.

There was also *Squalor Motel, Sperminator* and *Ken Chan the Laundry Man* . . . and in San Diego a double bill featuring *Hot Nazis* and *Huge Bras No. 4* ran for 155 weeks.

Meanwhile, back in the suburbs, Henri Pachard was still big. In the same week when he won the "best film" award in Hollywood, another one of his films—*Climax*—opened to generally high-style reviews at the Sonomarin Adult Drive-In theater, on 101 in Sonoma County just over the Marin County line, six miles north of Novato.

I drove up there the other night in a rented 280 Mercedes with Maria, who had long been a fan of Pachard's.

The entrance, marked only by a huge, white, hand-painted billboard that says "Now Open," led down a long gravel track, and then we came on a toll booth, where an elderly Third World gentleman was selling tickets for $6 each—even at three o'clock in the morning, with only six cars on the weed-covered lot, and "Hot Lips" just finishing up. . . . *Climax* was still to come.

The popcorn stand was closed, and when I asked where I could get a cup of coffee, the ticket man said, "Nowhere." No services were provided, he said, except for the image on the screen.

All the speakers had been torn off the posts long ago, and a sign at the toll booth instructed all patrons to turn their radios to 540.

"How long have you been operating here?" I asked him.

"Twenty years," he replied. "We love the business. This is art," he said. "The money makes no difference. I was here in the old days, when we ran *Pink Flamingoes*."

Climax, the new Pachard film, was clearly one of his favorites and he was not surprised to hear that Henri had just won the big prize in Hollywood.

"I have known him for years," he said. "We are in the sex business."

June 30, 1986

Slow Day at the Airport

It was late on the afternoon of the Fourth when I boarded Flight 346 for Denver, which had the look of a comfortable ride. The plane was almost empty. There were 20 or 30 people spotted around the 200-seat passenger section, and not many were sitting together. Most were men, who seemed vaguely ashamed to be seen there.

Who are these men? And why are they flying alone on the Fourth of July?

Normal people don't spend the Fourth of July on airplanes, except in unfortunate circumstances. There are a lot of better ways to spend the national holiday than hunkered down by yourself in the far corner of a white-plastic widebody 767 cabin, 37,000 feet over Utah, muttering into a tape recorder or making entries into a ledger. There is nothing stylish about it, nothing chic or trendy or hip.

Flight 346 originated in San Francisco and arrived in Denver around sundown. After that, it went all the way to Dulles International in Washington, arriving sometime after midnight, . . . and then would come the 50-minute limo ride to the nearest motel, probably in Arlington, where guests are routinely hassled for illegal whiskey and suspected violations of the drug and sodomy laws.

Which was none of my business. I was getting off in Denver, and I had a lot of newspapers to read before then. I was not in the mood for random conversation.

The only other people on the plane were a half dozen or so off-duty pilots: "deadheads," as they say in the business. They were sitting mainly in the outside aisle seats, along both sides of the fuselage, all of them dressed in full uniform like emperor penguins, but none sitting together.

There was no feeling of camaraderie on this flight, which was fine with me. I was in the grip of another malaria flashback; nothing serious, but it had left me feeling weak.

I was halfway down the aisle when I felt a hand on my leg and heard a voice just below me saying, "Hello, Doc. What are you doing here?"

Ye gods, I thought. What now? I looked down and saw that it was one of the pilots, a clean-cut Aryan boy of about 29, who was now reaching up to shake hands.

He was wearing a snappy blue pilot's blazer, with gold-striped epaulets and silver wings on his chest and in his lap he was holding a professional pilot's black leather map case. "It's been a long time, Doc," he said. "Where are you going from here?"

"Home," I muttered, not pausing to chat. The malaria was taking over. There was something familiar about his face, but I couldn't remember his name.

We took off precisely on time. I stretched out in my two-seat section by the smoking window and unrolled my newspapers.

After 10 minutes or so, I finally remembered the pilot's name. He was a major drug smuggler. His code name had been "The Fat Man," when he was one of the highest-priced pilots in the business.

The last time I saw him, he was flying Lear jets in and out of Aspen, wearing turquoise bracelets and gold bhat chains around his neck. . . . But he had dropped out of sight for a while.

My own business had taken me elsewhere in those years. . . . But I remembered him now, and I was not surprised when—not long after we'd reached cruising altitude, after the passenger safety film and the in-flight telephone instructions—I looked up from my *New York Times* and saw him standing beside me.

"Hello, Julian," I said. "Sit down. Have a drink. What are you doing in that uniform? I thought you were in prison."

He grinned and sat down, adjusting his legs to accommodate the two black leather map cases he was carrying with him. They were identical, about the size of a small TV camera, and looking very expensive.

We talked for a while, trading notes on our mutual friends. A few were dead, and others were locked up or crazy. "I got out just in time," he said quietly. "The business got too vicious. There was an undercurrent of treachery." He looked wistfully off across the cabin, and tears welled up in his eyes.

"Thank God for my old lady," he said. "She's the one who made me go straight. She gave me the ultimatum."

"That's incredible," I said. "I'm amazed. You actually quit the dope business?"

"Absolutely," he replied. "It was either that or go up in flames. It got so I couldn't even trust my family."

"Your wife?" I asked. "She was always an evil bitch."

"No," he said. "It's her brother. He's crazy on speed. Twice!" he muttered. "Twice he tried to kill me."

I shrugged. "These things happen," I said. "Many have been killed, as you know."

"Yeah," he rasped. "But I have to meet the pig tonight, at the airport, and pay off some money I owe him. There may be trouble," he said, bashing his fist into his palm. "Can you help me out on this one?"

"What?" I said. "Are you crazy? You want me to go out and fight?"

"No violence," he said. "I can handle the payoff by myself. Just take this stuff and meet me at the La Cantina bar in about 10 minutes." He lifted one of the black leather cases into my lap. "These are my maps and my instruments. I don't want to be carrying them if I have any trouble at the gate." . . . Which happened, almost immediately after we came up out of the passenger chute. Two men who appeared to be

Spanish grabbed Julian, who was clutching his other map case, and dragged him into the men's room.

It was horrible, but I wanted no part of it. I never even looked back on my way up the hall to La Cantina—where I waited for more than an hour.

When he finally arrived he was frantic to get his hands on the map case. "Thank God!" he shouted. "This is what we wanted. Now let's get out of here."

"Forget it," I said. "We missed the last plane."

"What?" he said. "Are you crazy? There is no last plane in this business." He tossed a hundred-dollar bill on the table for the waitress and shouted again, "Let's go. I have a charter standing by."

Which was true. By sundown we were on a Lear jet into Aspen, and Julian was carving up his map case with a Swiss army knife, jerking packets of fresh green money out of the lining.

"You swine," I said. "What was in that other bag? What did you give those people?"

"Krakatoa cigarettes," he said. "They got a whole case."

"Horrible," I muttered. "You dope fiends are all the same."

July 7, 1986

Lester Maddox Lives

"Contrary to ongoing and recent media reports you will find the Report is well-balanced and completely deferential to the freedoms outlined in the First Amendment."

—Henry E. Hudson, Chairman,
Attorney General's Commission on Pornography

It was calm in the mountains last week. The winter was finally over but summer was not quite with us. The rains came every afternoon, along with the occasional rainbow, and there were lightning storms at night. A local man was convicted in District Court of incest, and another was arrested for harassing women on downtown street corners for what the Aspen Times called "lewd suggestions . . . and obscene, abusive language."

The river was high, there was no moon and the roads were slick with new mud. Even the drunkards stayed home. The bars were empty and the business climate was grim. Nazi Jay went to Reno to find a woman, and Tex went down on his Sportster at 80 mph, ripping the flesh off his arm.

But nobody cared. Not even Ed Bradley, who stayed hunkered down in his condo with a fat young girl from Missouri despite rumors out of New York that CBS was planning to fire 700 people on Monday. But nobody knew who they were; the names would be released at a press conference some time next week, along with the latest ratings.

It was a good week to stay in bed. Some people tried to play golf, but it was hopeless. The course was like a peat bog. The longest and finest approach shots dug two inches into the green like falling bullets, and balls were washed off the fairways by rushing water. The clubhouse bar was closed for the second straight year—this time for reasons of bankruptcy—and the swimming pool was covered with a layer of slimy green fungus.

But it was good to be home, despite the angst and the schizoid weather. The sun would come again, they said—or at least before Labor Day— and the Dow Jones stock market index was making another run at 2,000. Krugerrands were still selling in New York and San Francisco for $349, and in Aspen there was a long waiting list for no-risk, low-level balloon rides at $150 an hour.

The fat boys were finally in charge, and they had their own set of priorities. In Washington, the U.S. Supreme Court upheld the sodomy laws of Georgia, along with the right of local police to make felony arrests in the bedroom of a private home, regardless of probable cause or even a valid warrant.

Ed Meese dropped the second big shoe by releasing his huge and long-awaited "Final Report" of the Attorney General's Commission on Pornography, the leading edge of a new White House–based assault on almost all forms of sex in America except the act of procreation.

It was a good week for preachers. As the Falwells and Swaggarts jabbered about vengeance, and as Pat Robertson counseled vengeance with a smile, Big Ed just laid back and said it didn't really matter to him how things got done, just as long as the vengeance was total. He had a list, he said—since 1964, when he worked as a deputy prosecutor in Oakland and Berkeley, during the time of the Great Confusion.

The court's decision and the Meese report were applauded by hard-core evangelicals—an essentially fascist constituency—and also by former two-term Georgia Governor Lester Maddox, a longtime foe of Sodomites.

Maddox is a legendary bigot who once tried to keep black people out of his cheap fried-chicken restaurant by passing out hickory ax handles to white customers, as they came through the door to eat supper.

No more wretched example of high-powered White Trash exists in America today than Lester Maddox. When the Great Scorer comes to write against Lester's name, he will get the same chance as Knute Rockne. There will be no talk about whether he won or lost but how he played the game. And there will be a special dung heap in the low-rent section of hell for that brute.

Maddox came out of retirement, as it were, to denounce sodomy once again and to call for the forced exile "to Cuba or Moscow" of Atlanta TV mogul Ted Turner, president of TBS and several other networks. Turner's sponsorship of The Goodwill Games, a sort of off-year Olympics featuring head-to-head competition between U.S. and Russian athletes, convinced Lester that Turner was in fact a bedrock communist who was working overtime to sell out his own country and the Kingdom of God.

We have all come to live with the fact that Ronald Reagan is more popular now than John Wayne ever dreamed of being. He rides a white stallion and chops wood on Sunday and his wife hates sex and drugs. These things are taken for granted and admired by almost everybody. Reagan's most recent approval rating in the Gallup Poll was 68 percent, the highest figure enjoyed by any president since Gallup went into business and perhaps even higher than George Washington.

These things happen. Tiny Tim was the most popular man in the world at one point; he got married on the Johnny Carson show. The famous bank robber Willie Sutton was a folk hero at the time of his death. And millions worshiped Gorgeous George, the original bull-fruit wrestler who paved the way for Muhammad Ali. . . .

But there is something distinctly different in the idea that Lester Maddox is once again a major voice in national politics, despite his legacy of shame. It is somehow worse than Richard Nixon getting re-elected and moving back into the White House.

Some things are unacceptable, regardless of partisan politics, and the inexorable rise and rebirth of swine like Maddox is one of them. . . . The man would embarrass South Africa. They would probably take away his passport and restrict him to the company of people like Idi Amin or Dr. Joseph Mengele. If Lester Maddox lives, something far better has died.*

July 14, 1986

Sex, Drugs and Rock and Roll

"Let their way be dark and slippery: and let the angel of the Lord persecute them."

—Psalms 35:8

My friend Cromwell just returned from Palm Springs, where he got rich in the windmill business. People call him a wizard now, and he travels first-class at all times. . . . When the thousands of "honored guests" assembled on the deck of the aircraft carrier USS John F. Kennedy for the viewing of the July 4 fireworks in New York Harbor, Cromwell was among them—wearing a black silk suit and chatting amiably with the other guests, as they smiled and sipped champagne.

There are a lot of ways to get invited to White House cocktail parties these days, but being suddenly rich is still the best one. Cromwell is not comfortable in his new role, but he understands the rules and he has a very keen sense of discretion.

* (On July 30, 1985, Maddox announced in Atlanta that he feared he may have contracted AIDS from blood products he was given at a Bahamas cancer clinic.)

He had come back to his home on the mountain in the last week of June, arriving just before dawn with a convoy of four vehicles, two trailers and five motorcycles. They had driven across Utah all night at top speed, running with halogen lights and full radar.

I heard the rumble of their engines when they were still a mile down the valley. It was like the roar of approaching Cigarette boats, or a herd of wild beasts on the veld. By the time I got out on the porch with a shotgun, they were already on me. . . . And then they were zooming past, like a ghost train, without a hint of a flash from the brake lights or the honk of a horn.

I sat on the porch for a while and watched Mars, a red ball hanging low in the sky about 220 degrees south. . . . And then I went back inside and called Pat Buchanan at the White House, but they said he was caught in a traffic jam on the Key Bridge and his breakfast with the president had been canceled.

"Bad business," I said. "I guess this means he's finished."

The woman laughed. "You know better than that," she said. "Mr. Buchanan will outlive us all. He will never be finished."

Which is probably true. Buchanan has bounced back from more tragedies than Irving Fryar and Oil Can Boyd. He has lived in the hot center of national politics for more than 20 years—writing speeches for Agnew and Nixon—and now he is director of communications for the White House and a special assistant to President Reagan. He controls the news, or at least tries to, and he is doing a pretty good job of it.

"Look," he said in a recent interview with a *USA Today* reporter. "It's a Reagan revolution. We're going to engage and engage and engage the adversary on issue after issue. That's the way you're eventually going to prevail."

There are bonfires on a lot of hillsides tonight, the sound of drums and wild hooting, people with serious scores to settle muttering at each other in the darkness. The yahoos are out there, and they think their time has come.

Cromwell agreed, when we had lunch the next day at the Tavern. He had abandoned all hope for traditional politics, and was preparing to leave the country for 10 years. "Ed Meese will be running the country until 1996," he said. "The climate will be ugly for everybody."

We agreed on this, and drank wine for several more hours. Just before we left, to ride back up the mountain on his new 4-wheel ATC, the Federal Express man arrived with a package for me.

"This is a heavy sucker," he said. "It comes from the Department of Justice, and this label says it's pornographic material."

"That's right," I said. "It's the new Meese Report. This is one of the first copies off of the press."

"You evil sot," he snarled. "I know this stuff. They should have locked you up a long time ago."

He laughed harshly. But then he started to yell when Tex jerked him up by the belt and dragged him off to the back room, bending him down by the neck.

The place was almost empty at the time, and the bartender paid no attention. One of the women got hysterical, but it was over in a matter of seconds.

There is an old and baleful axiom among smart lawyers that says "The weakest link in any civil-rights case is usually the defendant." Some will say "always the defendant," but that pushes the limits of cynicism.

In any case, the rule was back in the news last week when X-rated film starlet Traci Lords allegedly confessed to Los Angeles police investigators that she was 15 years old when she made the first of her recent string of big-money sex films.

The news sent a rumble of bad craziness through the pornographic film industry. The last thing they needed was to hear that one of their hottest young stars was in fact a runaway with a false ID. It is a felony in many states to use a minor in pornography. A Colorado couple was recently sentenced to 10 years in federal prison for selling lewd photographs of their children through the mail.

No sympathy was expressed for these people—not even in the foulest massage parlors or the all-night Loop joints below Broadway, where you can lock yourself in a closet and feed quarters into a steel slit, at 40 seconds a hit.

Ten dollars will not last you very long, at the Loops. The films are extremely short, and there is no plot. But they are generally harmless: Violence is not a popular theme with the Loop crowd, and neither is child pornography. Raw sex at high speed is what these people want for their quarters. They are not into flogging and pederasty. There is not enough time for it.

The indulgence of a full-bore criminal perversion is not an idle thing. It requires a deeper commitment—and an element of madness—that most tourists and salesmen don't really need, if all they want to see is a standard-brand middle-class orgy.

The Meese Report is very hard on these people, however. The panel recommends that all doors be removed from what they called "peep-show booths"—the Loops—so that "occupants" can be clearly seen, and observed by the general public, or at least the other customers, and discouraged from sexual activity.

It is a shrewd plan—for some jungle crossroads in Malaysia—but the concept of ripping off doors to prevent sex is going to be a hard one to sell in the more civilized jurisdictions. It might be OK for the bus stations, but not for the country clubs.

July 21, 1986

Welcome to the Tunnel

"We are in a tunnel. It's been rather dark, and will stay that way for quite a while."

—Hugh Hefner, *Playboy*

Well . . . the president took his drug test the other day, or at least that's what they tell us, and although the final results are still hazy because of possible complications arising from his urological medication, it is safe to assume that he passed. If not, he will get another chance.

Don't worry about it. There are a lot of strong drugs being used in the White House these days, as always, but they are not the ones The Gipper was being tested for. Traces of lithium or powerful antibiotics may turn up, but there will be no mention of crack, ecstasy or black Lebanese hashish.

The president uses only *legal* drugs, the products of a multibillion-dollar industry that at one time or another has peddled almost everything from pure cocaine hydrochloride to thalidomide. There is a human growth hormone on the market today—by prescription only—that could pump Nancy Reagan up to the size of John Madden in about three months, if that's what she really wants.

There are drugs available that would grow a thick mat of hair, or even quills like a porcupine, on the chest of Raquel Welch in less time than it took Luther Burbank to grow a crop of mutant tomatoes behind his house in Santa Rosa.

All things are possible, if you know the right doctors—or even the wrong ones, for that matter, like the quacks who run experiments in state prisons on convicted sex offenders, hoping to render them harmless. The genitals of a wild boar can be withered down to where they will fit nicely into a one-ounce bar jigger, if necessary. . . . A small Mexican child can be made to look and behave like William "Refrigerator" Perry of the Chicago Bears.

Not everybody is in favor of these blind leaps into medical and physiological darkness—but there are always a few who will persist in pushing the limits of science, in the name of some greater good, and it is hard to keep them under control. It is well to remember that they laughed at Thomas Edison, and that Albert Einstein was regarded for most of his life as a useless malcontent.

It is also worth noting that a new F-111 attack bomber costs $30 million, or about twice the price of the recently proposed "electric security fence" around the U.S. Capitol in Washington, to make it safe against Libyan "death squads" and fanatics from the Islamic Jihad. '

Nobody mentioned that one for a while, but it is presumably still on hold—the back burner, as it were—awaiting action by Congress. The terrorist menace has eased off momentarily, in deference to newer and meaner things like the War Against Communism in Nicaragua, the War On Drug Lords In Bolivia and the War Against Almost Everything in Mexico except tacos.

There is also the War on Drugs, the War on Sex and the continuing War on Democrats—all conducted with considerable style and vigor from the action-packed War Rooms in the White House, where Pat Buchanan is definitely earning his salary as communications director.

There is not much doubt about who has seized the high ground these days. These people have been doing their homework on just about every issue in sight except the genuinely disastrous national debt, which is mounting into the trillions. . . . But The Gipper is not concerned about that one; he will be long gone from the Big House by the time it hits, and solutions will be presumably left in the hands of lesser, queasier men—like George Bush, Bob Dole or even the Rev. Pat Robertson.

Jack Kemp might even want to take a whack at it. Ho, ho. That should be interesting. The whole Potomac River will boil like the Lake of Fire when that silly little hooter tries to bring his Trickle-Down, Supply-Side snake oil to the reality of the Pentagon spending a half-million dollars a minute on national defense for the next year.

If you think Jimmy Carter was funny, wait until you see Rep. Kemp ride out to do battle with a multibillion-dollar national deficit on a budget that would have shamed Herbert Hoover.

Even David Stockman calls it gibberish, and he was there when they originally cooked it up. Even a teen-age crack dealer can tell you that there is no way to cut revenues and triple expenditures without getting into the kind of problems that croaked Billy Sol Estes and the Franklin National Bank, along with the utterly bankrupt governments of Brazil, Argentina and Haiti.

But so what? The Gipper will be exercising his white stallion up on the mountain above Santa Barbara when those bills come due in Washington. . . . And he may be gone even sooner than we think: The hard-rockers who will be running the GOP long after Dutch has gone off to the great rancho in the sky are looking far down the road—toward another decade of leaky-fisted Republican dominance—and one of the things they see is a routine clause somewhere in the finer print of the 25th Amendment (and never mind the 22nd) that makes it mandatory for any vice president who succeeds a sitting president for emergency reasons to take office before Jan. 20, in order to be legally eligible to run for two terms in office.

That will be a little loophole—for The Gipper as well as for George Bush and the boys in the back room. Without a real candidate to follow Reagan's truly awesome act in the campaign of '88, they will be sorely tempted to short-cut the political process by creating a medical emergency before Christmas and putting George in charge during a moment of national fear, which is probably the only way he will get there.

Maybe not, but it is as good a bet as anything else on the political horizon right now. The Gipper might resist, for a while: he is feeling mean and he still has scores to settle in these last two lame-duck years— but so did John Wayne, and he also retired early.

We are in for some fast weeks in the passing lane. Hugh Hefner is right about the tunnel, and Ed Meese is still with us. In a generation of swine, the one-eyed pig is king.

August 11, 1986

Strictly Business

Phoenix—I was sitting by the pool at the Arizona Biltmore, waiting for a call from Gordon Liddy, and the big digital display sign above the cabanas said it was 104 at 3:16 P.M. The boy behind the bar was sprinting around like a big poodle, whipping up a corned beef on rye. I was drinking a gin and tonic and squirting sweat from every pore. It was a relatively mild afternoon on the desert, but to me it felt like death.

Meanwhile, on a small black and white TV behind the bar, another Local Boy Makes Good story was unfolding in front of our eyes. William Rehnquist—formerly of 1817 Palmcroft Drive, Phoenix—was hunching slowly but surely toward confirmation by the Senate as the next chief justice of the United States.

It was a big day for the Biltmore neighborhood. Just down the street, around the corner from where Paul Harvey lives, is the home of Sandra Day O'Connor, another one-time Phoenix lawyer who was recently appointed to the U.S. Supreme Court.

Down another nearby lane is the ranch-style home of Nancy Reagan's mother, Edith Davis. And not far away is the old Kleindienst place, where Richard used to live. . . . That was before Richard Nixon appointed him to be the 68th attorney general of the United States—the same job now held by Ed Meese, who comes from Oakland.

The old gang is scattered now, gone off in many directions. But the flag still flies in Phoenix—or at least in Scottsdale where the newest Big Kid on the block is G. Gordon Liddy, formerly of Washington, D.C.

Gordon is listed in the greater metropolitan Phoenix phone directory, 7909 E. Joshua Tree Lane, and the message on his answering machine leaves no doubt about who really ran the Watergate operation. The instructions are very precise: "We are gone now," it says. "Speak quickly and clearly. If you hear six beeps, your message has been erased."

The age of Rehnquist was about to begin. On Thursday he was endorsed by a 13-5 vote of the Judiciary Committee, despite last-minute revelations by his former personal physician that only a few years ago he was dangerously addicted to what, in the trade, they call "downers."

That is not a bad rap in Phoenix, or even in Washington. A lot of people get into downers; there are worse things—there is crack, there is Black Tar Heroin, there is PCP; if nothing else seems to work, you can always load up on a big syringe of Ketamine, a powerful animal tranquilizer for large cats and medium-sized primates, like chimps, gibbons and baboons.

It depends what you want. The judge—known as "Bill" to his friends in Phoenix—wanted only to get relief from a chronic back pain, which led to serious insomnia and caused him to need pills.

So what? There are some days when we all need pills. Rehnquist is presumably human, and if he needs a strong drug to sleep peacefully at night, who is going to tell him he shouldn't have it? Not me.

On Friday morning I had to fly to Toronto for a political meeting. The 10 o'clock flight was full, but I made emergency arrangements for a smoking window seat in the rear of the first-class section. There was some ugliness involved; we had to bump a senior airline executive and tempers flared for a while, but in the end it all worked out.

I was no sooner settled into my seat when I was joined by a man named Squane who said he worked for the Justice Department—the Federal Bureau of Prisons, in fact, and his job was to "acquire sites" for new federal prison facilities, which he said were desperately needed.

"We are already running 51 percent over capacity," he said. "The situation is getting out of control. We have twice as many people in the federal prison system today than we did five years ago." He nodded solemnly. "In 1981 we had 24,000," he said. "Today we have 41,000, and we're running out of space."

The idea seemed to depress him, and he hunkered down in his seat. "And it's going to get a lot worse before it gets better," he said. "Starting next year, there won't be any such thing as *parole* anymore. When we get the final report from the Federal Sentencing Commission, going to prison will be automatic for anybody who gets accused of anything except jaywalking."

He asked the stewardess for another large glass of wine. "You think it's bad now?" he said with a baleful stare off into the distance. "Well, you wait until all of a sudden there's no parole, no probation, no appeal. . . . By this time next year we're going to have mandatory sentencing guidelines for all federal judges. . . . They'll be like robots, just punching out the numbers on a card: One joint? Three years. Three grams? Nine years. . . . One pound? Forty years and a flogging." He paused and stared down at his hands.

I felt embarrassed for him, but the feeling passed quickly. "Wait a minute," I said. "Let's get a grip on ourselves, here." I tapped him knowingly on the elbow. "It was *you,* Charley. . . . It wasn't the goddamn stork that arrested all these people. No. It was you—you and that monster, Ed Meese."

I tapped him again, a bit harder. "How much money do you make?" I asked him.

He stared at me.

"Never mind," I said. "It's not important. All I really want to talk to you about right now is what kind of money you people are paying for the acreage you'll need for all these new prisons."

"We're flexible," he said. "We have plenty of money. And what we don't buy, we can always condemn and seize under eminent domain." He shook his head sadly. "I'd hate to see it come to that," he said. "But we really have no choice. It's a national tragedy, and we can't let this scum run around loose, like they do now. The time has come. They must be eliminated."

"Not necessarily," I said. "I have a few acres out in the Rockies that I think you people could use. It would make a fine prison."

"Why not?" he said. "If you call me in Washington on Monday, I think we can do business."

"Wonderful," I said. "I can provide a nice environment for these criminals. We can put them to work, restore their self-esteem."

He agreed, and when the plane finally landed in Chicago we shook hands. . . . and that's how I got in the prison business. *Res ipsa loquitur.*

August 18, 1986

Midnight in the Desert

It was midnight when I got back to Phoenix; the temperature was 103 and there was no sign of life at the baggage carousel. An elderly man with a whisk broom told me the conveyor belt had been shut down earlier in the evening by a bomb scare.

No baggage had come down the chute since the emergency, he said in broken Spanish. It had all been "torn up by the dogs," then taken out and dumped in the Salt River.

I took the news calmly and went upstairs to the airport lounge, which was still open and doing a lively business. People who looked like they hadn't been on an airplane since 1966 were slumped together on rattan couches, far back in the dim-lit corners. The bartender was too busy to talk, so I sat down next to a small man with a spade beard who was wearing a white cashmere jumpsuit. He was reading the sports page of the *Arizona Republic,* laughing distractedly to himself and tapping a gold Ronson lighter on the bar.

He smiled at me. "Are you ready for Herschel?" he said. "Are you prepared for a whole new world?"

"You bet," I muttered. "What do you have in mind?" I was not in a mood for subtleties; my luggage had just been officially destroyed by wild dogs.

My new friend was excited about the recent acquisition of former Heisman Trophy winner Herschel Walker by the Dallas Cowboys. He said it made Dallas a cinch for the Super Bowl, that Herschel would tear up the league and gain 2,000 yards.

"Ridiculous," I said. "He'll be lucky to gain 500. Dallas won't even win their division."

"What?" he screamed. "Are you crazy? Walker is bigger than Jim Brown and faster than Bob Hayes. He will stomp them like bugs. I'd bet my wife on it."

"Nevermind your wife," I said. "What else do you have? I'm in the real estate business. Do you have any property?"

"You fool," he said. "My wife is the most beautiful woman in Scottsdale." He rolled his eyes up at the ceiling. "What do you *want?*" he moaned. "I have property, I have money, I have a gold Mercedes 600 downstairs. . . . As Jesus is my witness, brother, I am the richest man south of Camelback Road." He gestured wildly toward the exit.

"You see all those parking lots out there, brother? I own them. I make so much money that I have to carry it home in buckets every night."

I understood. It was like dealing with the Oak Ridge Boys. "OK," I said. "Let's do it." I reached into my satchel and pulled out a packet of new Canadian money. "Here," I said. "Take this and give me your car keys." I reached out to shake his hand. "Walker will not gain 666 yards this year. Take it or leave it."

He grasped my hand eagerly. "You're on," he said. "Herschel will gain more than Walter Payton and Eric Dickerson put together. He will humiliate Mike Ditka. He will make Tony Dorsett obsolete."

We haggled for a while, then he called the bartender over to witness a signed document. His name was Eddie and I got the feeling he had been here before. He didn't flinch as I traded my packet of Canadian money for the signed title to the big Benz.

Eddie took a while to get the paper work together. My new business associate's name was Jack, he said. Jack Parker.

He got a chuckle out of that one, but it matched the name on the Benz title, so I kept a straight face and asked the waitress for a fork, which I bent into the U-joint position and folded casually into the palm of my right hand.

Jack seemed not to notice. "What kind of work are you in?" he asked. "You don't look like a real estate agent." he chuckled again. "Are you a Fed?" he asked. "Is that it?"

At that point Eddie came back and said I owed another $5,500 toward the Benz—even at four to one.

I lifted my fist and showed him the tines of the fork.

"That figures," I said. "Bring me a credit card voucher—a blank one." He fixed me with a sullen glance for a moment, then shuffled away. When he came back with the ticket, I laid it face down on the bar, on top of my platinum American Express card, and asked him for a ball-point pen, which I used like a rolling pin to produce an acceptable imprint. . . . It was an old massage-parlor trick that I learned many years ago on some half-mad night in the downtown TraveLodge.

Jack had no objections. The contract called for us to meet again, here in the bar, on the final day of the season, and one of us would walk away with both the money and the car—depending on Herschel Walker's rushing stats for the season.

"Forget it," I said. "He won't get 500 yards. They'll break his knees. He'll be crippled by Halloween."

Jack stared down at the big leather-mounted Benz key that he was rolling around in his fingers. "I was right," he muttered. "You are a Fed, aren't you?"

"Nonsense," I said. "I am just another businessman, like yourself."

"What kind of business?" asked Eddie.

"This kind," I said. "I am a professional gambler, and I will see you in December." I stood up and left a large tip. "It's getting late," I said to Jack. "I'm going to the Biltmore. Can I give you a ride anywhere?"

"Not really," Jack replied. "I have business in the other direction." He smiled pleasantly and stood up. "Damnation," he said. "I really wish you could meet my wife. She loves gambling."

He followed me out to the escalator and explained that I would find all the insurance and warranty papers in the glove compartment. "Don't worry," he said. "We'll be in touch."

I believed him. They killed Don Bolles in this town, and it is a long run from Phoenix to the Colorado state line. What now? I wondered. Just walk fast and stare straight ahead.

The car was exactly where he said it would be, a huge gold 600 with smoked windows. The key fit perfectly, and within minutes I was rumbling into the parking lot of the Biltmore.

The next morning I drove the Benz out to Wickenburg, where I traded it straight across for a new Jeep wagon and then drove north at top speed. It seemed like the right thing to do, given the utterly crazy circumstances. By sundown I was past Flagstaff. Nobody was chasing me and my mood was getting better with every mile. It was Saturday night in America, and I felt like a native son.

August 25, 1986

Down to a Sunless Sea

There are news reports out of Alaska about rampant alcohol abuse on the North Slope.

Where will it end? First there is crack on Wall Street, and now we have whole villages full of Eskimos turning their backs on the outside world and holing up by themselves to drink whiskey for weeks at a time.

Nobody knows how to cope with it. The price of oil has fallen so low that the Eskimos no longer have money, so they are retreating into booze. Five or six of them will load a whole pickup truck with cheap whiskey and go off to some shack on the far end of a remote ice floe and get hopelessly, savagely drunk.

This is a new development in the Klondike, or at least it is just getting noticed. Nancy Reagan has not gone after the drunkards yet, and there will probably not be enough time for it. The War on Booze ended 55 years ago, with the repeal of the Volstead Act. Whiskey is legal now, and the era of Prohibition is viewed by most historians as a wrong and unfortunate experiment.

But things are different now: This time the war is on *drugs,* and as the Reagan era winds down, it is taking on all the trappings of a holy war.

On Sunday, the president and his wife will make an unprecedented joint TV appearance, from the White House, for the purpose of "ridding the nation of drugs." It will be an extremely major statement, according to presidential spokesman Larry Speakes, perhaps the heaviest thing since John F. Kennedy's grim speech on the Cuban Missile Crisis.

Well, maybe so. We can only wait and see. They have been trying to shut down the opium dens in Singapore for 3,000 years. Every government since the Chang Dynasty has sworn to crush the opium trade, but nobody has ever made a dent in it. The price of opium is relatively the same today as it was in the year 900 B.C.

Kingdoms fall, empires crumble, powerful nations come and go. . . . But the opium market remains as stable as rice or gold. Nobody questions it; nobody asks why. It is a crop that grows every year in half of the known world and a lot of people want it. They *like* opium. They enjoy smoking it and floating happily into a dream world, and that is a hard habit to argue with.

It is an acquired taste, they say, and I have never had much luck with it. There is a lot of ritual involved, and you are always dealing with foreigners who may or may not take care of you, once the dragon begins to sing. You want to have a lot of disposable income and plenty of free time on your hands before embracing a serious opium habit. It is not a productive drug, as a rule.

But some of the exceptions have been spectacular. The poet Samuel Coleridge was one; he got into opium for a few years and wallowed crazily in the Behavioral Sink—but while he was down there he also wrote the "Rime of the Ancient Mariner" and "Kubla Khan."

> *In Xanadu did Kubla Khan*
> *A stately pleasure dome decree:*
> *Where Alph, the sacred river, ran*
> *Through caverns measureless to man*
> *Down to a sunless sea.*

How's that for a lead, Jack? Yeah. A lot of *sober people* will move instinctively to the back of the bus, to make room for whatever dope fiend wrote that one. Ronald Reagan could live another 200 years and never even dream lines like that. There are some jobs you can't hire out.

If George Bush could find a speech writer who could write like Sam Coleridge, he would hire him immediately and never mind his bad habits. On the fast tracks where you run without brakes, *all* of God's creatures are welcome. Nobody ever asked Gen. MacArthur how he came up with that "Old Soldiers Never Die" speech—yet it ranks with the highest ravings of Coleridge and Poe and whatever king-hell loon wrote the "Book of Revelation."

Perhaps they were all opium eaters. Who knows? It is an essentially benign drug, for those few who can properly afford it; and for the others it will always pose certain legal risks and career problems. Opium was big in the Orient before the invention of the wheel; it has traditionally been an embarrassment to the business community and a foul stain on the social fabric.

But so what? All they do is lie down and smoke. They become giddy and useless—but never violent or dangerous. . . . And it wasn't a gang of opium fiends who bombed Pearl Harbor and burrowed like crazy moles into caves on Iwo Jima, killing 200,000 Americans and countless millions of their own kind.

No. Those were the sober people, the smart crowd. They were Japan's best and brightest. There were no pictures of Tojo lying around on a bamboo mat with an opium pipe on his lips. He was too busy for that kind of foolishness. There were bombs to be dropped and throats to be slit. There was a whole world out there to be conquered; they had no time for opium.

Whatever style of logic may have prevailed in the corridors of the Japanese War Ministry in those years has never been totally explained—but it has never been linked to drugs, like the Nazis, or to any other cheap vice.

It was a need for oil and a lust for power and 10,000 people calling you "sir" and chanting your name like a prayer every time you went out in public.

They all wanted to be *on the team*. It was like doing the Super Bowl Shuffle, along with the Fridge and the rest of the boys. It was dumb, but it worked. . . . And it was not smart, in those days, to argue with anything powerful enough to crush Spain, China and France in less time than it took to age a good bottle of wine.

Dope fiends have always been with us, and they are guilty of many things, but a compulsion to rule the world has rarely been one of them. Power mongers are early risers; opium eaters sleep late. Tojo woke up with the sun, and Hitler was so paranoid that he never slept at all.

The Reagans have a style all their own. They say they sleep well at night. They are both utterly convinced that all drug dealers should be put to death by flogging. Not everybody agrees, but the train is leaving the station, and everybody from Tip O'Neill to Sonny Bono and Sirhan Sirhan is scrambling to get aboard. The fat is in the fire.

September 8, 1986

The Turk Comes to TV News

The whole CBS network went up for grabs last week, and it made a lot of people nervous. ABC and NBC had already been sold off in the past year to Big Business cost-cutters, and now the legendary monarch of the TV news business seemed on the verge of going belly up and being sold for salvage.

It was an ominous prospect. CBS has been the dominant force in TV news almost since the first days of television, when Edward R. Murrow could take on the accountants and the profit-takers and still get two hours of prime time for a prize-winning news special. Murrow's integrity and intensity are revered by TV executives today, but at the time of his best work he was regarded as a prima donna and a troublemaker.

Yet it is mainly on Murrow's reputation—along with heroes like Walter Cronkite, Eric Sevareid, Hughes Rudd and currently Bill Moyers—that CBS has traditionally been viewed as the champion of TV news.

This is no longer true. CBS net profits were only $27.4 million last year, down from $212.4 million the year before, and these numbers annoy the stockholders. In the era of Reaganomics it is not chic to hold low-net stocks. Anything short of 20 percent might be sniggered at by the Joneses.

The news is not seen as a good investment these days—except by those of us in the trade—and I am not the only one who broods on it. Sometime around noon on a bright afternoon last week I seized the phone and called another member of the tribe—Ed Turner, executive vice president of CNN in Atlanta—for a professional consultation.

HST: I've been a believer in CBS for all these years.

ET: Hell, I used to work there. . . . In the old days there were just three networks, and really there were only two because ABC was not a news factor. . . . Up until the '70s, you had two networks providing news programming. They were doing a half hour in the evening, but they were also doing one or two hours in the morning of real news. . . . Now there is so much more competition, because you have independents doing their programming, you have the cable movie outlets and you have the big and growing monster called VCR, where you don't even have to watch TV as a vehicle for your movie. You have more radio stations than ever before, you've got more magazines.

HST: How are you doing so well down there, then?

ET: Because we specialize. We provide a very perishable product.

It's called news. The other three entertainment networks have elected, and wisely so, to compete for those who want to be entertained.

HST: Why is "60 Minutes" rated so high?

ET: Because there's always a place for a damn good news program.

HST: What about "West 57th Street"?

ET: It is news that is edited and produced in a real zippy, snappy fashion.

HST: What about "20/20"?

ET: It's a more ponderous version of "60 Minutes" with Barbara Walters' celebrity interviews. She's done very well at what she does, but it's not news in the traditional sense.

HST: How about "Nightline"?

ET: "Nightline" is hard news. It's first-rate.

HST: Why did they cut it from an hour to half hour?

ET: The affiliates weren't carrying it at an hour and it was dying in the ratings in that second half hour.

HST: News is a drag on the economics of TV?

ET: News if it is properly handled by the managers can make a lot of money. At your local station it is probably the most profitable thing they do. At the network, it can go either way. NBC says it will lose $50 million on its news budget this year . . . This "1986" program, the NBC version of "60 Minutes," if you can believe this, this is their figure: They spent $21 million trying to come up with the format. I'd have to stand there until I rot and throw money out the window . . .

HST: I couldn't spend that much money on booze, drugs or anything else. . . . Is that Linda Ellerbee's?

ET: No, she's on a new show on ABC. It starts in a couple of weeks. "1986" has been on for a while, that's with Roger Mudd and Connie Chung.

HST: If they lose money, why are they starting new news shows?

ET: Going back a few years, for a long time, and by that I mean, half a dozen years, "60 Minutes" was a losing proposition. It could not draw audience if they'd pay people to watch it. Then they moved it to after the football game on Sunday night. And from that moment on, it has become the most profitable thing CBS does.

HST: Why is that? I know why I watch it. Those are my two things, football and news.

ET: Just what you said: You like news, you like football. It's at a comfortable time of the week when people are settling down in front of the TV set.

HST: Will network people be hired away for local stations?

ET: The local stations are getting more and more into network news operations and that is a major problem faced by the networks today. . . . The trend is for local stations to send their own person to that big story and satellite it back home so they show their own journalistic skill and they build their own image. For the 1988 Democratic Convention, there have already been request for parking for 280 trucks for individual television stations. . . . The technology has gotten so mobile to hit these new satellites that they don't need the networks like they used to. They can go do it themselves and look like heroes in their hometowns.

HST: Is this good news for us?

ET: Oh, yeah. Absolutely it is. The more the better for the viewer. The more volume you've got, the more opportunity you've got for someone like Bill Moyers to come along . . . It's a training ground for a lot of kids.

HST: So what do we have here?

ET: Your local news is going to get better, your network news is about as good as it going to get, the three network stars will remain stars, they'll have healthy audiences, but the action is no longer in those three shops in New York City.

HST: What are you people going to do?

ET: Live from everywhere. If the people explaining understand what the hell they're talking about, it doesn't matter how deep their voices are, it doesn't matter how pretty they are. If they don't understand what they're talking about they're going to be boring and they'll lose their audience and lose their jobs. The need for real journalists who can talk about what they know is going to grow as never before.

September 15, 1986

Bull Market on The Strip

Las Vegas—The dawn does not come up like thunder at the Stardust Sports and Race Book on Las Vegas Boulevard.

At six in the morning the hotel lobby is empty except for a handful of what they call "early crawlers" on The Strip—but the casino is humming with action.

The big boards never close in the Stardust. A wall of betting boards and TV sets half the size of a football field will give you the numbers on everything from the fourth race at Pimlico to the Bramble-Rosario fight and the baleful notation that Northwestern is 250-1 to make the Rose Bowl.

Bramble is 3-2 over Rosario—a good bet—and Camacho is 3-2 over Edwards.

So what? Who needs that kind of gambling?

A 3-2 bet is a hot tip when it comes from E.F. Hutton or the Chicago Board of Trade, but at this hour of the morning in the Stardust Sports and Race Lounge, anything less than 5 or 6 to 1 will cause sniggering in the front-row seats and cause people to slink out the side exit doors—and into the hot strange glare of the early morning sun.

No cabs are waiting out there on that lonely curb. A terrible windstorm flogged the boulevard last night and sent most of the smart people home early. The wind blasted palm fronds across the parking lot and at Circus Circus and blew me off a 12-foot hurricane fence on the far rim of the new parking lot at the Las Vegas Hilton.

A small man wearing a "Death From Above" T-shirt approached me near the Gai Mu poker pit and asked if I could put him onto some action.

I ignored him, but a man walking behind me reached down into his boot and zapped him with a 50,000-volt Nova XR-5000 stun gun.

The Soldier of Fortune boys are breaking down their trade show and exhibition at the Sahara, which we can see from the 18th floor of the Hilton. The pugil-stick tournament has ended, the terrorism seminars have dispersed, and the ammunition is mostly used up.

I went over to do my last-minute shopping. At most conventions, you end with up with vinyl notebooks, stick-on I.D. tags and retractable ball-point pens. Things here are different. Some of the souvenirs are expensive, and it can be dangerous to leave them behind. On the other hand, you can spend a lot of time in the Green Room at the airport if the metal detector is working, and even after you get out, there will always be red marks next to your name.

With this in mind, I spread out my purchases on the king-sized bed and tried to decide how they should be packed:

BAGGAGE MANIFEST

1. Three dozen tracers, some for the .357, others for the .44 Magnum. They cause a huge yellow streak to erupt from the front of your weapon. The blue-tipped ones are incendiaries.

2. 100 assorted Delta Press stickers, bearing legends including "Rob Someone Else," "Face Me—Face Death," "If You Come Through This Door You Will Be Killed/Si Vienes Por Esta Puerta Te Mato," and "God's Favorite Caliber—.44 Magnum."

3. One Galco International shoulder holster for Model 39 Smith and Wesson or the Beretta 9mm auto.

4. One authentic Rommel Field Afrika Korps hat, khaki, silk-lined.

5. 20 red aerial pyrotechnic flares, hand-held, burn 6.5 seconds.

6. Two books: "Get Even: The Complete Book of Dirty Tricks" and "Your Conduct in Combat Under the Law of War."

7. Two AlMar One Zero Special Forces/SOD knives, 9-inch blades.

8. One Soldier of Fortune 10th Anniversary poster, inscribed "Dear Hunter, Blow One Away For Me—Robert K. Brown."

9. One 100 percent cotton Rip-Stop Special Forces battle dress uniform, Vietnam leaf pattern.

10. One Steyr SSG P-II sniper rifle, 26-inch heavy barrel with synthetic stock of ABS "CYCOLAC" and Kahles steel-tube ZF84 6X scope.

11. One Dark Invader 3010 Night Vision System, including infrared spot illuminator/image enhancer with relay lens for 35mm.

12. One Soldiers of Fortune World Tour jacket, black nylon, extra large, with globe emblem and list of countries—Afghanistan, Angola, Burma, Cambodia, Costa Rica, Cuba, El Salvador, Grenada, Guatemala, Honduras, Israel, Korea, Laos, Lebanon, Nicaragua, Pakistan, South Africa, Thailand, Vietnam and Zimbabwe—where Soldiers of Fortune have "intervened."

13. One hardened steel spike—"looks like a pin—your best friend in a tight spot."

14. Two boxes of .45 ExCaliber wax pellets with brass cases—"a safe, easy and inexpensive alternative to real ammo."

15. Six Riot Buster smoke grenades, 2 inches in diameter, 4 inches long.

16. One 6 oz. can Envelope Compromise Spray, for detection of letter bombs.

17. One 120-foot nylon GI Critical Application rope.

18. One navy blue patch with gold-embossed lettering and emblem: "United States Secret Service."

19. One Ruger P-85 semiautomatic 9mm double-action pistol, with Sai case.

20. Two chrome octagon Samurai chains, each 21½ inches long.

21. One solid leather core hand-painted Cattle Baron Leather Co. bullwhip, 12 feet.

22. One sterling silver Revenge ring, skull motif.

23. One Bruggemann & Brand T-3F nylon triple canopy low altitude troop parachute, 22x13x10-inch pack, 330-lb. capacity, for tactical warfare.

24. One European stiletto, stainless steel blade, 4⅞ inches closed.

25. Aerospatiale AACP short-range anti-tank rocket, fully guidable, 4-second quiet time, low muzzle velocity, particularly effective in urban combat conditions, with Kevlar firing tube.

I finally got it packed, but the bell captain refused to touch it. Even my old friend Gene Kilroy from the Ali camp, now a ranking casino executive at the Hilton, wouldn't help. But just then Ken O'Brien hit Wesley Walker to beat Miami to overtime. The Race Book paid off in new hundreds and got me a limo to the airport.

September 22, 1986

The South African Problem

The boys in the Big House are rolling high this week. President Reagan—at the urging of unspecified "close advisers"—has vetoed a bill out of Congress, HR4868, which would impose real economic and political sanctions by the U.S. against the clearly atavistic nation of South Africa.

The details of the proposed sanctions are not especially harsh, but that is no longer the point.

The point is that Reagan has chosen to veto a bill that has wide popular support and heavy majorities in both the Senate and the House of Representatives—despite the distinct possibility that Congress might muster the necessary two-thirds majority to override.

The House, in fact, is expected to repudiate the White House Monday, and the Senate—which voted 84–14 for the bill in August—will have to vote once again later this week.

A two-thirds majority in both houses is required to override a presidential veto—which is normally a hard nut to make—but in the case of South Africa the House is already conceded and 20 senators will have to change their votes in public, for reasons that will be hard to explain.

This is, after all, an election year—and 22 Republican senators are running for re-election. Fourteen of them are first-termers and at least half of these are in trouble—along with a lot of other people, including a handful of businesslike Democrats.

The vote in the Senate will be interesting. It has been since the first vote endorsing the rape of Nanking that 20 senators have rolled over like weasels and exposed their softest parts, at the whim of a lame-duck president.

It will be an ugly scene and it will happen on live TV. They will be led down the aisle like fat eunuchs, each with his own foul excuse.

"I was drunk when I voted the first time—they told me I needed the black vote. . . . The president is a beautiful man, no matter what they say about my fund-raising problems."

These sleazy tales will abound, and a few will test the limits of contempt and human tolerance.

But it will still *be* hard to turn 20 of them all at once. That is an exercise in long numbers and hubris that we rarely see in politics these days.

It has been since the time of the Sun King and Cato the Elder that politicians have been so systematically humiliated in public.

This is no minor issue, no boil on the national flesh that will disappear with time and herbal medicine. The South African problem will not go away anytime soon. Those people are riding the tiger down there, and it is one of those rides that does not have the look of longevity. The whole nation will be gone, like Rhodesia, by 1988. . . .

And after that we will have those people on our hands, two or three generations of crazed Afrikaners who got chased off the continent by native black people. They will arrive by the tens of thousands at airports like Miami, Atlanta and Dallas, with letters of passage and crates full of burp guns and Krugerrands. Some will push north to Montana and Coeur d'Alene, Idaho, to hook up with the Aryan Nation and other white-supremacist cults. By the turn of the century—if Reagan has his way—expatriate Afrikaners will control huge sections of the American West, from the Black Hills all the way to the ocean.

Many people are nervous about this, but Ronald Reagan is apparently not one of them. He will be 88 years old by the time these curs come to power, and they will revere him as a living god. Nobody named Reagan will ever have trouble in the Western United States for as long as the land remains intact—or until the time of the Great Earthquake, when California slides into the sea.

This kind of talk might seem crazy or paranoid in Boston or Washington, but in places like Scottsdale and Bozeman and Carson City, it is no joke at all. There is talk in Texas of settling a million or more displaced Afrikaners in a long strip along the Rio Grande, as a buffer against the Mexicans.

The concept of Ronald Reagan as a master Mole for the Aryan Nation has not taken hold yet, in the centers of political power. Even his closest people still see him as a profoundly talented old man from Hollywood who will go down in history as perhaps the greatest salesman of his time. . . . But not as a philosopher-king or a serious political thinker, like all of those other presidents that he frequently quotes.

They view him more or less as they would view Willie Loman if he had wandered through the looking glass and became president of the United States.

In the meantime, Campaign '86 is limping along to what looks like a gambler's finish. The numbers have hung stubbornly at 50–50 all summer, but now there are rumors of a drift. The smart money is said to be leaning Republican in some of the critical Senate races like Colorado, Missouri and Florida.

Nobody in the business really believes these things. Polls are mainly the result of crude hypes and baffling contradictions among local wizards and poll-takers. . . . But that is the nature of politics, and if you believe the smart money these days you will bet 51–49 Republican.

There is another school of thought that says the upcoming Senate vote on HR4868 could change everything—that the certain humiliation that will hang like the shag of a dead animal on the necks of some of the weaker and more vulnerable GOP Senate candidates might cause them to be seen as shameless castrati in their own states.

Threatened incumbents like Paula Hawkins in Florida, Mack Mattingly in Georgia and the hapless dupe Slade Gorton in Washington will be *forced* to change their votes by presidential fiat.

But three is not enough. The boys in the Big House still need 20 new ones—in addition to the 14 hard-core GOP right-wingers who have already voted for it.

Fourteen is different from 34, and that extra 20 is going to be hard. A smart gambler would weep publicly about the terrible power of The President, and then look for something like an 8– or 9–1 bet against him. The real odds are not quite that high, and there are people in Washington who will tell you that he might even lose this one—which is not so strange a notion. Call it a gift at 3– or even 2–1 override, and a sporting proposition at even money.

September 29, 1986

Loose Cannon on the Deck

Presidential spokesman Larry Speakes said the United States has asked the Soviets to join in a news blackout during the Summit talks. . . . "The President believes that this is not the time for public rhetoric but, instead for private talk."

—Denver Post, October 4, 1986

Well . . . maybe so. Iceland is said to be a good place for private talk, and the Russians will probably go along with the news blackout scheme, if only because Reagan wants it.

Why not? The President appears to have serious things on his mind.

He is in a noticeably ugly mood, and not even his good friends in Washington are eager to send him off to Reykjavik to deal mano-a-mano behind closed doors with the cruel and devious Gorbachev.

Too many things have gone wrong, they say, and Dutch is not taking it well. . . . There was another botch in the Big House last week, or at least that's how it looked on TV. The traditional last-minute rollover did not happen when the Senate voted on the South Africa sanctions bill on Thursday, and the result was a high-profile public humiliation for the Reagan administration.

The final 78–21 vote to override the presidential veto was 13 short of what Reagan needed to avoid a major political embarrassment. It was the first loss of his career on a major issue, and the defeat was made more cruel when it came at the hands of the Republican-dominated Senate, where he has won almost everything else.

The numbers were so humbling, in fact, that they raised certain questions as to whether the long-running "Reagan Revolution" has finally come to a fork in the road—or if the whole thing is a high-stakes Ponzi scheme designed to maintain GOP control of the Senate in the '86 elections, almost exactly a month from today.

There is nobody in the White House or anywhere else for that matter who remembers the last time Ronald Reagan lost a serious argument with the Senate. The last time he got beat up in public was on "Death Valley Days," at least 20 years ago.

It was not easy to feel comfortable with the notion that "Reagan just finally blew out, like an old tire"—in the words of one Washington player who refused to have his name in print—but it was no easier to read shrewdness or slick politics between the lines of what looked like a stunning political defeat.

Even some of the most vulnerable of the GOP senators up for reelection this year voted against him. There was said to be a certain hollowness in the air when the roll was finally called. It was Dole, Laxalt, Denton, Armstrong and 17 others, including country gents and yahoos like Barry Goldwater, Strom Thurmond and Jesse Helms.

It was a diminished-looking crew that ended up getting stuck with this one, and none of them seemed to know why. . . . Every other time they had stuck like gum to the president, they had *won*, and enjoyed the fruits of victory. But this time Dutch had led them into shame and defeat, for reasons they couldn't explain, and it was making some of them nervous.

What were his motives? Why would he blindly defy public opinion and certain disgrace in Congress by vetoing a bill that even his own people knew from the start was a losing proposition?

The day after his crushing defeat in the Senate, Reagan was all over national TV. On ABC he was shown in direct confrontation on the White House lawn with what appeared to be the whole White House press corps.

There was no more of that old-timey stuff about tossing bon mots over his shoulder to appease the crude shouting of Sam Donaldson, as he and Nancy made their way from the chopper to their refuge in the East Wing. . . . No. This time he got mean, waving his fists distr ctedly and charging the camera too fast for the zoom lens, causing his face to look fat and unnaturally swollen.

The argument, that day, had to do with accusations from two American hostages in Lebanon that Reagan had abandoned them while bringing the whole weight of his presidency to bear on the Russians to engineer the release of tainted American journalist Nick Daniloff.

The President denied it, insisting angrily that dealing with presumably civilized enemies in the Kremlin was different from dealing with gangs of crazed Arabs from the slums of Beirut and Damascus.

He looked haggard and humorless, like a 76-year-old man who needed sleep. The past 48 hours had been uncustomarily naked of victory: The beating in the Senate had put him in a foul humor. And then, at almost the same time, had come news of ominous leaks from within his inner circle—which is always a bad sign in Washington: It means the big rats are beginning to leave the ship. Many secrets are sold in the last days of a lame-duck presidency.

In this case, Bob Woodward, this vicious creep from the Washington Post, had somehow gotten hold of a transcript filled with bad jokes and treachery from an Aug. 14 White House meeting between Reagan and his top national security advisers. . . . According to Woodward, the conversation was like something out of one of the old Nixon tapes, a crude mix of homo jokes and treacherous plotting against Col. Moammar Khadafy of Libya.

The idea of sending Dutch off to Iceland while still in the grip of some wrong-minded senile funk is not entirely popular in either the White House or the high-speed cubicles of the Republican National Committee. "He's been acting a little crazy," said one veteran oil industry lobbyist. "They're working him too hard on these fund-raising tours and now he's pissed off at everybody. He raised millions of dollars for these dirty little Senate candidates, and then they all ran like rats when he needed their votes on South Africa. They left him out on a limb like some old racist fool.

"Nobody in his right mind would let Reagan go off alone with that Russky up in Iceland," he said. "His mind is not stable. God only knows what he might say, or what kind of papers he'll sign.

"The man has nothing to lose," he went on, "and nobody will have any control over him. He can do anything he wants to, up there, and we could all be screwed to the floor."

October 6, 1986

Let the Good Times Roll

"LAS VEGAS, Nev.—An unidentified man, who hired a pilot, a witness and a photographer to videotape a stunt that apparently went awry, plunged from an airplane at 10,000 feet, and police Wednesday found the body of a man wearing a partly deployed parachute under a white dinner jacket. A car parked two miles from where the body was found had two flashlights aimed upward through the windshield and a Las Vegas map on the front seat."

USA Today, October 9, 1986

The Banshees screamed for a lot of people last week. It was an unnaturally grim string of days, like a flashback to the time of The Plague. Many were called, and many bit the bullet. The casualty list was long, and it was an interesting mix of names.

There was Bernard Kalb from the State Department, John Zaccaro from Queens, and Lyndon LaRouche from Virginia. . . . There was also Roger Clemens from Boston; John DeLorean from New Jersey; Yassir Arafat, formerly of Tunis; Dan Rather from Park Avenue; and, some genuinely hapless dupe named Eugene Hasenfus, who now resides in a bamboo cage in Nicaragua.

Others were not so well-known. There was a fisherman named Johann from Reykjavik, the philosopher-sheriff from Aspen and the third-base coach of the California Angels. The most obscure case of all—except for the sport from Las Vegas—was Donald P. Gregg, who turned up on the staff of Vice President Bush in the role of "black ops/control officer" for the botch in Nicaragua that resulted in the nasty spectacle of Hasenfus being led out of the jungle on a leash by a gang of smiling little men.

They will both go on trial very soon—Hasenfus by the Sandinistas, and Gregg by his own kind, the gray people, who will judge him by their own rules.

. . . Which are basically the same as our own, but they tend to be worded differently. In the spook world they use words like "departure" and "termination" in ways that would not be acceptable in the general business community.

"Departure," for instance, is what happened to those two American pilots who died when their plane was shot down by a SAM missile in Nicaragua, and "termination" is what will happen as soon as possible to Eugene Hasenfus, who somehow walked away from the crash, and now sits and squawks like The Raven above the doorway to Bush for President headquarters.

If he had died, he would have been a hero—like the others—but by allowing himself to be captured before he could chop out his own tongue or eat the Death Pill that he was supposed to be carrying at all times in the hollowed-out handle of his commando/survival knife, he became a huge and instant *liability*—a "loose end," as they say in the trade, with no future at all in the business he had chosen.

Even if he survives the trial without going insane or being hit like Lee Harvey Oswald by his own people, he will be better off marrying a Miskito Indian woman or even a fat young boy from some cannibal tribe in Ecuador than by crawling out of the courtroom, when the trial is finished, and catching the first plane north to Miami. No job will be waiting for him in that town. They will grab him out of the airport and put him in a canal full of alligators, and when his body turns up with the others he will get a minor mention in the local newspapers. "Former Mercenary Found Dead in Hialeah Swamp; No Clues in Brutal Murder."

Many of the people who were in bad trouble last week made the news for reasons that made a mockery of the old notion that "there is no such thing as bad publicity."

People like Richard Nixon and Wilbur Mills used to say that. But they are gone, now—after learning, the hard way, that it only applies to show business.

Dan Rather, still cranked up from his adventure in power politics at CBS, got all the action he wanted during a midnight stroll on Park Avenue when he was savagely beaten by two thugs because he failed to answer their first question: "Kenneth, what is the frequency?"

Nobody seems to know exactly what happened next, except that Rather was beaten like an egg-sucking dog for not knowing The Frequency.

At another end of the spectrum last week was a dispatch out of Cairo by *New York Times* correspondent John Kifner about PLO chieftain Yassir Arafat, who was recently expelled from Tunisia by presidential edict. The reasons were never made entirely clear, except as just another rumble in the harsh world of pan-Arab politics, but there was clearly far more to the story.

Ugly rumors out of Tunis had persisted for many months, but it is not in the nature of Arabs to speak publicly about essentially private things like adultery, debasement and treachery. . . . And when Kifner finally wrote the story and sent it, the *Times* did not reward him with the traditional bonus that normally comes with a scoop.

The headline on Page 3 said "PLO Moving From Tunis to Yemen," and the first nine graphs were intensely dark and political.

But paragraph 10 was different:

"A key factor, according to Arab diplomatic sources, was that the aging and ailing Tunisian president, Habib Bourguiba, had quarreled with and divorced his wife, Wassila, who was sympathetic to Mr. Arafat and the PLO. . . . The initial result, Arab diplomats said, was the loss of the villa set aside for Mr. Arafat."

Yassir has never been well-liked or popular in the Arab League nations. He is ugly and loud, and spittle flies off his lips when he talks. His beard is unclean and his eyes are like bags of dirty water. The starch in his uniforms get rancid after two or three days of soaking up fatty acids, and even good friends avoid him in private.

Even the most jaded and degenerate hacks in the Beirut Press Club could not bring themselves to sign their names to a story so repulsive as the saga of Yassir and Wassila. The shameful squatting in the night on the pillows of the presidential villa—in full view of the servants and sometimes even the press—was intolerable.

The story is over for now. At a press conference last Tuesday, Arafat announced that the new PLO headquarters would be either in South Yemen, East Beirut or Kharg Island.

October 13, 1986

A Death in the Family

"Throughout the centuries, the red fox has left a record symbolizing cunningness, sagacity, and courage. . . . It has left a mark on the pages of literature and legend, even to modern slang, which applies the name to sly, sharp-witted people: for example, 'He is a foxy fellow,' or 'He out-foxed me.' "

—New Hunters' Encyclopedia, p. 147

Well, folks, let me tell you a story about the red fox, and how I came to know him. It is a tale of treachery and violence and vengeance rarely encountered in a family newspaper—or even by me, in my own life, which has not been entirely free of these things.

But even dumb brutes can learn, and I have long since quit even violence, which I used to enjoy as a sport (but that passed when I realized that not everybody feels that way, and some people really want to hurt you).

Vengeance went the same way. It was fun to plot and to talk about, but the real thing required more time and energy than being saddled with a terminal disease, and not even the best vengeance ever paid the rent.

The English language is not crowded with words beginning with the letter "v" that suggest anything but trouble. After violence and vengeance, there is also vulgar, vicious, victim, vermin, vain, vacant, vile, vampire. . . . the list is long, with not a lot of smiles.

Right. And never mind these arcane drifts of language. We will leave them to villains and vissmongers like Edwin Newman and Robin MacNeil.

What we are talking about now is the hideous death in life of a red fox, considered by many experts to be one of the smartest beasts in nature.

"The fox has a distinct personality. His exceptional cunning, amounting sometimes almost to genius, has been responsible for many exaggerated stories of his extreme resourcefulness."

—Ibid.

But not from me. There is a whole nest of those vicious little red buggers about 200 yards across the field from my front porch, and I am now in the process of killing them. I got the big one a few days ago and the others have gone into hiding.

They went all to pieces when the old man finally returned from his last trip across the field. He was blind in both eyes and covered with a hard crust of feathers and peacock dung, and he was leaving a trail of blood from the stumps of his hind legs.

It was midafternoon and the carrion birds were just beginning to think about feeding, but they were not in any hurry. There is no lack of food around here. The peacocks eat well—even at 20 below—and so do all the scavengers. There is always plenty of wheat, cracked corn and French fries.

But not a lot of *meat,* which is what they really like. . . . They will eat anything that bleeds, including their own kind, like sharks in a feeding frenzy. If one of them gets wounded, he will be quickly devoured by the others. They eat the eyes and entrails first, and then they get into the meat.

"Certain outdoorsmen consider it a sin to kill a red fox; such enthusiasts view it solely as a coursing animal and are content to let it remain such forever."

—Ibid.

On any market survey with a "chic scale" from one to ten, the red fox will run about eight. He is a very stylish little animal, with a neo-valuable pelt and a social cachet on the level of mean horses and fast dogs.

Even George Washington loved the red fox. He "spent many happy hours running foxhounds over the wooded areas of his Mount Vernon plantation."

On some farms they will settle for lesser prey, like the *grey* fox—one of the lower and uglier strains in the *Vulpes vulva* family; it has eyes like warts and hair like the spines of a sea urchin, and a brain like a chicken on speed.

There is also the coyote, which is hunted or at least chased now and then by gangs of *nouveau riche* huntsmen in places like Vail and Palm Springs. . . . But it is not quite the same, because the coyote always wins.

He is not a vain little punk like the red fox, with its bitchy little temper and its pampered way of life. The coyote is a mean, solitary meat eater who will eventually kill any dog who can follow it far enough.

But I have never had a problem with coyotes, although the valley is full of them. In 15 years of relentless coexistence, not even a rabid coyote has ever come up on my front porch and killed one of the family animals, or even chewed up one of the peacocks.

The red fox had a different attitude. He was arrogant and greedy and rude, and somewhere along the line he developed a taste for Salisbury steak. He also killed the family cat and took to roaming brazenly in the yard and even up on my porch in broad daylight, sniffing around the peacock cage.

The Hav-a-Hart trap is a heavy metal box about 4 feet long, with doors on both ends and a nice little food tray in the middle. When the animal gets far enough in to eat the Salisbury steak, both doors clang shut and lock firmly. Escape is impossible.

When I found the red fox in the cage I talked to him for a while as I prepared a mixture of feathers and peacock dung, which I then began shoveling through the bars and into the cage with him. The fox became hysterical as he thrashed around in the mess, trying to bite off the end of the shovel. Every once in a while I sprayed him with liquid glue and then a final shot of Mace in his eyes before I let him go.

He looked more like a raccoon than a fox at that point. The glue had set up quickly, producing a layered effect with the dung and the feathers. The beast dragged himself out of the cage, yapping and howling, and ran awkwardly across the field in the general direction of his den in the briar patch.

On his way across the field, the hideous, stinking, half-blind, brain-shattered animal had to pass between two yearling peacocks who were pecking around in the grass for bugs, paying no attention to this thing that they didn't even recognize as a fox. I was stunned, however, to see the fox veer off his course and make a kind of staggering dumb-vicious pass at one of the birds. So I shot him from behind with a load of double-0 buckshot to help him on his way. The last time I saw him he was covered with blood and two huge red-tailed hawks were circling over-head preparing to take him into the food chain.

October 20, 1986

Back to the Ormsby House

EDITOR'S NOTE: Hunter Thompson's predictions for the U.S. Senate races have been startlingly accurate.

A few examples from his Sept. 1 column in which he called some of the key races:

"FLORIDA: Reagan family favorite Paula Hawkins is in serious trou-ble here. Gov. Bob Graham is a finely organized political hot rod. . . . He will beat her like the family mule.

"GEORGIA: GOP incumbent Mack Mattingly . . . is a Barbie Doll with no clear constituency and is not resting easy as the front-runner. As a 2–1 underdog, Wyche Fowler is one of the best bets on the board.

"MISSOURI: Former GOP Gov. Kit Bond has a huge name recogni-tion advantage over current Lt. Gov. Harriet Woods. Odds: 3–1 Bond.

"COLORADO: Tim Wirth, a high-profile congressman and proven Kennedy-style vote getter in House races, is said to be in trouble from GOP Rep. Ken Kramer. Don't bet on it. 7–5 against Kramer.

"NORTH CAROLINA: Terry Sanford is overdue to win an election. . . . 3–2 Sanford.

"NEVADA: Even the boys in the back room are wringing their hands about this one. Paul Laxalt . . . is giving up a seat that is rated 50–50 between Republican Jim Santini and Demo Rep. Harry Reid. Laxalt is too much a classic party man to give up a Senate seat unless he thought he could guarantee his successor. But he may be wrong. Odds: 3–2 Reid."

Gary Hart is on TV again. This time, it is "Nightline," and he is paired with a very haggard-looking Paul Laxalt, the ex-senior senator from Nevada, who has suffered through a very long day. Until Tuesday, sometime around noon, Laxalt was a contender. He was known as "the president's best friend," and also the master tactician who had orchestrated both of Reagan's winning presidential campaigns. . . . He was a mysterious figure, of sorts, a career politician from Nevada, with many notches on his gun: former Republican National Committee chairman, former governor, former lieutenant governor—and, as of midnight on Tuesday, a former blue-chip presidential candidate.

—*Ye Gods, here is Ed Zschau, live, from his headquarters in Santa Clara. He looks weird as he approaches the microphone. I assume he is here to make the obligatory concession statement, but there is something odd in his eyes that makes me feel uneasy; it is the wild hungry stare of a deeply crazed low-rent politician who thought he had actually won. It is like watching Roberto Duran raise his fists above his head and grin stupidly at the referee while saying, "No más, no más. . . ."*

—Laxalt, the slick and shadowy Gray Eminence of the GOP power structure, the Cardinal Richelieu of his time, looked like the best bet in the '88 field until Tuesday, when the U.S. Senate seat he was giving up to run for president somehow slipped out of his grasp and was seized by the Democrats.

It was just one of those things, said Laxalt, but in fact it was a monumental disaster for the GOP and for Laxalt's chances of ever living in the White House.

Laxalt would now have to slink back to his suite in the Ormsby House in Carson City, a notorious lounge and casino favored by rich pols and state senators. It had long been his headquarters and his club and his refuge, but on Tuesday night it was surrounded by a crowd of mean drunkards, and many were calling his name.

It meant he was finished in politics. He would never be trusted again.

Old women who worked the night shift scrubbing floors in the Ormsby House cursed his name and mocked him for losing his power

Nor will we be seeing very much of Ronald Reagan for the next two years. A lot more of Sam Donaldson's questions thrown against the prop wash of the presidential chopper will go unanswered, and Dutch-watchers will have to be content with long-lens shots taken from outside the ranch.

The old boy has been shaken by this one, utterly humiliated after peddling himself across the country in an effort to pacify the crop of whining, wall-eyed first-term senators he installed six years ago. They were crumbling beneath him, jabbering about the polls and "Star Wars" and their parking spaces on the Hill.

"This is a make-or-break election," he told a gaggle of fat, surly tobacco farmers in North Carolina three weeks ago. "Losing control of the Senate will mean more than just economic hardship for our people.

"The safety of our neighborhoods and the security of our country are also at stake."

Well . . . we'll see. James Broyhill, the object of Reagan's crazed doomsaying in North Carolina, is gone, along with the Republican Senate, and now a vengeful Robert Byrd and his 10-seat Democratic majority is preparing to give the president a vicious beating.

The Republicans even had to endure the disgrace of Harold Stassen's latest loss in Minnesota. Nobody knew what he would run for next, but he was rumored to be considering a run for president in '88 in light of the Laxalt fiasco.

November 5, 1986

The Garden of Agony

"He is a man of splendid abilities, but utterly corrupt. He shines and stinks like rotten mackerel by moonlight."

—John Randolph

The political business was booming last week, but only for certain people. The pros and the pols and the serious players werre doing very nicely; with 34 Senate seats, 36 governorships and 435 House seats up for grabs, the politics business was turning over millions of dollars a day in what the staff lawyers called "fast money."

Which is nothing new in the politics business. Even George Washington needed cash in the final hours; there is always something, from feeding the horses to keeping the phones from being cut off. It used to be cash in brown bags, tight greasy little bundles of 10s and 20s, but now it comes by computer, with no fingerprints. It comes in vast amounts and it comes constantly, and in the New Politics of the '80s it is the main factor in almost every political campaign.

We are not talking about the petty cash drawer. The fast money now is what gets people elected. It is the stuff that can make a 5 percent difference in the polls in the week before Election Day—far more than any great speech or high truth or great issue. These things are all extras, compared with the candidate's access to money.

When Hubert Humphrey was running for president in 1968 and saw in the final hours that he was losing badly, his last desperate act was to switch his position on the war in Vietnam, hoping to win the anti-war vote that he needed to beat Nixon. . . . It failed, but not by much, and a whole generation of young politicians took notice. Selling ideology was not enough to win elections—not even when you pawned it in public for a mess of pottage. One field organizer told me, "Hell, I got more votes for Hubert by standing on a street corner and handing out $20 bills than Hubert did by telling that disgusting lie."

He works now as a political consultant in Washington, for $1,000 a day, for either party or any candidate who can afford him. "Things are different now," he told me last week. "The only thing that matters now is money. It's so much worse than it was 10 years ago that you don't even want to hear about it. This town is worse than it's ever been. These new people have no shame. It's like living in a whorehouse. I'm getting out."

Then, one afternoon late last week, I got a call from my old friend Patrick Caddell, one of the ranking pollsters and wizards in the business, who stunned me by saying that he also was "quitting politics."

"Don't lie to me, Patrick," I said to him. "You were born in this business. It's your life."

"No more," he replied. "The whole political system is a disaster area, and it's getting worse. There are some very sick people in the business today. It has gone from The Best and Brightest to the Worst and Meanest. I got into politics because I believed in things; now I'm getting out for the same reason. It got so bad that I was feeling dirty all the time. I finally had a shower built into the office, but it didn't do any good."

A top staff adviser to one 1988 presidential candidate explained the situation in terms of pure numbers. "The PACs have put $342 million into the (House and Senate) races. And we both know what that means. You know whenever money changes hands in this business, 10 percent of it disappears. That's at a minimum. I'm being conservative. Overseas, it's 50 percent."

There is so much new money in town now that it's passing into the hands of staff as well as members of Congress. It used to be just the members who would salt it away. Now it's routine to buy the staffers too.

"It's mostly cash and cocaine," he said. "They're all into it here. You can't win without doing it."

The Senate campaign in California this year was more expensive than the whole Nixon campaign in 1972. Some people were horrified, but others called it cheap at almost $20 million—which was still $10 million cheaper than a single F-111.

Nevertheless, it was a serious amount of money, and more than half of it was spent by Ed Zschau, until this year a no-name congressman with a fat little high-tech money factory, a Potomac jones and the political instincts of a hammerhead shark.

The Republicans viewed Alan Cranston as "vulnerable" this time around, and there was no time to waste. Zschau survived a vicious six-way primary by taking the high ground, nosing his way into position as "the most moderate" of the pack, and not talking too much about certain parts of his voting record, which put him somewhere out there with the Jesse Helms boys.

But when the real fight started, Zschau scrambled back toward the right, undeterred by some nasty Cranston spots calling him the "flip-flop" candidate . . . and it seemed to work. In September, Cranston's pollster told him he had a 12-point lead, but Zschau's camp said it was never more than 5, or maybe 6. . . . Zschau kept gaining through October, and the stories about his company doing business in South Africa didn't hurt his numbers a bit. . . . After all, he was with Dutch on this one.

Last week, it was being whispered in Washington that Cranston was in real trouble, and just five days before the election, independent pollsters declared it a dead heat.

It was an amazing comeback that insiders attributed entirely to Reagan's fund-raising appearances, which raised $1 million each. He made another one on Saturday in Los Angeles, and if you believe in the new math of politics, that could translate into just enough points to put Zschau over the top. The same thing could happen in Colorado and Nevada, which were also considered "too close to call."

Tuesday's elections may not be a de facto "referendum on the president," as his White House handlers keep telling us, but it is certain to be a referendum on the new Money Politics of the '80s.

If the theory holds, all this talk about Democrats winning enough of the close races to regain control of the Senate has been a pipe dream from the start. It was one of those big white lies that had to be told and nurtured and fondled openly in public like some kind of special secret, because it was necessary. Nobody comes to fund-raising parties for candidates with a chance of winning. This is the '80s, Jack. You want my vote? How much money do you have?

November 3, 1986

White Trash with Money

Phoenix—my phone in the Biltmore rang shortly after midnight, but I paid no attention to it. There were only two people in Arizona who knew I was in town, and one of them was there in the room with me. The other was in Cell Block 6—"Death Row"—in the State Prison about 60 miles south of here in a small town called Florence.

It is better not to answer the telephone under these circumstances. Wait until the message light comes on, then call the operator and give yourself an option. . . . And when Maria called down to the desk, moments later, I heard her say, "Mr. Parker? What? From Sky Harbor? Herschel Walker? Are you sure you have the right number?"

I was only half-listening, but when she gave me the message I felt an eerie sensation crawling along my spine. "Do we know anybody named Jack Parker?" she asked. "From the airport parking garage? He left a message that says, 'Herschel Walker has 522 yards after 10 games. Call me on Sunday night after the San Diego game.' What is this? Are you gambling again?"

It took a few seconds, but then I remembered the name. "Ye gods," I muttered. "How did he find me here?" I had met him at the Phoenix airport—the Sky Harbor—a month or so earlier, and he had given me his gold Mercedes 600 as security when I bet him that Herschel Walker would not gain more than 600 yards rushing this year. I was so sure of it that I had long since traded the Mercedes for a Jeep Wagoneer in Wickenburg, and never expected to hear from him again.

It was one of those crazy little bets that you make now and then in this business—usually in situations of personal impairment—and now the Cowboys were coming up against San Diego on Sunday, and all Herschel needed to crack the 600 mark was a middling good day against a 2–8 team ranked nearly last in the league against the rush.

The situation looked grim—especially now that Parker had somehow found me through five or six layers of deep cover. How was it possible? And if Parker could find me, what about the others?

My nerves were a bit tense at the time. I had come to town on some very delicate business and I was registered in the hotel under the name "Walker." There already had been two threats made against me, if I ever showed up in the state, and I was being careful to stay out of sight. Phoenix is not one of those towns where threats of violence are taken lightly. Too many people have been croaked here—blown up, slit open, locked up, kidnapped, and otherwise flogged, ruined and destroyed for seemingly trivial reasons.

There is a unique kind of thuggery and crude vigilante "justice" that thrives here, which is different from most other places except maybe Tijuana, Sicily and the slums of downtown Manila. It used to be called "Old West," or "frontier-style justice," but in the brand-new fast-buck Sun Belt prosperity of places like Tucson and Phoenix it has developed into something entirely different.

Michael Lacey, editor of the *New Times* in Phoenix, has been grappling with the "New West" mentality for almost 10 years, and he still finds it baffling. "How many communities can you go into where there are absolutely sensational murders . . . what's more sensational than sticking six sticks of dynamite under a reporter's rear end and blowing him through the car? . . . You've got the Wild West mentality, with what's going on out here. . . . But what you've really got is the Wild West *dissolving,* and yet these guys still think it's kind of cowboy-oriented to hang around with hoodlums and punks; you've got so many new people coming in here that they don't even know or care if the water they're drinking is fresh or whether it's some kind of filtered effluent. . . . All they care about is making money. . . . They don't care about a situation where a local journalist is blown away for simply *writing* about these things. . . ."

Lacey was talking about the worst crime in Arizona since the days of Winnie Ruth Judd, the notorious "tiger woman" who chopped up her victims and sent them off to Los Angeles in trunks.

"Don Bolles, a long-time investigative reporter for the Arizona Republic, was gravely wounded June 2, 1976, when a homemade bomb attached to his car exploded in a midtown hotel parking lot.

"Bolles, 47, made several statements to those who rushed to his aid. Some heard the reporter name the Emprise Corporation, the Mafia and someone called John Adamson as those responsible for the explosion. Bolles had spent years investigating Emprise—then co-owner with a local family of Arizona's six dog tracks—and had written about the firm's ties to suspected Mafiosi. John Harvey Adamson was a 32-year-old alcoholic, a con artist and a man who made his living as a burglar and a thief.

"Police charged he had lured bolles to the Clarendon—by promising to provide information about an alleged land-fraud scheme. But while

Bolles waited inside the hotel, Adamson attached the bomb under Bolles' car, then drove to a nearby bar, where he called the reporter to cancel their late-morning appointment. Moments later, as Bolles was backing out of the parking space, the bomb was detonated by a remote-control device similar to that used to operate model airplanes.

"Bolles died June 13, eleven days after the blast ripped him apart. He was survived by seven children and his wife, Rosalie. Adamson was arrested on a first-degree murder charge within hours after Bolles died."
—*New Times Special Report June 1986*

The case remains unsolved, and this year is the 10th anniversary. There have been trials, convictions, appeals, destruction of key evidence, raw treachery and allegations of criminal involvement by high political figures like Sen. Barry Goldwater and former Gov. Bruce Babbitt, who is now a presidential candidate.

The Bolles saga is one of my reasons for coming back to Arizona this time—but that is another story, and we will get to it later.

In the meantime, Sunday afternoon came up like thunder out of San Diego . . . and Herschel Walker gained only 15 yards against the Chargers, which left him at 537, and subject to a season-ending injury like the kind of thing that happens to people in Phoenix.

I did not return Mr. Parker's call, and I left for New York on Monday. There was no need to talk—at least not until next week, when the Cowboys will be mauled like stray dogs by the Redskins.

November 17, 1986

The Lord and a Good Lawyer

Political gibberish is not a purely American art form, like jazz and safety blitz. But in only 200 years we have raised it to a level of eloquence beyond anything since the time of the Caesars or even Genghis Khan. . . . And Paul Kirk's utterly meaningless assessment of

the Democratic Party's current strategic position vis-a-vis the 1988 presidential campaign won him instant recognition in Washington among
those ranking political insiders responsible for making nominations to
the Gibberish Hall of Fame.

It was one of those statements that had to be made. Nature's abhor-
rence of a vacuum is nothing compared with the way the editors of *The
New York Times* feel about the need for a major front-page political
story on Thanksgiving Day. Accordingly, the *Times*' internationally ac-
claimed cuisine critic, R. W. Apple Jr., was called back from the food
beat in London and Paris and Rome and given the task of firing the first
big journalistic salvo of the 1988 presidential campaign.

Neither Kirk nor anybody else in the Democratic Party had expected
to be put very suddenly and with no real warning at all in a position of
having to even think, much less talk to *The New York Times*, about
having to "seize control of the national agenda" this far ahead of Election Day in 1988. That was not supposed to happen for at least another
year.

The Democrats' game plan, until then, was to lay low and talk like
The Universal Underdog—just another bunch of good guys and athletes
who got victimized by the cruel ignorance of Ronald Reagan—and then
emerge in the winter of '88 with a fistful of tangible solutions and two
or three viable, charismatic contenders who almost certainly could beat
George Bush or any other Republican.

But now the president, far too used to letting used-car dealers from
San Diego run the country, had looked the other way while Ollie North
ran a brisk little gun-running outfit to finance his Central American war
out of the basement of the White House, and the few Democrats who
were reachable when Johnny Apple called as the holiday weekend began
were uneasy.

They felt strangely out of place, like Mike Tomczak or Turk Schonert,
thrust into starting roles they hadn't played for years. Barney Frank,
apparently worried that his party members would drool all over themselves in some sort of presidential feeding frenzy, counseled moderation,
saying, "There's no point in us trying to reform the NSC . . . there's
no way for us to keep cowboys like North off the staff. It's not wise to
try an institutional solution of personal defects," thereby earning a place
of his own next to immortals like Hubert Humphrey, Al Haig and Yogi
Berra.

Never mind that Dutch was too old and too guilty to duck this one.
Apple got Fritz Mondale to sound just as scared as he did two years

ago: "If people think our party is quite happy to hurt the country for its own advantage, the country will turn against us, and it should turn against us."

Despite the Democrats' pessimism, there was movement in the winter book numbers last week: The boys in the back rooms in places like Vegas, Washington and Moscow were making serious adjustments in their early line odds for the 1988 presidential race. Recent events had "changed the current picture," as they say in the politics business, and the names on the chart were changing.

Most of the big losers appeared to be Republicans—not only the senators who lost their membership in what has been called "the most exclusive club in America," but other key figures and once-powerful champions of the Reagan revolution, like Vice President Bush, former GOP Sen. Paul Laxalt from Nevada, and even Reagan himself, who suffered such grievous political losses that his once-magic "image" changed from John Wayne to Ratso Rizzo in the space of three weeks. He not only lost control of the Congress, a huge chunk of his personal credibility with the electorate, the personal trust of Secretary of State Shultz, and the respect of the entire Japanese nation, but also about 88 percent of his own sense of humor.

Reagan had gone out on the campaign trail day after day for almost three months and begged the voters in places like Fresno, Baton Rouge, Reno and a tin hangar at the Denver airport to "stay with" him and his warriors in this critical midterm election, or otherwise they might risk a disastrous public repudiation of his whole presidency and everything it once seemed to stand for.

The voters responded by rejecting almost every big-time politician in the country who had made the mistake of identifying in public with Reagan. Many were croaked and few were chosen. The Senate went Democratic by a margin that not even the most pessimistic jades in the White House had thought possible; the president was confused and humiliated by the Russians when he stumbled up to Reykjavik, Iceland, for a hopelessly ill-conceived "summit conference," and two weeks later he found himself mired in a shocking scandal that suddenly loomed larger and more dangerous than Watergate.

After all, Oliver North is not a Cuban burglar. He is a lieutenant colonel in the United States Marine Corps, although his chances of making bird colonel seem dim this week. . . . It would have been a quiet ceremony, in the Rose Garden perhaps, with the president pinning on his eagles. . . . Now, he's looking at five to ten at Leavenworth unless he can find a good fixer, and he's trying: "My plans are now to trust in the Lord and a good lawyer," North said Saturday.

So what? What about Diamond Don Regan, whose deniability has more gaps than Rose Mary Woods could produce? And Ed Meese, who gave North a few days to shred things in his office before sending in the G-men (obstruction of justice, anyone?) and now is reportedly considering stepping aside in favor of an independent prosecutor, perhaps somebody not so chummy with the president?

And what about the big dogs? Reagan, who tells us he slept through the whole thing, and Bush, who has Max Gomez, Robert McFarlane and half of Saudi Arabia hanging around his neck?

Perhaps Bush should quit first, so Reagan can find his own Jerry Ford to hand off to—maybe Bob Dole, or Pat Robertson—but make no mistake, they should both resign. This one's not going to get any better, and Dutch should duck out before the Democrats wake up and the new Congress smells blood.

December 1, 1986

Ronald Reagan Is Doomed

"We can't afford a weak American president who will be in office another two years."

—West German spokesman

German politicians were not the only ones worried about the bent legs of Ronald Reagan last week. There were sounds of babbling and scrambling all over Washington, as many gentlemen of a distinctly rodentlike persuasion either quit or got pushed off The Ship. The Reagan Revolution was beginning to look like a second-hand Studebaker with bald tires.

Presidential spokesman Larry Speakes was not the first to go over the side, but his decision to leave government service and seek work in the private sector was seen as a major sign. His new job will be as communications director for Merrill Lynch, Pierce, Fenner & Smith, a brokerage conglomerate. Speakes will triple his White House salary "by jumping to Wall Street," according to "CBS Morning News," and he weakly denied all speculation that his departure had anything to do with the specter of President Reagan being driven into an exile worse than Nixon's by the fallout from the fateful "Iranian Transaction."

The Big Guy is in big trouble on this one, and he will probably not survive it. He has been a hero all his life, but this time is going to be different. John Wayne is dead, and so is Ronald Reagan. This is the last reel of his last movie, and it is not going to end like the others.

He is a 77-year-old man who was once the best salesman of his time, but now he is like Willie Loman. His friends have deserted him, his wife has turned mean, and his enemies are no longer afraid. The same people who once called him "the greatest American president since George Washington" now regard him as senile—a weak and crazy albatross around the neck of The Party.

The GOP will not win another general election in this century. Ronald Reagan has served his purpose, and now he is left to wander naked and alone, like King Lear, "a poor, infirm, weak and despised old man."

There are players in Vegas today who will tell you that the odds against Reagan serving out the full four years of his second term have dropped from 13–1 to as low as 7–1 or even 6–1 in the last 10 days.

Why should he? The man has done his work. For the last 20 years he has functioned brilliantly as the flag-waving front man for a gang of fast-buck Southern California profit-takers who no longer need him. "Ron is a genuinely nice guy," said one of them recently, "a truly decent man. But let's face it—all he needs for early retirement, right now, is one good case of the flu." It's entirely possible that he may never come back to Washington in January, after Christmas break.

The Lear connection is all too clear in Reagan's case. He is an "idle old man, that would still manage those authorities that he hath given away." (Act I, Scene iii).

There is, in fact, a school of thought in politics that says Reagan is the only *innocent* player in this degraded, low-rent movie. Some people will tell you that Ed Meese is another one, or that George Bush could pass for smart or human. . . . (but they lie).

Why were all these people—the president, the attorney general, the vice president, the president's national security adviser and his top aide, the whole ranking insider/elite administration Republicans—so desperately and totally committed to a cause called "the contras" in Central America that they would risk the whole reputation, credibility and the possibility of a humiliated Nixonlike place in history just to send just another $30 million to a fat, inarticulate Latino yuppie named Adolfo Calero in Nicaragua?

Was it worth another Watergate?

Another horror in history for the GOP?

Who is Danny Ortega? And how dangerous is he? Is he so bad that a whole generation of professional Republicans would risk *everything* (their lives, their truth, their sacred honor, etc.) to wipe him out *now?*

Who are these "contras" anyway? And why do they need so much money? Are we dealing with berserk patriots? Or common Texas thieves?

Who stood to gain by this hideous political conspiracy? Who had the motive?

Certainly it was not Ronald Reagan. The last thing in life that he needed was a scandalous nightmare of lies, crimes and gigantic money-laundering to haunt the last days of his once-splendorous presidency. No amount of money-profit from a massive and illegal arms deal with *anybody*—and especially not the cruel and fiendish Ayatollah Ruhollah Khomeini of Iran—could have drawn Reagan into this plot. It was a no-win situation.

Bush, on the other hand, had *everything* to gain by it, and very little to lose. His chances of becoming president of the United States in 1988 were never good. He was, of course, the vice president. . . . But he had no friends in politics, or at least not the kind he needed: Not even Reagan was going to endorse him; it was going to be another one of those humiliating scenes like Nixon had to go through with Eisenhower in 1960, when he was treated more like a stray dog than the Heir Apparent.

Nixon lost that election to John Kennedy by a margin so thin that you couldn't even see it, and he knew in his heart that his life would have been different forever, if only Ike hadn't laughed at him.

"We have seen the best of our time. Machinations, hollowness, treachery and all ruinous disorders follow us disquietly to our graves." That is also from Lear: Act I, Scene ii, and Bush should have it tattooed on the palm of his left hand, as he plots his campaign for the presidency.

He will, of course, need a slush fund—not unlike the one Gordon Liddy and Maurice Stans put together for Nixon in 1972. There is *never* enough money when you have to run for president as a contemptible underdog.

Bush is no stranger to big-time politics. He has been around the track more than any single man except Nixon, who once assigned George to head up the CIA, where he got a crash course in deep-cover "black" operations like the Iranian Transaction.

He is also the only top-level official in Washington—except perhaps for CIA Director William Casey—with provable connections to all the others involved, from Robert McFarlane and Oliver North to Israeli intelligence and Prince Fahd of Saudi Arabia and Calero.

The Senate Intelligence Committee will be holding public TV hearings on the arms deal this week, and by Friday afternoon the odds on George Bush being our next president will be about 33–1.

December 8, 1986

God Bless Colonel North

"It was no big deal. They were only small shipments."

—Manucher Ghorbanifar, Iranian arms merchant,
"Nightline," December 11, 1986

The man was on network TV, lounging on a silver lame couch in Monte Carlo with Adnan Khashoggi, the richest man in the world . . . and he was chatting casually with Barbara Walters about how he and his sloe-eyed pal "Shoggi" had arranged the disastrous arms deal that was threatening to destroy the presidency of Ronald Reagan.

Manucher Ghorbanifar, an international type, was not especially concerned with the panic in the White House. The real problem, he said, was that he and Shoggi hadn't been paid the first dollar of their 33 percent "brokerage fee." They had put a lot of time and hard work into the deal, he said, and now they were getting stiffed: What began as a sort of non-profit loss-leader operation had become a nightmare of rotten publicity for otherwise decent businessmen.

The whole thing had been bungled, he complained. Jews and Canadians had become involved, and even Filipinos. There was an embarrassing lack of professionalism on the American end, he said bitterly; it was giving the whole weapons business a bad name.

The international arms trade is an ugly business, and giddy foreigners with no pulse are not the only ones involved in it. As of last Jan. 17—according to a recent UPI dispatch out of Washington—the list of international arms merchants was expanded to include household names like Meese, Casey, Regan and Bush.

That would be the attorney general of the United States, the director of the CIA, the White House chief of staff and the vice president, who is also the current front-runner for the GOP presidential nomination in 1988. They are the ones who "participated in drafting the FINDING," issued Jan. 17 by President Reagan as a formal "intelligence authorization" ordering a U.S. arms sale to Iran, and providing legal justification for the sale.

Nobody seems to know, for sure, just how much money was involved or where the money went. Estimates range from $12 million all the way up to $2 billion—but none of the boys involved will admit receiving a dime of it: Not "contra" bagman Adolfo Calero or the Friends of Oliver North or even Manny and Shoggi.

These details are still shrouded in mystery—where they will remain until sometime in January, when the Congress comes back from vacation to bite the bullet.

In the meantime, a hellbroth of terrible pressures will be building up in Washington. The holidays will not be a merry time in the White House. There will be nothing under the tree but ashes, switches and subpoenas. Whatever remains of the unhappy Reagan family will be lucky to make it to Andrews Air Force Base while they still have helicopter privileges.

When this one finally unravels, it will make Watergate look like a teen-age prank, and Richard Nixon will seem like just another small-time politician who got wiggy on greed and cheap gin. This foul "Iranian

Transaction" will go down in history as the worst thing that happened in Washington since Wilbur Mills went crazy and burned half the city in 1814.

In the White House, head gorgon Patrick Buchanan went wild with hatred and rage. It was all *deja vu* to him. He had been there before, in uglier times, when the same gang of weasels that he called "The Nattering Nabobs of Negativism"—the pinkos and the press—had savagely destroyed *another* Republican president, and left Buchanan unemployed.

That was the Watergate scandal, a truly hideous episode in his life, a stunning repudiation of everything he stood for. When "The Boss" turned out to have been guilty as a street pimp all along, Buchanan felt betrayed. "It's like Sisyphus," he wrote. "We rolled the rock all the way up the mountain—and it rolled right back down on us."

But that was in the old days. Buchanan survived Watergage by slipping through the cracks. Agnew pled *nolo* and Nixon resigned in shame. . . .

And now Patrick is back in the White House, as "Director of Communications" for another crooked president—although he really doesn't see it that way.

"What liberalism and The Left have in mind," he warns, "is the second ruination of a Republican presidency within a generation."

It is an ugly prospect, and nobody can say for sure why it's happening. Why has every Republican president since Abraham Lincoln been so crooked that they need a brace of Secret Service men to help them screw their pants on every morning?

From Ulysses S. Grant to Big Bill McKinley and Warren Harding, they were all so dirty that they could barely sleep at night.

Even Ike had Sherman Adams. "I need him," he said. "And nevermind his morals."

Nixon was genetically criminal. Agnew was born wrong. Ford was so utterly corrupt that he made millions by pardoning Nixon, and Reagan is beginning to take on the distinctly Spanish physical characteristics of the Somoza family, formerly of Nicaragua.

Buchanan is the only living human who was deeply involved in both The Watergate Scandal and this new horror, 10 years later, which he lamely tries to call "Contragate"—as if it were nothing more than some kind of overzealous slippage into True Patriotism that could only have been committed for the right reasons.

Which is not true. There is a lot more to this twisted Iranian Trans-action than some game of Capture the Flag at a military academy that somehow got out of control. Buchanan is in trouble on this one, and by Groundhog Day he will be gone, once again, from the White House—seeking work in the private sector, along with his current boss Donald Regan. They are both expendable, at this point, and neither one will need food stamps when they finally go over the side. Regan will go back to Wall Street, and Patrick will be back on TV, cursing the press and the lintheads for $1,000 a day.

Adm. Poindexter and Col. North will be sharing a cell at one of the nicer federal prisons, and Dutch will retire to the Sky Ranch above Santa Barbara with his wife and his dog and probably Michael Deaver, who will soon be sucked into the maw of the Federal Witness Protection Program and will need a reliable sponsor for his new way of life as a wood-chopper.

December 15, 1986

Orgy of the Dead

It was Friday night when we finally blew up the Jeep. The explosion shook the whole valley and sent chunks of red shrapnel flying over the house and all the way back to the White River National Forest. All traffic stopped on the road and the elk herd scattered in panic.

But not for long. It was over in 22 seconds. Nobody was injured and no animals were killed, despite the ominous presence of Russell Chatham, the famous meat-eating artist from Montana.

Russell is also a famous chef—and wherever he shows up, things die. He will jerk a tarpon out of the sea or an antelope off the prairie, just to get his hands on the meat.

It is a cooking fetish, hooked up with a high sense of art and a wolflike hunger for anything that drips blood. . . . And when he heard we were about to set off a huge bomb in the midst of an elk herd, he flew over from San Francisco a day early.

But there was no meat on that day, for Russell or anyone else. The only thing that died in the blast was the Jeep, which had fought valiantly for something like 55 hours against the crude and stupid death that we finally inflicted on it.

The bomb was huge, by local standards. It was four sticks of Iramite, a brutal plastic explosive known as "Super Dynamite" in the trade, wedged under the hood of an old red Jeep Wagoneer, equipped with a 278HP V-8 Chevy engine and four *new* studded whitewall Michelin XAS mud & snow tires . . . and it was what they call in The Business "an extremely dangerous wrap."

Which was true. The old steel Wagoneer, a relic from some earlier and better day when Jeeps were still built like small tanks, had withstood the assaults of some of the meanest and best-equipped boys in the international violence business. It had been packed full of dynamite, soaked down with gasoline and then blasted at point-blank range for two hours with flares, full-auto, and .50-caliber tracer/rockets from a newfangled $2,500 single-shot sniper rifle that was brought over the mountains from Boulder by some wild boys from Soldier of Fortune magazine.

But nothing had worked.

The 12-gauge "high-impact" shotgun flares, designed to explode in a blaze of phosphorus at precisely 150 yards, fluttered limply to earth in the tall grass of the pasture at less than half that distance, setting fire to old fence posts and hay bales. . . . The full-auto M-16s were utterly useless, spraying bullets all over the landscape and hitting everything except the Jeep, which had been set up only 100 yards away.

It was a series of horrible jokes. The big rifle—a custom-built item weighing 29 pounds and mounted with a scope so precise that it was "guaranteed" to hit a watermelon at 3,000 yards—turned out to be worse than a Roman candle in the hands of a drunken teen-ager.

It was advertised as "state of the art" in terms of accuracy, impact, flash suppression and no recoil, a totally modern weapon. . . . But the first person to fire it, local sportsman and ski merchant Dan Dibble, fell away from his shot with blood spurting out of his forehead from a terrible recoil-whack that split the flesh between his eyes like a blow from a nine-pound hatchet.

He bled all over the house for two or three hours, and his shot was at least 8 feet over the target—a huge ball of fire that landed somewhere up in the snow.

The Soldier of Fortune boys were embarrassed, but none of them could do any better.

These were big-time shooters and the cream of the hired mercenary crop, with access to any weapons they wanted—in Woody Creek or Angola or Nicaragua—and somehow they failed to hit the dynamite or anything else that would give us the massive explosion we were looking for.

The only break in the long afternoon of truly crazy incompetence came when one of the mercs managed to hit the front seat of the Jeep with a tracer/incendiary round, and set the upholstery on fire.

We were gripped by a feeling of ugliness when the target failed to explode. Nobody knew how to explain it. The Jeep was still smoldering, but the bomb refused to go off . . . and it would stay that way for the next 50 hours, a living bomb that nobody could go near.

The mercs pulled out quickly, taking their used brass with them. We chased them down the road as far as the tavern, where they tried to seek refuge and pass for normal tourists.

The fat one locked himself in the men's room, but Tex kicked the door down and dragged him out by the hair.

The one who called himself "chief" fled out the back door and tried to hide in the bowels of the trailer court. Two others barricaded themselves in the Laundromat and threatened to commit suicide unless they could talk to Ed Bradley and make the whole story public.

They were still there when the tavern closed at midnight, and the Jeep was still on fire in the back pasture.

The dynamite was still simmering on top of the DieHard battery, and one of their women had run off with their Power Wagon, heading back to Boulder at top speed.

When I went back home, around three, a surly crowd was still gathered in front of the Laundromat, jabbering distractedly and chanting Sandinista slogans.

The nightmare went on for two more days and nights until finally on Friday afternoon, my neighbor George Stranahan, the famous beef rancher, came over with a fistful of blasting caps and blew the Jeep into thousands of small red chips. "Merry Christmas," he said as he left. "There's more world news on Page 2."

December 22, 1986

The Year of the Pig

"This may be the generation that will face Armageddon."

—Ronald Reagan, *People* magazine

Nobody from the White House was arrested or even indicted over the Christmas holidays, but it had the look of an uneasy truce and there was nobody in national politics who thought it would last much longer.

Congress comes back next week, and the pace will pick up dramatically. Many heads will roll before Groundhog Day. There will be film clips on the evening news of broken men being led into courtrooms by vacant-eyed lawyers carrying satchels of affidavits and mysterious tape recordings. Huge fees will be sheduled, and politicians will be trundled through the streets below Capitol Hill like doomed aristocrats being hauled to the guillotine during the French Revolution.

The new year will almost certainly be strange. Even Pat Buchanan has jumped into the 1988 presidential race now. He was talking to Evans and Novak on TV the other day, and seemed to have no problem confirming the rumor of his candidacy.

I was stunned. The republic is definitely on shifting sands, at this point. . . . But not everybody is worried: Khashoggi's people and the crowd from Merrill-Lynch etc. that keeps moving in and out of the White House at ever-increasing salaries are not especially concerned about the drift. . . .

But the awkward truth is that three times in the last 20 years one of the two major parties has put forth presidential candidates who were so utterly crooked and publicly corrupt that they had to be removed from office for dark reasons. . . . And two of them were re-elected to second four-year terms by massive popular acclaim.

Nixon won 48 states in 1972, and Reagan won 49 in '84. The voters loved them, but they were both as crooked as screwworms, and even their families and closest friends were finally compelled to denounce them. . . . Gerald Ford, the only one of the three *not* re-elected, was a different case entirely. He was dragged into office at the last moment— appointed, in fact, by a shamelessly criminal president who would have done time in federal prison if somebody hadn't pardoned him. That was Ford's job, and he took a nasty beating for it in 1976, rejected by the voters in favor of the yahoo governor of Georgia.

It was like one of these ugly "police scandals" that they keep having in New York. Some people flee to Bermuda and others commit suicide or surrender their lives to rich foreigners.

There are a lot of things that can be said of Jimmy Carter, but nobody ever called him "crooked." He was never accused of a felony, or even a misdemeanor. . . . And neither was Lyndon Baines Johnson, the only other Democrat elected to the White House in the last 26 years. . . .

That was 1960, when John Kennedy beat Richard Milhous Nixon and paid for that victory by having his head blown off in Dallas. . . . And the only crimes Jack Kennedy ever got accused of were bringing cocaine and naked women into the White House for a few hours a day—usually at lunchtime, when they frolicked around the once-elegant White House swimming pool. . . .

Which no longer exists. One of Nixon's first official acts upon taking office was to order the pool filled up with bricks and turned into a nasty little press room with no air conditioning, and it has been the same way ever since.

Nixon was said to fear water, and Ford was apparently no different, and Reagan has not been seen on a beach or even near a pool since somewhere back in the '50s when he was selling light bulbs for General Electric.

The time has finally come, now, to find out how smart Ronald Reagan really is, and the spectrum of possibilities is surprisingly broad.

If he comes back to Washington after his brief holiday visit back home to Santa Barbara, he will be *dumb*. . . . If he comes back to the White House and tries to hide out in the East Wing and claim he can only vaguely remember even meeting a man named Oliver North, he will be *stupid*. . . . And if he returns with his fists clenched and his teeth on fire and a John Wayne kind of madness to take on both Congress and the Press and even public opinion for the next two years, he will be *crazy*.

That is about it, for the options. He is looking at a no-win situation, and so are all the others. . . . But Dutch is the only one who can still quit and get away with it.

George Bush can't even run, much less hide. He will be lucky to get off without doing time in a federal prison and doing pushups on some filthy asphalt basketball court every morning with people like Vice Adm. Poindexter, Gen. Secord and the apparently berserk Marine Lt. Col. Oliver North.

They will all be locked up, and they will take many others down with them. . . . Attorney General Ed Meese and brain-damaged CIA chief William Casey are already targeted for humiliating felony/conspiracy prosecutions, and at least 33 people on the White House "staff" will be charged with baffling crimes and forced to turn to Jesus to escape jail. . . . Even Pat Buchanan will go this time, despite his bizarre run for the presidency. They are all guilty as egg-sucking dogs.

Gary Hart and Jesse Jackson will be trapped together in the White House for at least the next five years, and by the time of the presidential election in November of the year 2000, the "Reagan Revolution" will be noted by an asterisk in the history books—like The New Frontier and the heinous personal disfigurement of one-time Attorney General Ed Meese, who will be living by then on a barge in some slough on the outskirts of Antioch. . . . Joe Kennedy will be president in 2001, Mexico will no longer exist, and the states of Wyoming, Montana and Idaho will be fenced off as a white-trash penal colony. . . . There will be a chicken in every pot and every honest farmer will have 40 acres and a mule.

December 29, 1986

Mixup at the Hospital

As Reagan and his wife, Nancy, boarded Air Force One for their trip home, a reporter shouted. "What will '87 be like?"
"Great," Mrs. Reagan replied. "Better than '86," the president added.

Who else but Sam Donaldson could have done a thing like that? To stand on the hot tarmac at the Palm Springs International Airport with a small Sony microphone in your hand and *shout* such a ghoulish query at the president of the United States and expect to get an answer. . . .

Only Sam. It is a very special art, and he is good at it. Sam is the White House correspondent for ABC News, and when it comes to cutting through the muttering haze of a presidential press conference— or even a "nonverbal photo opportunity" for the afternoon wires—Sam has no peer in the business.

I can still hear his wolf-like howling in my dreams. . . . Once you have stood next to Sam at a press conference and heard him suddenly utter one of those wild barking cries at the president, it will stay in your memory forever. It is one of the reasons I had to quit covering the White House. No civilized human should have to live with a noise like that.

But Ronald Reagan will. The new year was barely 24 hours old when he got the first shot: "What will '87 be like?"

What indeed?

Well, Sam . . . I guess I'm glad you asked that question. Because I am, after all, the president, and I am heading back to Washington, now, to celebrate my 76th birthday on Feb. 11. . . . But *before* that, Sam, I will be forced to undergo another neopublic colon operation, and confront a horrible plunge in my *approval rating* numbers in the public opinion polls. I will also say farewell to a few trusted old friends who are also in the hospital with cancer. . . . What the hell do you *think* '87 will be like? You brainless jabbering brute! I should have had you assigned to Soweto a long time ago. How are your hemorrhoids? Are you still drinking? And what about your son? Is he *learning* from the prison experience?

These are not exact quotes, but they will do, and a transcript would be just as ugly. Reagan has always had a Nixon-like hatred for the press—

even back in the old days, when he needed them—but now, in these last tortured hours of his presidency, he sees no reason to hide it.

And why should he? He is an old man with decent instincts and a truly enviable record as president that might still shine in the history books—if he quits the presidency tomorrow and gets out of town while there's still time.

That is harsh advice, but I offer it without malice and in fact with a certain affection (or perhaps sympathy, or maybe true *recognition*) for one of the true warriors in the business. He has been a more effective politician than Hubert Humphrey and a better actor than Charlton Heston.

And Humphrey, widely regarded as one of the true warriors in his own right, couldn't even get elected—and in the end, despite many accolades, he was generally viewed as an embarrassment to the trade.

But Hubert got off easy, compared with what Reagan will go through if he decides to take the Nixon trip. Even Evans and Novak are worried about it. On TV the other night they were consoling each other with a slightly built, rheumy-eyed young man named Mitchell Daniels, the "chief White House political adviser" and "main architect," they said, "of President Reagan's most recent senatorial campaigns."

Young Daniels was guardedly optimistic, despite the foul fruits of his last project—a tragic and humiliating beating of the president, as well as the party. . . . He is a flimsy little yuppie who looks like something that got rejected at birth, in the throes of some mixup at the hospital, when the mother had to choose between it and some healthy-looking fetus that turned out to be Patrick Buchanan.

"Take the strong one," she said. "He will have a long life and be a comfort to me in my later years."

Well . . . maybe so. Mr. Daniels also said that both the party and the president were in far better shape than people seemed to think, despite the shocking hemorrhage of numbers in the wake of Oliver North and the fatal "Iranian Transaction."

"We are OK," he said. "I can assure you of that."

But it didn't seem that way to some of us. Daniels seemed no more "OK" than Bernhard Goetz. He will never get over what's wrong with him, and neither will Ronald Reagan.

They will be like the 49ers, the doomed victims of some unimaginably hideous wreck that will never come closer to being properly explained than The Rape of Nanking or the Springhill Mine Disaster.

They should all be fired. Candlestick Park has been a nest of dope fiends and waterheads from the very beginning. The whole structure should be plowed under, for landfill.

It is getting harder and harder to pay serious attention to the news these days. A new snowstorm has swallowed up the jeep in the back pasture, and the county animal control officer is hot on my heels with some kind of class-action complaint regarding "the torturing of wild animals."

"I know it sounds crazy," the newly elected sheriff told me at a banquet last week, "but they're demanding a full investigation. . . . Ye gods," he muttered, "what the hell are you *doing* out there, anyway? Didn't I warn you to stay away from those animals? Now I have to make a goddamn *formal* report! . . . What am I supposed to tell these people? That you insist on torturing animals? That we've tried to stop you, but we can't? No!" he shouted. "I can't tell them that!"

"I know," I said. "Don't worry. It's all nonsense."

"What?" he yelled. "Nonsense?" He chuckled bitterly. "Oh no," he said. "That's not what it says in this complaint! Or in that crazy thing you wrote for the newspaper!"

"You fool!" I said. "That was a *political allegory*. The fox was Pat Buchanan. He's the White house communications director . . ."

"What?" said the sheriff. "You expect me to actually write something like that?"

"No." I said, "but you can tell the animal control officer to write it." Which was true, and that is how we left it.

January 5, 1987

The Gizzard of Darkness

We drove north in the darkness toward Ignacio—just the three of us, huddled nervously in the cab of the old BMW 3.0 coupe. There was a light fog hovering around the towers of the Golden Gate Bridge, along with some stains of fresh blood on the deck. . . . There had been a massive collision a few days earlier.

Driving the bridge has never been safe, but in recent years—ever since it became a sort of low-tech Rube Goldberg experiment for traffic-flow specialists—it has become a maze of ever-changing uncertain lanes and a truly fearful experience to drive. At least half the lanes are always blocked off by flashing lights, fireballs and huge generator trucks full of boiling asphalt and crews of wild-eyed men wearing hard hats and carrying picks and shovels.

They are never gone, and the few lanes they leave open for what they call "civilian traffic" are often littered with huge red Lane Markers that look like heavy iron spittoons and cause terror in the heart of any unwitting driver who doesn't know they are rubber. . . . Nobody wants to run over one of those things, except on purpose, and in that case you want to take out a whole stretch of them, maybe 15 or 18 in a single crazed pass at top speed with the door hanging open.

We were not brooding on these things, however, as our little car sped north through the light midnight traffic toward our strange destination in Ignacio. . . . It was Saturday night and we were running late; our appointment with the Clairvoyant had been for 11 P.M., but a bizarre call from Washington had held us up.

The story, this time, was that CIA Chief William Casey—a key figure in the mushrooming Iran/Nicaragua scandal—had long since been "disappeared" by his CIA cohorts, and that the elderly gent now sequestered behind a screen of CIA bodyguards in a penthouse suite at Georgetown University Hospital is not Casey at all, but some cleverly crafted *impostor*.

"It's only a dummy," said my source. "They're going to shoot him full of cancer or some kind of animal poison just as soon as they can get him alone—and then they'll call a presidential press conference to announce that Casey lived and died as a true American Hero—who unfortunately went to his death with all the secrets of the Iranian Weapons Transaction and Oliver North and the criminal guilt of President Reagan still locked in his crippled brain.

"That will kill the whole case," he explained. "They will blame it all on Casey, and then bury that poor old wino in a closed casket and call for a New Beginning."

My informant is rarely wrong on these twisted, top-secret stories from the dark side. But they tend to be hard to confirm, and this one was no different.

I finally gave up and decided to lay off of political stories for a few days. My old friend Heest, a disbarred attorney, suggested another option. He was on his way "up the road," he said, to visit his personal psychic in Ignacio, to get some legal advice. He was facing charges of felony assault in Oakland for stabbing a stranger in the buttocks with a fork in a waterfront tavern, and his lawyer had quit for reasons he refused to discuss.

Not even the public defender would touch it, he said bitterly, so he had decided to turn his case over to his psychic, who had never let him down. "She is harder than cheap nails," he said, "and she draws all of her wisdom from *Michael,* who is very sharp about politics—maybe she can help you out on this Casey thing."

"Who is this *Michael?*" I asked him. "Does he have any links to The Agency?"

Heest laughed distractedly, but I could see he was getting frantic. He had suffered a broken wrist and loss of vision in one eye, as a result of the stabbing incident, and he was helpless to drive his own car. "Please *help* me!" he screamed.

"Don't worry," I told him. "I'll drive. . . ."

It was long after midnight when we finally got to Ignacio, where the psychic was waiting impatiently. She was a nice-looking woman of 39 or so, wearing a stylish white dress and no shoes. There was nothing about her home to suggest a lifetime of witchcraft.

Heest had gone to pieces. It was not his first offense he was well-known in Oakland as a savage drunkard and a wife beater. "What does *Michael* say?" he whimpered. "He's the only one who can help me now."

The woman stared at him for a moment, then she uttered a long sigh and fell back in her Spanish-leather chair. Her eyes rolled up in her skull until only the whites showed, and her lips moved soundlessly, as if talking to birds in her sleep.

Then she came slowly awake and gazed around the room with a faraway look in her eyes. "Michael says he cannot help you now," she said in a low voice to Heest. "He says you will spend the next two years in an extremely confined environment—probably at Folsom Prison."

"What? Heest screamed. "Oh, God, NO!" He leaped up from his chair and staggered out of the room. We heard him retching outside on the lawn.

I dragged Heest into the car and left him sucking feverishly on a bottle of green chartreuse. . . . I went back inside, but there was still no sign of *Michael,* and I demanded to know where he was.

"He speaks to us from the *astral* plane," she said. "But tonight he is here in the room."

Suddenly, the whole thing became clear to me. These people were on a different frequency—like Mr. Kenneth from Park Avenue—and this creature called Michael that Heest had tried to pass off as some kind of hermit political guru was in fact not a person at all.

He was, according to one of the occult handbooks she had on the floor among a pile of stones, "composed of 1,050 individual essences, ex-humans so to speak, who have lived on the land part of earth."

Well. . . . I thought, why not give the bugger a shot? Maybe he knows something. "Where is William Casey tonight?" I asked her. "Is there any truth to these rumors that he is not where he seems to be?"

She seemed puzzled, so I gave her some of the details and she passed them along to *Michael* wherever he was—and his answer came back like a rocket.

"You must be crazy," she said. "This man is the director of the Central Intelligence Agency. Of *course* he is where he seems to be! What are you trying to do—get me arrested?" She stood up and waved a fat silver stone at me. "Get out of my house!" she yelled. "I've seen your kind before!"

Heest died in the back seat somewhere along the way back to town, so I dropped him off with Capt. Hanssen at the harbor master's shack on Scott Street, where his body was burned with rubbish.

January 12, 1987

Crazy Patrick and Big Al

"I happen to believe if I could get nominated, I could be elected."

—Alexander Haig

They laughed when Big Al tossed his hat into the ring, but nobody is laughing now. As the race for the 1988 GOP presidential nomination gets bogged deeper into shame and confusion, the name "Haig" rises faster to the surface. "The General" has always been a slow starter, but those who have dealt with him at close quarters will tell you that he is capable of extreme bursts of speed in the stretch.

Not for long, they say—but there are times when "long" doesn't matter, and those are the times when people who thought they were *born* fast have looked back over their shoulder and seen Big Al coming on them like a panther with hot breath.

There is no noise, at first, they say—but all of a sudden you hear a weird mix or drooling, jabbering sounds, and then you get seized from behind by a thing with no real shape, and ridden down like a sheep.

There is nothing slow about Al Haig. He once got promoted from major to brigadier general in something like 68 seconds. That was in the good old days, when he went to work for Henry Kissinger and needed a fast promotion so he could wear the right kind of uniform to the White House.

It was like a Mason Williams film. Haig became a general so fast that most people thought he had been one all his life. It was one of those battlefield promotions that seemed *right* at the time, and it was never officially questioned . . . except by Richard Nixon, who thought it was very humorous.

On those restless nights when he drank gin with Kissinger in the Lincoln Room, he often joked about Haig. "How many stars can we grow on that boy?" he would ask, while Manolo brought the martinis and Henry scanned the stack of daily action-memos from his ambitious personal assistant, Gen. Haig. . . .

And Nixon, meanwhile—between bouts of falling to his knees and praying drunkenly for help to the portrait of Abe Lincoln on the wall— would try to speed-read the latest screed from Patrick Buchanan, his long-time personal speechwriter and ax-man, who had recently been assigned to handle what they called "the Agnew problem."

And now, less than 20 years later, we have Cruel Crazy Patrick and Big Al, the Wild Boys, roaming around Washington like a pair of Foam Frogs in heat, laying 3,000 eggs every night and cranking up a genuinely mean ticket—Haig & Buchanan, Buchanan & Haig. What does it matter? "We will kill the ones who eat us, and eat the ones we kill. . . ."

WINTER BOOK UPDATE: GOP

Robert Dole 3–1
Patrick Buchanan 4–1
Alexander Haig 8–1
George Bush 11–1
Gerald Ford 13–1
Jack Kemp 22–1
George Shultz 33–1
James Baker 34–1
Howard Baker 40–1
Paul Laxalt 44–1
Evan Mecham 59–1
Pierre DuPont 66–1
William Armstrong 70–1
Pat Robertson 188–1
Harold Stassen 100–1
The Field: Frank Sinatra,
Roy Cohn, Henry Kissinger,
Dennis Hopper, Richard Nixon, etc.

There is not much doubt about the real strength of the GOP ticket this year. It will come down to a choice between the Fat People and the Wild Boys, with nobody who can pass for human in either camp. Big Daddy is gone now. Ronald Reagan will never again ride the elephant; he is the oldest man except Footbone Willis who ever lived in the White House, and he has been a great gift to The Party. . . .

But eight years is enough, for these people, and they will be lucky to hang on for that long, while Oliver North is alive. "The Colonel," as they call him, is like one of those Doberman guard dogs that Hermann

Goering used to have, and when people stared at the beast they would look at each other and say, "Thank God that dog can't talk."

The Iranian Transaction had caused major movement on the GOP chart since that story broke in November. The party became polarized on issues entirely different from the ones Pat Robertson understood, and now he is gone, leaving the evangelical right wing of the party virtually naked of leverage and clearing the decks for Realpolitik heavy hitters like Dole, Haig and Buchanan.

George Bush has slipped badly. He is no longer the front-runner, and he will be totally off the board if he ever gets subpoenaed to testify about his role in the Iranian Transaction. His fingerprints are all over it, but so far he has slipped the noose . . . and last week he somehow managed to put his press secretary, Marlin Fitzwater, into the role of White House spokesman to replace Larry Speakes. Washington insiders were stunned. It was like Clyde sending Bonnie to represent him in court. Bush is doomed, but he is still dangerous.

The only "experienced" and plausible man for the job is Gerald Ford. Nixon has worked hard to regain respect, which might pay off for Jerry. Pardoning Nixon now seems fairly benign, just good party etiquette, in comparison with the current treachery.

The big loser in the last six months has been Paul Laxalt, who failed to elect a Republican successor for his Senate seat. Although Nevada is full of cheaters and losers, they are not widely loved.

Shultz has the face of a president, but he may not be genetically suitable to the Republicans.

If the Republicans have a future beyond 1988, it may be lurking like the ghost of Hermann Goering down in Arizona, where newly elected Gov. "Ev" Mecham is making Buchanan seem like a bleeding-heart wimp. Mecham's first official act was to cancel Martin Luther King's birthday as a paid state holiday. It embarrassed everybody in the state except the KKK and the Nazis. Even Barry Goldwater was horrified.

The rats never die. Every time they abandon one ship, they have to move to another—and this time it is the new *USS Arizona*.

January 19, 1987

Trapped in Harding Park

When Parker called from Phoenix I almost lost my grip. Once again he had found me in truly obscure lodgings. Last time it was the Arizona Biltmore, and now it was the El Drisco in San Francisco, a place where *nobody* can be found.

But Parker's people had no trouble running me down. There was a matter of $26,000 that I owed him on a bet regarding the rushing yardage of Herschel Walker, in his first year as fullback for the Dallas Cowboys. . . . Parker had won the bet, but not by much, and now he was eager to double up and get cranked on a sort of logarithmic basis, on the Super Bowl.

He was a Broncos fan; his wife had been somehow involved with Dan Reeves, when he was a running back for the old North Dallas Forty, and Parker's sense of loyalty had grown stronger over the years. He wanted to bet big on Denver. His faith was pure and his eyes were wild with greed.

He also wanted to buy the Boathouse Lounge, a long-abandoned roadhouse on the banks of Lake Merced—a place in the classic Raymond Chandler style, straight out of "The Big Sleep," or maybe some early Bogart saga. . . . It is a seedy place, but a powerful sense of drama seems to hover on it, a feeling that *almost anything can happen in a place like this*. . . .

Which is true. Parker, a profoundly wealthy parking lot magnate from Phoenix, had heard rumors about the Boathouse Lounge all the way from Scottsdale, where he lived on the edge of a golf course.

Money meant nothing to Parker, he said, but he felt that he could do gambling business only somewhere on a golf course, where there was no possible chance that somebody might overhear his conversation. It is a normal kind of attitude in Phoenix, where normal people and even journalists are routinely whacked, slit, strangled with their own small intestines and blown into clouds of pink meat, for reasons that seldom seem worth arguing about.

Parker wanted to watch the Super Bowl in a place where nobody would recognize him, or preferably not even speak English if they did. I suggested an obscure "sports bar" down the coast in Pacifica, a place normally lost in the fog belt, but with 15 or 16 TV sets and a state of the art telex gambling wire straight from the Churchill Downs Sporting Book in Las Vegas.

We ended up at the Harding Park golf course, at Benny's place, where we set up on the edge of the putting green a big TV set that I'd brought from the O'Farrell Theatre, plugged into a 200-foot extension cord, so we could watch it far out on the grass.

The Broncos were 9-point underdogs all week, but Parker refused to take points. We settled on $33,000 as the valid current price for his Mercedes 600 that he'd given me many months ago as "security" for our flaky bet on Herschel—and on that basis he said he wouldn't mind going double or nothing, with maybe a few side bets now and then.

"Wonderful," I said. "We will bet on *every play, every down,* every pass or run or fumble and even the exact hang on punts." We started with the first flip of the coin, which Denver won and which cost Parker the first of many, many $100 losses for the day.

By halftime it was clear that the price-bettors were not in an entirely favorable position. The nine-point gamblers' bulge that had looked so shrewd and menacing after the first 21 or 22 minutes was beginning to feel a bit queasy, after that hideous doom-struck little fruitbag, Rich Karlis, missed two straight field goals—one with the ball snapped from the 6-yard line.

The margin that should have been 16–9 or at least 13–9 was just a single point, and the weight was beginning to shift.

By the middle of the third quarter it was clear that the mean boys from New Jersey were simply too big for the Broncos, who averaged about 20 fewer pounds per man. . . .

The Denver pass rush—normally a speedy gang of sack artists and gamblers—couldn't get anywhere near Phil Simms.

By the end of the third quarter, with just 50 seconds left, the score was 19–10 . . . and then 26–10, exactly one TD over the spread and a long, mean quarter to go.

With 5:57 to go, Rich Karlis hit a field goal, but it was meaningless. It was another disastrous rout—the same kind of flogging that humiliated the 49ers.

By sundown Parker had lost $71,000, but it didn't seem to faze him. He felt he could get most of it back playing golf, where he maintained a 6 handicap and played frequently in the pro-am tournaments.

We went out on the back nine and hit the fat irons for $1,000 a shot on 16, 17 and 18. He played with the feverish intensity of a dope fiend or a man who had nothing to lose, and somehow he picked up three or four strokes on me. I didn't have the heart to flog him any longer. On

17 I had one of the most elegant attack shots of my life—a 220-yard 7-wood that went over a huge cypress tree and hit the pin on one bounce, but before Parker saw it I kicked it away in the rough and said I'd lost my ball. It seemed like the right thing to do.

The real horror came when we finally packed up and tried to drive back to town. It was getting dark, and the dim, orange lights from the shotgun range were bouncing gently across the lake. We could hear the flat boom of the big duck guns in the darkness as we drove slowly off the course and back toward Highway 1.

Parker was the first to flip out when he saw the big Master Lock and the chain around the gate, which had been wide open when we got there. "Mother of God!" he screamed. "I knew this would happen! They're waiting for us out there! It's a trap!"

"Nonsense," I told him. "There must be some mistake. All we have to do is call the police. We'll ring up the Taraval Station. They're only five minutes away."

"You crazy bastard!" he screamed. "I knew I couldn't trust you!" And then he disappeared into the wilderness, leaving everything behind him except his Harley-Davidson chain wallet and a matchbox full of blue MDMA capsules.

We never saw him again. About six minutes later a brace of police cars arrived, along with two carloads of wine-drunk teen-agers who taunted me unmercifully from the other side of the fence. "You dirty little sots!" I snarled at them. "Someday you'll be on this side!"

They were soon rousted by Officer John Probst, along with his partner, Paul Guinasso, who opened the gate and set us all free . . . except Parker, who took off like a rat through the trees.

January 26, 1987

Expelled from the System

"Hamilton Heights High School students who refuse urine tests when suspected of drug use for a second time will be expelled. Students testing positive can enter rehabilitation programs. . . ."

—*USA Today*, February 6, 1987

Sam Nunn was big on TV last week, and so was Ed Meese—along with Joe Biden, Terry Waite, Ted Kennedy and Carlos Lehder Rivas, the alleged "cocaine kingpin" from Colombia. There were also Arab arms dealer Adnan Khashoggi and White House Chief of Staff Donald Regan.

It was a mixed lot, for sure, and the only thing they all had in common was same-color backstage passes for the 1988 presidential campaign. They will be among the Players, the huge and crazy cast of this Thing that is looming before us.

The word among big-time political thinkers is that this one is going to be a genuine "watershed election," one of those uncommon moments where the lives of a whole generation will actually be altered forever, right in front of their own eyes.

These moments are rare. The last real one came in 1960, when John F. Kennedy punched through the fog of the "Eisenhower years" and the "Silent Generation" to upset then-Vice President Richard Nixon and snap the spine of an era that had gone on for too long.

This *generation*—the one that is in or out of college right now—seems fated for one of the lower slots on the ladder, as generations go: somewhere in the Great Wah of history between the time of Herbert Hoover, Warren Harding and Ulysses S. Grant.

A recent study of today's college students concludes that they "seem to have no confidence or willingness to extend their knowledge." They are bored by almost everything, says researcher Thomas Kopp of Miami University in Oxford, Ohio, and they are also boring people. More than any other generation, he says, they are dogmatic and uncreative, motivated more by desire for good grades than excitement for learning.

There are other hazards that plague this generation. The heavy hand of The Law has caught up with almost everybody, and even the innocent are plagued by lawyers and health inspectors. No generation since the crazed "McCarthy Era" of the 1950s has had to struggle with such a grim historical albatross.

Which of us can look back on even the worst and wrongest of our high school years and say that we ever faced anything as bad as being grabbed on the way to home-room by a big man in uniform, dragged into the nearest bathroom and forced to urinate into a jar, for reasons that might scar you forever?

Who knows what that dingbat principal in Arcadia, Ind., had in mind when he ordered his students to submit to random drug/urine testing? In the old days it was just a matter of being caught smoking cigarettes in the band room or drinking beer at lunchtime in the parking lot—and these crimes were *serious,* at the time, but they were not so serious as to get you *expelled from the system forever*.

That is the hallmark of the Reagan administration—a Punishment Ethic that permeates the whole infrastructure of American life and eventually gets down to George Orwell's notion, in *Animal Farm*, that "all animals are equal, but some animals are more equal than others."

Which is fair enough, in some years, but even in the worst ones it is not a fair thing to lay on teen-agers who are constantly flogged by the idea that any small deviation from The Rules might get them expelled, branded like lepers and cost them their "place in line" for the rest of their lives.

Both Thomas Edison and John Dillinger were expelled from high school. But they didn't let Dillinger come back, and the rest is history— the same kind of history that Ronald Reagan's "supply-side," "trickle-down" political philosophy has inflicted on these poor bastards who are coming of age in the '80s.

It is a grim time to be growing up. An NBC News/*Wall Street Journal* poll found that "one in three single people say they would ask a potential partner to be tested for the AIDS virus." And "safe sex," the meanest oxymoron of our time, has taken root on TV with such a vengeance that even Oprah Winfrey endorses it.

"Thirty-four percent of singles said they would ask a potential partner to take a test for AIDS," said a Page 38 piece in the *Washington Post,* "and 15 percent were undecided." It was a bare 51 percent of respondents that said "they would not ask a partner to be tested for AIDS" and "a 56 percent majority of singles that said they would ask a new sexual partner for his or her "sexual history" before agreeing to "have sex" and even then "63 percent said they would insist on using a condom."

Well . . . maybe so. Rubbers are big business these days, along with "rehab," D-rings, and other forms of punishment associated with the Republican mentality.

It is a terrifying thing to have to confront, at the age of 15 or 16. The only living American who seems to have come genuinely and even happily to grips with the New Ethic is former Secretary of State Henry Kissinger.

The president's wife, in her role as main spokeswoman for the administration's War on Drugs—headed until now by Vice President Bush—has created so much pressure on a whole generation of confused pimply teen-agers who may or may not "Say No to Drugs" that the last half of the '80s seems destined to produce another *generation of criminals* like the one that got caught on the cusp of the '60s, when the Jell-O-conformity of the Eisenhower Era finally created so many socioeconomic rejects that it eventually became fashionable to be one. . . .

That was when "the '60s" began—first the Beat Generation, and the New Frontier, then civil rights marches, the Vietnam War, and finally the national nightmare of hippies, free sex and the worship of drugs in all forms, including the fried skins of bananas.

It was a wild time. The great pendulum swung with a vengeance, and San Francisco was the crossroads for most of it. . . . which might happen again, very soon, with the prospect of Warren Hinckle running for mayor. There is another one of those Ninth Waves coming, just over the Chinese horizon. Nobody knows what it means, but in the end it will probably not be much different from the others. If Hinckle has his way, there will be a condom attached to every copy of *The Examiner* on sale in any street box in San Francisco, or even Oakland.

Why not? Let the million flowers bloom. We have done it before, more than once, and it was always a lot better than getting drafted or purified or hanging around a Merrill Lynch office all day, to get two cents on the dollar.

February 9, 1987

Gone with the Wind

I was talking to a journalist from Arizona the other day, and he said we should all be careful about jumping to conclusions about this hideous scandal that is hovering over the White House. "We can't just treat this like a remake of Watergate," he said. "This one might turn out to be entirely different."

"You're right," I said. "This will be more like the Carson Sink."

"Nonsense," he said. "That had nothing to do with politics. It was a strange animal 'die-off' of some kind, a mysterious environmental disaster—even biologists are baffled."

"Not really," I said. "They know it was poison, and it killed everything it touched."

Which is more or less true. The Carson Sink is a national wildlife preserve, where all of the animals died or at least most of them, and the few that survived straggled off across the desert to poison other places. There were geese, egrets, coots, ravens, ducks, blue herons, white pelicans and something like 3 million fish. . . . "This used to be a nice place," said one local. "We used to come here and feed the birds. Now we can't even eat them."

That will not be the problem in Washington. Cannibalism is still fashionable there, but it is more in the nature of a local art form than random feeding on flesh, and the food chain is so full of poison that the natives have long since developed powerful immune systems, and many appear to thrive on it.

Both William Casey and Robert McFarlane, for instance, were eaten so quickly that some people compared them to the deadly poison Fugu fish, which is considered a rare delicacy in Japan, eaten only by ranking gourmets.

Casey, former head of the CIA, was eaten within hours of his first and final exposure to the dread Iran/contra toxin. He was gone so fast that nobody even talked to him, consumed by reports of a brain tumor that allegedly rendered him speechless.

McFarlane, a former national security adviser to the president, survived a bit longer than Casey, but he eventually met the same fate. Not long after he went before the Senate Intelligence Committee and uttered testimony that seemed damaging to President Reagan's credibility, he fell into a funk and swallowed 30 Valiums in what was called "an apparent suicide attempt." It failed, and he is now "resting comfortably," they say, in the maximum security tower at Bethesda Naval Hospital, down the hall from William Casey.

McFarlane will not be there for long. They will be needing those beds pretty soon, when the investigation gets rolling and the other boys from the White House start testifying under oath. Valium sales will soar, and the stomach pumps at Bethesda will be kept cranked up at all times. By late spring the VIP ward will be so crowded that it will look like one of those nightmarish hospital-in-the-street scenes out of "Gone With the Wind." . . . There will be uncontrolled howling and weeping, and many patients will be chained together like common criminals, with numbers inked on their foreheads and subpoenas attached to the backs of their gray pajamas with super glue and duct tape.

The last big whack to hit Washington was the Watergate scandal, which ripped many people out by the roots, including Richard Nixon and a whole cast of top-level villains from the staff of the White House and the national Republican Party. . . . Many of these went to prison, some were crushed, and a few of the worst and most dangerous became obscenely rich.

But that is where the parallel ends. Gordon Liddy was the Bad Boy in the Watergate crowd—the meanest of the mean—but all he did was commit a few burglaries, shred some papers and shoot out a street light in front of McGovern for President headquarters on Capitol Hill. . . . And for that he served four years in prison, where he wired his jaws shut and took full advantage of a federally financed "phys/ed program" that got him certified as a sixth-degree Black Belt in karate by the time of his release.

But all Gordon did was follow a set of queer orders, steal a few documents and threaten to cripple anyone who objected. His main crime was scaring people, which ranks very low on the felony schedule and exists in a whole different world from the genuinely major crimes that USMC Lt. Col. Oliver North is eventually going to have to answer for.

Gordon Liddy was cruel, but he never did anything even remotely like running a neo-Nazi shadow government out of the White House basement, skimming millions of dollars off the top of illegal arms sales to hostile foreign governments or selling weapons to a hate-crazed international terrorist like the Ayatollah Khomeini in Iran, who was paying North millions of dollars for TOW missiles with one hand while admittedly using the other to finance the 1983 bombing of the U.S. Marine barracks in Lebanon, which killed nearby 300 of North's people.

That is a long way from "Semper Fi," and there is a steel bed with D-rings already reserved at Bethesda for the eventual presence of Ollie North. He is hiding behind the Fifth Amendment now—along with his one-time boss at the White House, former NSC chief Vice Adm. John Poindexter.

But that dike will not hold forever, and when it finally breaks there will be bodies all over the landscape hanging grotesquely in the tangled branches like the coots and the cormorants and the bloated white pelican carcasses in the trees around Carson Sink.

Many will be called, and more than a few will be chosen. The Presidential Suite at Bethesda is on 24-hour standby status, as always, and there is a posh corner ward full of needles, pumps and other powerful instruments that has been set aside in the name of Vice President George Bush. He is fatally allergic to Valium, they say—but before this Iran/contra nightmare is over he is going to need a very strong medicine.

There is nobody in Washington who believes that these cowboys and lackeys and geeks like North, Poindexter and McFarlane were acting *on their own*—that they were running that whole monumentally crooked circus without the consent of Vice President, White House heir apparent and ex-CIA Director George Bush.

No. There are limits to the art of damage control, and this one will not be dismissed as some kind of "environmental mystery" like Carson Sink, or a low-rent burglary like Watergate.

February 16, 1987

New Blood on the Tracks

"Now what these gentlemen did, in terms of their advice to the president, I have no idea."

—Marlin Fitzwater, new White House press manager

The saga of Marlin Fitzwater is a tragic one. He is a genuinely big time political operative, Ronald Reagan's new press secretary and chief media spokesman for the White House. . . . He clawed his way to the top in a truly evil business, a savage trade that will eat some of its best and brightest practitioners.

The last White House press secretary who really *thrived* in the job was Pierre Salinger, who worked for John F. Kennedy in the early '60s. Pierre was good. He was trusted on both ends—by Big Jack and also the press people, and his brain was extremely *quick.* If you ever got bored with hanging around your desk in the White House press room and started feeling too smart for the job you were stuck with, all you had to do was get uppity at one of JFK's weekly press conferences:

If Kennedy didn't flog you, Pierre would . . . he was a player, and he would give you all the action you wanted, and when Mr. Salinger was quoted in the *Washington Post,* it was usually on Page 1.

But Pierre had to quit when JFK was murdered. He now lives in Paris and covers Europe for ABC. He set a standard, in terms of style and tone, that none of the hacks who came after him could match or even understand . . . until Jim Brady came along in 1981.

Brady was a class act, but he didn't last long in the job. Some pimply young geek named Hinckley put a bullet into his head, and another one through Ronald Reagan's armpit. . . . Big Dutch survived, but Brady was shot through the brain and was soon replaced by Larry Speakes, a shallow-brained, mean-spirited, pot-bellied yuppie from the bowels of Mississippi. . . . The only fun Speakes ever had in his job was when he had to formally deny that President Reagan had called one of the ranking journalists in the White House press corps a "son of a bitch."

Speakes mopped the sweat out of his eyes with a blue silk handkerchief. "You must be deaf," he said to the reporter. "What the president actually said was, 'It's a sunny day and you're rich.' "

Some people laughed, but Speakes was not among them. And neither was Marlin Fitzwater, who was then employed as press secretary for

Vice President George Bush. Fitzwater was being groomed for the job he always wanted—the main nut, the voice of the president, heir to the throne of Jody Powell and Ron Ziegler.

It is a nasty job, but they rarely get put in jail. Ziegler *walked,* somehow, through the darkness of the Watergate scandal—and so did Patrick Buchanan, who was guilty as 16 dogs (and who will also walk out of the Iran/contra scandal because he was only a speech writer, they said, and he never got near the money).

But if real justice were done in this world, Patrick would be chained ankle-to-ankle with Oliver North and forced to hitchhike together like Siamese twins from coast to coast on U.S. Highway 6, which runs in a twisted line from the George Washington Bridge at the top of New York City to the lip of the Malibu pier . . .

Number 6 is gone now, swallowed up in the huge gray web of the new interstate highway system; they changed the numbers and laid concrete over the old two-lane blacktop, but U.S. 6 still shows on old highway maps that they used to give away free at the Gulf and Sinclair stations.

On most days it is a waste of time to read the newspapers, but last Saturday was not one of them. The front page of *The New York Times* reads like the Book of Revelation. From left to right, across the top of the page, it was a chain-link indictment of some doomed and twisted vision of the old American Dream:

Column One began "REAGAN UNAWARE OF ANY COVER-UP, A SPOKESMAN SAYS" . . . The spokesman, of course, was Marlin, and the best he could do was, "As far as the president is concerned, there is no cover-up. He certainly was not aware of any."

Next, for comic relief, a beady-eyed single-column cut of Dennis B. Levine, the scandal-ridden stock-swindler turned stool pigeon, with a caption slugged SENTENCED. He got off with two years in prison.

Back to business: "U.S. SAID TO PLAN FOR AID TO EGYPT IN ATTACKING LIBYA." The deck gets to the meat of it: "Reagan Reportedly Approved Help in 'Pre-emptive' Raid if Tripoli Made Threat." The Fitzwater denial is relegated to the jump page: "There was no policy or plan to do that that was put in motion."

Then, the real zinger: A two-column picture of Mario Cuomo, a hand over his eyes, despondent, with one of the most vicious cutlines ever—one brief line: "Q: And what about the Vice Presidency?"

Honored with the top of Column Six was "The Brazilian problem," as bankers refer to it: "BRAZIL TO SUSPEND INTEREST PAY-MENT TO FOREIGN BANKS. DEBT TOTALS $108 BILLION."

All this pushed more world-class stories below the fold: "Regan and Mrs. Reagan Feud over President's Work Load," "Senate Panel Told of Weaknesses in the Control of U.S. Arms Sales," and, for dessert, "Judge Gets Poisoned Candy; Man He Sentenced Arrested."

It had the look of bad news and big trouble for Marlin Fitzwater. His life was going to turn strange and awkward, as more and more of his people were taken off to jails and federal prisons. . . . Marlin peaked about five years too late; that job he always wanted and that fine office full of teakwood and soft Spanish leather in the West Wing of the White House was suddenly beginning to look more like a jail cell than the Room at the Top his mother always told him he would have.

They were guilty. They were *criminals,* and many would be sentenced in the same pinstripe Ralph Lauren suits they used to wear when they swapped war stories about Egypt and Bangkok and commando raids in the Congo after hours in the Oval Office.

U.S. Marine Lt. Col. Oliver North will probably do three years in Lompoc for his role in the treacherous Iran/contra scam, and people like Regan and Casey and Poindexter will also spend time in prison—just like the boys from Watergate, who were also big hitters in the White House.

But Marlin's main problem will be Dutch, The Old Man, The President, The Great Communicator, Ronald Reagan. As the foul evidence unfolds, even his own people like Ed Meese and John Tower are forced to confront the awful possibility that the president is guilty of major crimes and may have to be locked up.

February 23, 1987

The Lake of Fire

"A good tree cannot bring forth evil fruit, neither can a corrupt tree bring forth good fruit."

—Matthew 7:18

There was blood in the water in Washington last week. There were human remains on the sidewalk outside Duke Ziebert's, and the hallways in the White House basement were slick with human scum. Even The Gipper was bleeding, and George Bush was walking around like a man with both wrists slit and trying to ignore the blood.

"Hey George—what's that red stuff dripping on your shoes? Is that *blood?*"

"What? Are you crazy? That is *oil,* my friend—pure red petroleum iodides, for the blisters on my legs."

Indeed. And before this thing is over George will know agonies far worse than simple gout, or leech fever, or even the heartbreak of psoriasis. There is already talk among his neighbors up there in Kennebunkport about strapping him onto one of those old-timey dunking stools and letting the local boys have a go at him. . . . *Put him under a few times, Frankie, give him the two-minute cure, and maybe then he'll admit he was running the whole thing, all along.*

Good old George. He stood behind the president, right or wrong—and he even said he'd been one of the first to know about—and even to *approve* of—the malignant Iranian Transaction, although he never knew Eugene Hasenfus personally. That privilege was left to his staff people: Donald Gregg and the late Max Gomez, who died in the crash of that same C-130 that Hasenfus walked away from and brought the rain down on everybody.

But nobody is worried about George now. He will get his, soon enough—and in the meantime he was formally replaced as the official GOP front-runner for 1988 by former long-shot candidate, ex-Sen. Howard Baker from Tennessee, who was selected by party elders to seize the reins of power in the White House from the wretched Donald Regan, Reagan's Rasputin-like chief of staff, who was forced out of the White House for monumental negligence and sent back to his natural base on Wall Street, in the shadow of Ivan Boesky.

So the bogeyman is gone now. Regan was a swine from the start and a failure at his job—as the Tower Report documented, line after merciless line—but his last act on the job was an honorable thing, although it was not widely interpreted that way by the cannibal crowd in Washington.

By hanging on as long as he could, if only for two or three weeks, he took massive enemy fire on his own position and sacrificed what little was left of his own reputation and gave Dutch time to get away—just like he always did in the good old days, when he still thought he was John Wayne.

God only knows who that poor old man thinks he is now. Old actors never feel guilty for crimes they committed at work—because all they ever really did was play roles, and that was all Reagan did as president. He is going to have a hard time understanding some of the things that are going to happen to him when he starts getting treated like Richard Nixon.

That will happen. The Tower Report was only the tip of the iceberg. It takes its name from the ex-senator from Texas who once employed Robert McFarlane as a staff assistant, before he got promoted to his last job of record as Ronald Reagan's national security adviser.

McFarlane has been a loose cannon on the White House deck for a long time, the only one of the Iranian Transaction insiders who has come forth to testify against the president's fragile credibility.

But then he tried to commit suicide by taking what they called "a drug overdose." It was only 30 or 40 hits of Valium, they said, which impressed the Georgetown crowd, but Jim Morrison would have laughed it off as a chaser.

Mac seemed like a flake, a Dope Fiend of some kind. . . . And yet, when the big boys from Tower Commission went to Bethesda Naval Hospital to take his sworn testimony that clearly contradicted the word of the President of the United States, they believed Robert McFarlane's admittedly kinky version of events, instead of Ronald Reagan's.

It was bad news for The Gipper. All of a sudden, he was getting a busy signal every time he tried to ring the Secret Service hangar and order up the presidential helicopter, for a trip anywhere.

Even his personal pilots were giving him the fish eye. If he wants to get out of town now he will need a Rasta wig and some black leather overalls.

U.S. Marine Lt. Col. Oliver North is emerging now as the Charles Manson figure in this hideous scandal that crawls like a plague of maggots on the White House. Ollie was a *player;* there is not much doubt about that—and now that he is getting desperate he has taken to quoting the Bible.

On Friday afternoon, after the Tower Report pictured him as a fanatical thug, he was telling White House reporters to have a look at some verses from the Book of Matthew, specifically Chapter 5, Verses 8 and/or 10 from the Sermon on the Mount—or the Beatitudes, as North said, if they wanted to know the real truth about his awful situation.

Verse 8 says, "Blessed are the pure in heart, for they shall see God" . . . and No. 10 goes like this: "Blessed are those who are persecuted for righteousness' sake, for theirs is the kingdom of heaven."

Ollie takes a certain comfort in these glitzy New Testament dictums—which on some crazy shameless level seem to suggest that he may in fact be like Jesus.

Well . . . all things are possible in this world, but there are also a few more chapters in the good Book of Matthew than the ones Ollie had on his palm card:

"GIVE NOT THAT WHICH IS HOLY UNTO THE DOGS, NEITHER CAST YE YOUR PEARLS BEFORE SWINE, LEST THEY TRAMPLE THEM UNDER THEIR FEET, AND TURN AGAIN AND REND YOU."

That is Matthew 7:6, and it is not the brutal, pagan image that Col. North will want to lay on a jury of his peers—especially the God-fearing ones—when his time finally comes in the dock.

The bell has rung for the wild boys in the White House basement.

March 2, 1987

So Long, George

"I had a dream the other night: I got a hit off a left-handed pitcher. It was a clean hit, and I kept runnin' and runnin' and I kept on runnin', but I never could get to first base."

Negro League veteran, on television, February 11, 1987

"Before this thing is over George will know agonies far worse than simple gout, or leech fever, or even the heartbreak of psoriasis."

Hunter S. Thompson, *San Francisco Examiner,* March 2, 1987

Big George bit the bullet Sunday night, and it was a powerful thing to see. There was a fast and terrible speed to it that was almost biblical—like the Book of Revelation, where the rivers fill with blood and the seeds of the land turn to poison and men will gnaw their tongues for pain.

At midnight on Friday, George was the main man in the Republican politics and the certified front-runner for the GOP presidential nomination in 1988 . . . and sometime around noon on Saturday, only 12 or 13 hours later, he was down in the ditch with all the other low-rent crooks and fixers and hustlers like Wild Bill Casey and Spiro Agnew and crazy Bob McFarlane, who made such a silly attempt at suicide that even teen-agers laughed at him.

The hammer came down very suddenly, when George was just starting to feel uppity. After 16 weeks of laying back in the weeds like a dirty little animal, he suddenly came out swinging. . . . They showed the whole thing on national TV, from the time he emerged from his slick-silver White House jet airplane on the runway at Nashua, N.H., until 13 hours later when a cruel combination of his son manque from Miami and some dingbat doctor from Guatemala named Castejon set him up for a felony bust and three or four long years in a cage like the ones they used to put bears and big snakes in, at some federal prison like Eglin or Lompoc or the new windowless dungeon in Phoenix.

It was an ugly scene. George had just received word that big-time political pollsters in Georgia and 11 other Southern states had made him a huge and prohibitive favorite to sweep the whole thing on Super Tuesday in the first week of March '88 by winning so many state primary elections all at once that nobody could ever catch him. Maybe Dole would take Kansas and Al Haig had a lock on New Orleans, but Big George would be the guaranteed winner.

That was on Saturday. George went wild with joy and ordered up a six-pack of California Coolers for his staff . . . and then he called his son, Jeb, in Miami, who told him about the letter.

"What letter?" said George. "I never sent you any letter."

"Oh no," said Jeb. "Not me. It's the one about Oliver North—that deal you fixed up with him with Dr. Castejon."

George went stiff, then dropped to his knees like a wino and wept openly in front of his staff people.

The jig was up. And even as they screamed and bitched at each other, the Miami Herald was already on the streets, with the Bush-Castejon correspondence on the front page.

It was a felony crime, and George had signed his own name to the letter that would introduce Ollie to the evil Castejon. The shrewd and treacherous vice president was no longer clean, and if he hung around in New Hampshire much longer they would probably lock him up. He was doomed.

George went out on a limb, as they say—full of all the slick hubris and dark yuppie instincts that got him up there where he is today—and somebody with a really fine feel for politics decided to chop him down.

It was the same day that John Gotti, the accused Mafia chieftain, was acquitted in New York by a jury of his peers and went free on the streets like any other plumbing contractor with six bodyguards and a steel-gray Cadillac limousine waiting outside the federal courtroom and a closet full of tailor-made suits and two beach-white overcoats made from the skin of unborn wolves.

George Bush does not dress in that style. He is, after all, the vice president, and until the *Miami Herald* got a very sudden handle on him and whipped it out in the form of a doomsday-style copyright story in Sunday's early edition and every syndicate wire in the nation, George was looking almost like he might be the next president of the United States.

That was before he spoke with the raven, who told him "nevermore."

The bird arrived sometime around midnight, according to White House sources, and George was not ready for it. He went all to pieces when the beast flew into his window and croaked at him repeatedly, "Nevermore."

It made no sense at the time—although it was in fact March 13, a

Friday; and also the night of the full moon . . . but George is not a Moon Child. He was born under some other star. June 12, 1924, in fact. And he is marked with the sign of the chicken.

George prospered, nonetheless. He went to Yale and made friends in national politics—so many, in fact, that he was soon offered jobs like U.S. ambassador to Beijing, national chairman of the Republican Party and director of the Central Intelligence Agency, by Richard Nixon.

That was in the good old days, when real men were still running the White House and the president roamed the hallways at night with a beaker of gin in his fist, raving and jabbering at huge oil portraits of Abe Lincoln and John Philip Sousa while Henry Kissinger followed him around and made notes.

Nixon was a bad drunk when he got his hands on a pint of gin, and in those last ugly days when his whole life was draining away like hot Jell-O and all of his boys were being hauled off to prison by federal marshals, he came more and more to love his gin.

His brain was gone, by then, and on nights toward the end it was only the butler, Manolo, who kept him from getting busted for public drunkenness.

On some nights he wanted to drive—maybe over the bridge to Virginia or down to his private dock on the river where he kept the presidential yacht tied up—The Sequoia, which he used as a personal hideout where he could gamble all night with his friends.

Reagan seems to have no friends—only Nixon, who calls him every day in his new role as the heir apparent to the doomed and disloyal George Shultz.

March 16, 1987

Doomed Love in the Rockies

I was just settling in to watch the presidential press conference on TV last Thursday night when my phone rang. It was the hot line number, a sure sign of trouble. . . .

Never mind that, I thought. I am working. I can't be disturbed at this time. This might even be Reagan's last press conference. He had not been looking good recently; he seemed about 110 years old and utterly disoriented at all times. . . . His eyes had a viscous, jellylike appearance and he had taken to letting his hands flap crazily at his sides when he walked down the halls of the White House, even when photographers were present. Some very goofy-looking photographs had turned up in the press room, but none of the newspapers would use them, for fear of alarming the public. . . .

My phone was still ringing as Reagan made his appearance. I tried to ignore the noise, but after 30 or 40 rings I got nervous and picked it up.

It was Tex, from the trailer court, and he sounded frantic. "It's Loretta!" he shouted. "She's dying. You better get here quick, Doc, and bring the chloroform."

"What?" I said. "Are you crazy? Call me back after the press conference."

"No!" he screamed. "She's going *out!* This is it! I already have her in the bathtub."

Ye gods, I thought. What now? And why chloroform? But I had no choice. Tex was a dangerous brute and Loretta was a drinker. . . . and if she died, I would be named as the Family Doctor and flogged in public.

It was an evil situation, and I had somehow become a slave to it. On my way outside to the Jeep I picked up a pint bottle of No. 417 chloroform from the medicine tank. It had been around a while, but I felt it was active.

The blizzard was still raging and the road was slick with black ice. When I arrived at Tex's trailer I heard sounds of screaming and high-pitched cries from inside. The door was ajar, and I found them both in the bathroom. Loretta was lying in the bathtub, and her eyes were rolled back in her head. Tex was on his knees beside the tub, trying to keep her head above water. He seemed hysterical, "Why did you do it?" he screamed. "I can't stand to see you die like this!"

The bathroom was full of water, and I could see flecks of blood on the tile around the tub. Loretta made a low crying noise and tried to sit up in the water, but Tex lost his grip on her and she fell heavily sideways.

When Tex saw me in the mirror he went all to pieces and began sobbing, unable to get his breath. He reached behind him and lifted a tall bottle of green Chartreuse to his lips, then he poured two large jiggers and gave one to Loretta. "Here, honey," he said. "Drink this. It can't go on much longer."

She swallowed the green liquid . . . and then she jerked straight up in the water and began retching horribly.

"She's dying," he said calmly. "We can't help her now. It's the booze. She finally went too far."

Loretta groaned desperately and tried to speak, but Tex suddenly stood up and began hosing her down with a high-powered shower massage unit. The water made a cruel thudding noise as it beat down on her stomach.

Tex was still jabbering about Death and Whiskey and Punishment, then he asked if I'd brought the chloroform. "We'll need it by morning," he said quietly. "Toward the end she'll go into convulsions."

Then he seized my arm and pulled me out of the bathroom. "Don't worry," he said. "She'll be OK, but she has to keep taking her medicine."

"Medicine?" I said. "What is it?"

"Vitamins," he replied. He showed me a handful of thick white tablets that looked vaguely familiar. "She needs two more right now," he said. "I want to teach her a lesson she'll never forget."

Suddenly I understood. "You swine!" I snarled. "You evil bastard! These are not vitamins. This is Antabuse."

"Why not?" he said. "I tried everything else."

It was ugly. Antabuse is a brutally powerful emetic that is only triggered by alcohol and only used by terminal drunkards who know they will die if they even think about drinking any more whiskey. It is like wiring a pipe bomb to your transmission that will only explode if you shift into reverse.

I felt dirty and wrong for just being there. Tex wanted to keep the chloroform, but I packed it up in my kit and left quickly. It was still snowing.

By the time I got home the presidential press conference was over, but Reagan had enjoyed it so much that he seemed reluctant to leave.

On his way down the hall to his quarters he paused long enough to drive another savage spike through the heart of George Bush, confirming on camera that his loyal vice president and one-time heir apparent was at least as guilty as Poindexter and the lunatic Oliver North.

Bush denied it, but his lies only made him seem sleazier. His face has become swollen and he is said to be plagued by a growth of dead fatty tissue on his back, which is gathering in a lump in the area between his shoulder blades and prevents him from walking normally. He avoids TV interviews and new White House chief of staff Howard Baker has warned him to stay away from the Rose Garden on any day when the president is scheduled to meet visiting dignitaries or appear for a photo opportunity with the media. "They don't want him around," said one Washington journalist. "That thing on his back is growing so fast that he's beginning to look like the Hunchback of Notre Dame."

Bush has never been known for his ability to command personal loyalty from his staff people or even his family. Not even Republican politicians want to be photographed with him, and in recent weeks the desertion rate was beginning to look like a run on a Brazilian bank. . . . First his own son betrayed him in incriminating personal correspondence that showed up in the *Miami Herald,* then Arab arms dealer Adnan Khashoggi went sideways on him by offering to produce canceled checks to prove George was lying when he said he had never solicited illegal contributions for the "contras" in Nicaragua, and finally the president trashed him on national TV. . . . But all that was as nothing compared with the filthy shoe that dropped Monday when Manucher Ghorbanifar announced that he was now eager to testify before Congress and tell everything he knows about the dark underbelly of the Iran/contra affair, including "who is lying and where the money went."

Many heads will roll in Washington when that happens and there is no joy tonight in the home of George Bush. They will soon be loading him up on the tumbril with others and carrying him off to the guillotine.

March 23, 1987

The Scum of the Earth

American Life in the '80s . . . A man called Oral: Freud Wept, God cried, Even the Devil was Shamed . . . How Low, O Lord, How Low?

"And the Jews' Passover was at hand, and Jesus went up to Jerusalem, And found in the temple those that sold oxen and sheep and doves, and the changers of money sitting: And when he had made a scourge of small cords, he drove them all out of the temple, and the sheep, and the oxen; and poured out the changers' money, and overthrew the tables; And said unto them that sold doves, Take these things hence; make not my Father's house a house of merchandise."

—John 2:13–16

The TV preachers were all over the news last week, fighting desperately with the forces of Satan and the shame of their own kind. It was a crisis for The Holy Church, they said, and also for the revenue stream. The devil himself had somehow got his hands on God's throttle and now the boat was running out of control, aimed for the rocks at top speed. The wages of sin had taken a sudden upturn.

All the big boys went public, locking arms in a phalanx of righteousness that included almost everybody in The Business except Pat Robertson and his one-time protege, the dirty little degenerate Jim Bakker and his wife, Tammy, a confessed dope addict.

That is extremely harsh language to describe the essentially minor crimes that the ill-fated Bakkers were finally accused of committing in the course of their 17-year marriage and their rise to fame and prominence as co-hosts of a nationally syndicated religious TV operation called "The Jim and Tammy Show." It was harmless enough, on its face—not much different from "Leave it to Beaver," except that it reported revenues of $129 million last year—and if Tammy got deep into Valium and Jim got naked and crazy with a church secretary for a one-night romp seven years ago, so what? The White House and half of the corner offices in Manhattan would be empty for the next 100 years if we held our presidents and big-business executives to standards like that. . . . Betty Ford ate so much Valium she finally had to start her own hospital, and even Richard Nixon kept a lanky Chinese woman on a houseboat up the river from San Francisco.

No. The Bakkers went down for other and darker reasons. They were guilty of crimes against nature—or at least the nature of their own kind—and in the end they were eaten for the same reasons and by the same kind of power-crazed cannibals who ate Spiro Agnew, James Watt, Wilbur Mills and who will soon eat the remains of Michael Deaver, who was once Nancy Reagan's best friend in the White House and the closest adviser to the president.

These things happen. We are living in cheap times, and the fast lane is littered with some very expensive wrecks. Mike Deaver will go to prison, along with ex-heroes like USMC Lt. Col. Oliver North, the recently demoted Rear Adm. John Poindexter and former Air Force Maj. Gen. Richard Secord.

The only survivors will be whores, Black Priests and mean dingbats like former Interior Secretary James Watt, who recently accepted a job on the new board of directors of the PTL Club.

The Bakkers were doomed and Robertson was laying low, as far out in the weeds as he could crawl without abandoning all hope for his 1988 presidential ambitions. . . . But now, creeping up from the smoking ruins of the once-holy PTL Club like some hair-shirt golem from a Baptist vision of Hell, was the shrewd and pious Rev. Jerry Falwell, a long-time foe of the Bakker/Roberston combine and current religious adviser to Vice President Bush, another 1988 candidate.

Lonely George had found trouble again. He has the instincts of a dung beetle. No living politician can match his talent for soiling himself in public. Bush will seek out filth wherever it lives—going without sleep for days at a time, if necessary—and when he finds a new heap he will fall down and wallow crazily in it, making snorting sounds out of his nose and rolling over on his back and kicking his legs up in the air like a wild hog coming to water.

Not everybody noticed the Bush/Falwell connection in the sordid PTL Club affair. In the White House it was seen as a welcome diversion, from the daily nightmare of the Iran/contra scandal, a kinky little gang war between big-ticket preachers that might keep the president off the front pages for a few days. Nobody could say for sure what it meant, but it was a hell of a lot better than reading about Michael Deaver's indictment on perjury charges or Poindexter taking The Fifth, once again.

Oliver North was momentarily quiet, Fawn Hall was still refusing to pose naked for *Playboy*, Bobby McFarlane was secure in a drug-free environment somewhere south of Arlington, and Dutch had been sent off to polish his repartee among sixth-graders in the schoolrooms of Columbia, MO.

There was no joy in Mudville, but the great eyes of the network cameras were focused south, as it were, on the preachers, who were acting like a gang of baboons.

The newspapers called it a "holy war," a snake's nest of greedheads and crazy-rich preachers fighting savagely among themselves for TV rights to the Jesus market.

Oral Roberts was on TBS, live from the Prayer Tower in Tulsa and still begging for more money. His son, Richard, of the Abundant Life Prayer Group, was telling his audience to send "your one-time gift of $15 to keep PTL on the air" while continuing to hammer the faithful with reminders of his own family crisis. Just because Oral talked his flock out of the $8 million ransom price that he said God had put on his life with a deadline of midnight on April Fools' Day didn't mean the battle was over.

Oral still needed more. God's price, said Richard on TV, was not just $8 million, "but $8 million above and beyond our normal operating expenses."

In other words, God was talking net—not gross—and he wanted his eight big ones in a brown bag by the midnight hour on April Fools' Day.

And he *will* get his money, there is no doubt at all about that. Oral Roberts is a greed-crazed white-trash lunatic who should have been hung upside down from a telephone pole on the outskirts of Tulsa 44 years ago before he somehow transmogrified into the money-sucking animal that he became when he discovered television.

March 30, 1987

The Losers' Club

"He's a gentleman, maybe that's his problem; he's such a beautiful man."

—Sen. Alfonse D'Amato, R-N.Y., describing Sen. Terry Sanford, D-N.C., *New York Times,* April 3, 1987

Hubert Humphrey would have crawled all the way to Camp David for a compliment like that—but it never came to him, because he was not a beautiful man . . . And neither is Terry Sanford, who was one of Hubert's favorites.

Alfonse was lying, but he did it with a certain cruel grace that made Sanford seem like a churl. In truth, the 69-year-old freshman senator from North Carolina was the ugliest thing in Washington last week. He made a whimpering fool of himself on the floor of the Senate and shamed the term "liberal" so badly that even Patrick Buchanan felt sorry for him.

Buchanan, the new *eminence horrible* of the swaggering, bull-fruit far-right wing of the GOP, was quoted earlier in the week as saying: "This Democratic Congress lacks the stomach to go in for the kill."

It was one of those lines that will come back to haunt a man in Washington—and in Patrick's case the words were barely out of his mouth when they came back around on him like a boomerang.

On Thursday the new Democratically controlled Senate voted 67–33 to override Ronald Reagan's veto of the federal highway bill, and to give the silly old fool a taste of the whip that he will not forget for a while. He is finished in politics now, and he has Buchanan and Terry Sanford to thank for it.

On Saturday he ran off to Canada like one of those Vietnam-War draft resisters from the '60s and hid his head in the snow like an ostrich. The hog had died in the tunnel, and the "Reagan Revolution" was over.

Buchanan wept the real tears of a gut-shot warrior, but Sanford only giggled and flapped his hands like a eunuch. They were lily-white hands, soft and plump—the hands of a failed Southern liberal who had some-how voted three different ways on the same bill within the space of 24 hours.

Even Hubert Humphrey was shamed, all alone in his unquiet grave down in the depths of the River Styx. Not even The Happy Warrior had ever tried to vote *three* ways all at once. Any good liberal could handle *two*, he often said—but not *three*. It was a crime against nature, like sodomy.

There was a whole crop of new members in The Losers Club last week: Along with Dutch and Patrick and Dumb Uncle Terry, there was also Mary Beth Whitehead, the U.S. Marine Corps, Dwight Gooden, Jimmy Carter, Pope John Paul II, Howard Baker, Derrick Coleman, Terry Waite, Michael Deaver, William Rehnquist, and the Rev. Gary Heidnik from Philadelphia, who was busted on something like 55 counts of rape, murder, kidnapping and forced cannibalism.

It was a bad week for ministers. Heidnik's basement in midtown Philly was found to contain two mentally retarded black women chained naked to sewer pipes, and another one trapped in a slimy concrete pit . . . They had been living for months on "cheap dog food and minced human flesh," according to *Newsweek*. The reverend was hauled off to the downtown Philadelphia jail, where he was brutalized by angry inmates, who said there were some crimes they could not tolerate.

The erstwhile George Shultz and his shattered Department of State seemed to feel the same way. The new U.S. Embassy in Moscow was revealed as a snakes' nest of sex, violence and disastrous treachery—mainly on the part of trusted USMC security guards, who ran utterly wild at all times on booze and marijuana with women of any persuasion they could get their hands on, including female KGB agents who gained access to everything in the building, from the ambassador's safe to the CIA code room and the station chief's top-secret list of every Russian in Moscow on the payroll of U.S. intelligence. All were doomed instantly.

"Our people kept disappearing and our codes were constantly being broken," said one diplomat, "but nobody could figure out *why*." Every time one of the red-alert, fail-safe burglar alarms in the embassy was set off by KGB agents getting into TOP SECRET files, the sex-crazed Marine guards on duty explained it away as just another routine glitch in the brand-new, high-tech, maze of incredibly complex wiring systems.

"Don't worry about it," the Marines told the nervous staff investigators. "We have everything under control. All we need is to work out a few bugs, just a few little kinks in the system."

It was the state-of-the-art electronics, which the hapless Republican ambassador couldn't quite understand. He was just another one of Reagan's rich pencil-necks who didn't want trouble.

Not even the White House could handle it. The whole squadron was recalled at once and locked up in brigs from Camp Pendleton to Quantico, the main Marine base outside Washington. Two were charged with "espionage," a death-penalty offense, and the others were busted down to latrine scrubbers and sent off to the same federal prisons that will soon welcome ex-Marine Corps heroes Oliver North and former National Security Adviser Robert McFarlane (USMC-Ret).

The whole Marine Corps should be disbanded, finished off with other useless relics like the Sea-Bees, Hitler Youth and the Lafayette Esquadrille. The USMC has been useless as tits on a boar hog since 1951, when they led the famous "Inchon Landing" for Gen. Douglas MacArthur and saved America from total disgrace in Korea.

That was 36 years ago, and since then they have done little more than hang around foreign embassies like drunken peacocks and get the nation in trouble. The U.S. Army's 1st Airborne Division could eat the whole Marine Corps for breakfast and take the rest of the day off for beer and volleyball. The only solution to the "Marine problem" now is to croak the whole corps.

Abolishing the Marines would have no real effect on national military preparedness, and it would cut $10 billion or $12 billion off the bloated national defense budget—which now must include the almost $4 billion it will cost to raze the entire new U.S. Embassy compound in Moscow and build another one—a huge concrete igloo with no windows, or maybe a deep underground bunker like the ones Albert Speer used to build. All we really need over there is a roomy place with no bugs or spies or sex-crazed whiskey-wild whores from the KGB, or even the ghost of a U.S. Marine. *Res ipsa loquitur.*

April 6, 1987

The Loved Ones

"It appears that the guys in the short pants are doing the same thing the guys in the long pants on Wall Street were doing."

—*Denver Post* columnist Buddy Martin, April 18, 1987

There are some weeks that only a bull-goose loony like Jonathan Winters can enjoy, and last week was one of them. Many prominent names were back in the headlines, almost all for wrong reasons, and a full moon hung in the sky. By sundown Friday the banshee had screamed for more stiffs than the morgues could hold, and the jails were filling up like cheap hotels in Calcutta.

When Winters was faced with a similar sitaution in *The Loved One*, he wept tears of greed and frustration, then turned his face upward and begged for help from On High. . . . "There must be *some* way," he moaned, "to send these stiffs into space."

The front of the week was slow, except for a rash of disclosures about John Hinckley's strange correspondence with some of the worst and craziest murderers of our time, including Ted Bundy and Charles Manson. . . . Hinckley's shrink was about to send him home for Easter, by himself, but the visit was croaked by a storm of protest from the Secret Service.

The President was out west in Santa Barbara, playing happily with grade-school children and others of his own kind, but there was not a lot of public support for turning Hinckley loose in the airports with a wallet full of hundred-dollar bills and snapshots of Bundy and Manson.

Air travel is already a nightmare for anybody who can't afford to lease their own Learjet, and the odds against getting anywhere in the country on a commercial airline—especially on a Friday afternoon—are getting longer and longer.

Even a 22-minute commuter flight might go sideways on you at any moment: A rain cloud can mean sitting on a runway for three hours at temperatures worse than most saunas, and then getting arrested by FAA security guards for trying to smoke a cigarette or asking why your luggage was sent to Key West, or even weeping helplessly in a manner that worries the stewardess and fits some kind of "emotional distress" profile that means you might stab the pilot in the brain with a rat-tail file and start jabbering in Arabic. . . .

These horrors are real, and the last thing anybody needs on top of the standard-brand hazards is the idea that the crazy-talking little four-eyed freak sitting elbow to elbow in the middle seat might be John Hinckley, the kid who shot the president and mutters distractedly about collect calls to Ted and Charlie.

Hinckley was out of the headlines by Friday, pumped full of Thorazine and wrapped in a maze of black straps, brass zip-locks and D-rings in some basement room with no phone, and there were big red "F" stamps all over the outline for the essay he was planning to write about how I spent my Easter vacation.

Nobody needed it, and by that time the great eye of the national news had turned in other directions. The lull was over, and by Friday night there was fat going into the fire from coast to coast. . . . Huge rats swarmed out of the wood piles and chewed crazily on human flesh in some very fashionable neighborhoods, from the sunless canyons of Wall Street to City Hall in Atlanta and then west across the time zones to Gary Hart's headquarters in Denver and the chic meat racks along Camelback Road in Phoenix.

Good Friday was one of those cruel, life-shattering days when people who normally go skiing or play tennis on weekends found themselves being shoved by mean strangers down the hallways of their own office buildings and through the lobbies of their own condos with their hands behind their backs in chrome-steel handcuffs and not even a dime in their pockets for calling a lawyer from some pay phone in a tank full of tattooed men with crusted blood on their heads.

This is what happened to a lot of high-style bond traders, stockbrokers, pro basketball hot rods and other Gucci/Rolex boys last week, when the wheels of white-collar justice began rolling at fearful speed.

Ralph Lauren was not busted, but many people who claimed to know him personally were arrested and locked up like common criminals. In New York it was a gang of young stockbrokers from slick brokerage firms such as Prudential-Bache Securities Inc. and New York Depository Trust, who were said to share a taste for cocaine, and forgot that it was not quite legal.

The same thing happened in Phoenix, where some of the boys who make $2,000 a day in the winter for playing basketball against people like Larry Bird and Magic Johnson were busted by a local grand jury for allegedly buying a gram of cocaine now and then from a waiter in a local pesto palace. . . . They were all ruined, disgraced and banned for the rest of their lives from professional basketball in the civilized world except Israel, Sicily and the Philippines.

It was cocaine again, in Atlanta, where State Sen. Julian Bond and Mayor Andrew Young were engulfed in a shameful scandal that forced both of them—two of the major civil rights activists of our time—to jabber wildly on national TV and deny rumors that Bond's wife had flipped out and accused them both of being junkies.

There were no drugs involved in the Gary Hart bust. It was mainly a matter of flogging the lips off the presidential front-runner, if only to give him a taste of his own blood. Former political allies got federal marshals to seize $30,000 in receipts from a Hart fund-raiser in Hollywood Wednesday night. Then the *New York Post* called him a sex fiend who should have been put long ago into debtors' prison, and even his old friends called him weird.

These things happen, in politics. It's the meanest game in any town, and when it comes to the presidency of the United States, *there are no rules* . . . as Attorney General Ed Meese found out last week when somebody he was sure he could trust forever turned him in to the *Washington Post* for what he thought was a secret midnight meeting with former CIA chief William Casey, who is currently listed as brain-dead. Meese is looking down the barrel at multiple felony charges like conspiracy, perjury and obstruction of justice, and will almost certainly spend time in prison, along with U.S. Marine Lt. Col. Oliver North, Navy Rear Adm. John Poindexter and retired Air Force Maj. Gen. Richard Secord.

The Phoenix Suns will win the NBA title before any of these criminal swine will go home again. Meese will put his fingerprints on more license plates than Caryl Chessman before he slinks back home to Oakland.

April 20, 1987

The Death Ship

Louisiana officials ordered the barge out of state waters last week, saying a dark brown substance was dripping from the bales of garbage into the water. They also expressed concern that discarded medical supplies found among the trash might be infectious.

—Associated Press wire report, April 25, 1987

A man named Peterson came through the Valley last week and said he needed some whiskey. He said he was a road man for The Fabulous Thunderbirds, so I said, "How much do you want?"

The deal was done quickly. It was an early morning load out of a local place, and by noon the next day Peterson was on the road to Montana with a trunkload of cellophone-wrapped quarts. He was arrested in Grand Junction about six hours later for Drunk, Disorderly and Assault; and all the whiskey was gone. He wanted $5,500 to get him out of jail, and when he talked to Maria on the telephone she asked me what to do.

"Nothing," I said. "Nothing at all. Tell them to keep him until The Fabulous Thunderbirds come for him."

That was four days ago, and we have not heard from him since. The West is full of these thugs. You can't leave your screen door unlatched at night without wondering if somebody like Ted Bundy or Gary Gilmore or Perry Edward Smith might come wandering in to chop on somebody.

We live with these things. But not for long. I ran a check on Peterson and told the sheriff that he'd said he was a friend of a man named Cruse, from Palm Bay, Fla., who had just gone crazy and shot a bunch of people in a local supermarket, for no apparent reason.

First reports put the death toll at 12, or maybe 18. Nobody knew for sure. The killer was initially indentified by local TV journalists as *two* young white men with flaming red hair who had somehow come together and been trapped in the Winn Dixie Supermarket while attempting two separate armed robberies.

It was gibberish, of course. The Palm Bay killer turned out to be an elderly gray-haired sot from Louisville, with no friends in the world and a bad habit of shooting at children as they crept across his front lawn.

It was a cheap and savage story, like most of the others last week. . . .

On Sunday, I talked to a man named Harrelson in Bay Minette, Ala.

He was finally back home, he said, after a fast and terrible week in New Orleans, Tampico and Veracruz, where he had come to grips in a very personal way with some of the truly nightmarish aspects of the International Garbage Crisis.

Lowell Harrelson is the president of National Waste Contractors Inc., a previously obscure Alabama company that used to be in the business of shipping loads of municipal garbage up and down the East Coast on steel barges he leased out of Jacksonville—and until last week it was a nice way to make a living.

But the situation is different now; National Waste got tracked down and formally identified as the legal owner of 3,100 tons of festering garbage from the suburbs of New York City that is still floating around somewhere in the Gulf of Mexico like some poison heap out of hell that will never be allowed to dock anywhere.

It has been turned away from ports in North Carolina, Mississippi, Alabama, Louisiana, Texas, Cuba and Mexico. . . . Not even Haiti will allow the monstrous thing near its shoreline, for *any* amount of money.

It is like a death ship, a sinking hulk full of shame and disease, being towed back and forth through the sea lanes by a hired tugboat with a crew on the verge of mutiny and a captain going crazy with fear. The cargo—62,000 pounds of rotten meat, human excrement and unspecified toxic wastes—is so foul that it can't even be sunk in the deepest holes of the ocean.

The captain and the crew had to be warned by radio every 20 or 30 minutes by international maritime authorities from seven nations that they would all face long prison terms if they even *thought* about abandoning ship. The president of Mexico sent gunboats and attack helicopters to patrol the Yucatan coastline and turn the scow back to the east, toward Cuba, where Castro warned that the whole crew would be peeled alive like bananas if they came anywhere near Cuba—even in rubber life rafts, trying to peddle some tragic story about losing the barge in a hurricane.

Angry mobs roamed the beaches of Haiti, waving voodoo canes, and Jamaica radioed the captain of the doomed tug that he should be prepared to go down with his ship, if it sank in the open sea. There are very strict laws against dumping toxic scum in the ocean.

Meanwhile, back home in Alabama, poor Harrelson was still answering his own telephone and insisting that "the media is making a big joke out of this thing," and that he would "have a realistic solution to this problem by Monday afternoon."

When I spoke with him on Sunday he seemed vaguely hysterical. Why was he being treated worse than Hilter, he asked, when his only crime was trying to make an honest living as a garbage disposal contractor?

"Well, Lowell," I said, "you have a new problem on your hands. The garbage market is changing."

"What do you mean," he snapped. "It's a respectable business. I buy it up North and sell it down South for landfill. It's a good deal for everybody."

"No more," I said. "The raven has croaked for you, Lowell. The garbage dumps are full. You can't sell that stuff anymore."

"I know," he said. "It's horrible. I can't get a drink in New Orleans anymore. They hate me over there."

Louisiana, in fact, had been Harrelson's Waterloo. Gov. Edwin Edwards, no stranger to the criminal court process, looked at Lowell's barge and called it too filthy to tolerate. The half-mad captain hauled anchor at midnight and fled down the river in darkness.

Harrelson, meanwhile, had gone down to Tampico with a big bag full of green money and tried to arrange for a dumping site there, but the Mexican government would have none of it.

By Sunday he was back home in Bay Minette, plotting strategy with his lawyers—and his death ship was still lost in the fog somewhere north of Cozumel. The Coast Guard had grown wary of the case and dumped it off on the U.S. State Department, where the doomed and disloyal George Shultz would have to deal with it.

"Don't woory," Harrelson said. "By tomorrow I will have the solution. That's all I can tell you right now. This thing has been hard on my family. Call me tomorrow at my office."

April 27, 1987

The American Dream

I make my living off the evening news
just give me something, something I can use
people love it when you lose
they love dirty laundry

—Don Henley, "Dirty Laundry"

"In speeches and interviews, the party leaders said they are encouraged by a string of recent good news breaks for their side, in particular the scandals in the White House, on Wall Street and among television evangelists, who have generally supported Republican candidates in recent elections."

—Wire report on last week's caucus of the Democratic National Committee in Santa Fe

That was last week, but things are different now. The River Styx has jumped its channel about three times since then, and the world is a different place. Julius Erving is gone, along with the Bradley Fighting Vehicle, Jim and Tammy Bakker and Kentucky Derby favorite Demons Begone, who died on his feet in the backstretch at Churchill Downs and had to be taken away in the dreaded "horse ambulance," with blood pouring out of his nose.

The last time a thing like that happened with a horse was in the Preakness, when a spectacular little filly named Riva Ridge collapsed on the track and had to be "destroyed" in front of 100,000 racing fans and 66 network TV cameras.

The crowd went crazy with grief when a nameless black groom in a white jump suit came out on the track and fired a huge 240-grain .45 bullet through her head. . . . They buried her in the infield, with a big crane digging her grave almost exactly where she fell, and the wailing of one lonely bugle was the only sound you could hear in Maryland on that gray afternoon.

Lt. Col. Oliver North (USMC) did not hear any high lonesome music when the white van came for him last week, and neither did Gary Hart. They died like dogs, for no good reason at all—or at least no real reason except craziness.

There was no way to explain it. Oliver North apparently moved into the White House basement about five years ago and turned himself into something worse than the mad Dr. Frankenstein. . . . He was given control of everything he could reach, from the president of Israel and secret U.S. Army bank accounts in Switzerland to the CIA and George Bush and the home phone number of the Chinese defense minister . . . until he finally hooked up with a truly savage little criminal named Carl "Spitz" Channell, who used him for years as a sort of billion-dollar Judas goat and then finally turned him in.

The Boss called him Ollie, they said, and he had a cost-plus Q-level expense account that even John DeLorean would have envied . . . but that, too, was last week, before all of his ex-buddies turned on him and said they knew he was criminally insane all along.

Navy Admiral John Poindexter rolled first, and then Spitz. . . . Next week it will be his old pal Gen. Secord (USAF Ret.) and ex-National Security Adviser Robert McFarlane, who has attempted suicide.

Secord will be the first witness this week in Washington, and McFarland will be the second. Channell has already pleaded guilty to felony tax fraud and named Ollie as his co-conspirator.

Gary Hart was whacked by a very different kind of craziness last week. He was caught between a rock and a hard place, as they say out here in the West—accused on the one hand of having no pulse, and on the other of being a sex fiend.

That is a very hard dollar, in most precincts. The voters are not comfortable with such massive contradictions. How can a man appear to have no human feelings and be as cold to the touch as a lizard, and also maddened by a wild and ungovernable lust at all times? No man since Caligula has pulled off a trick like that. Is it possible for a former United States senator and current odds-on favorite to be the next president of the most powerful nation on earth to have the face of Abraham Lincoln and the soul of Jerry Lee Lewis?

Questions like these are not popular on the presidential fund-raising circuit, and Gary Hart is not good at handling them. He has a very Calvinist sense of humor, and 15 years in the shadow of Warren Beatty have not been healthy for him. When it comes to "womanizing" in Washington, Hart is an amateur. Four generations of Kennedys have roamed naked and crazy like satyrs on Capitol Hill, and Wilbur Mills wallowed and howled like a rhino in the Tidal Pool with a mainline stripper from Boston named Fanny Fox . . . but nobody called them perverts, and only a few people called the police.

But Gary has not had the same kind of luck. He is, after all, both a preacher and a lawyer—degrees in Law and Divinity from Yale. That is a fearful mix, and it did not prepare him well for the events of the weekend.

Only a week earlier in Los Angeles, he'd been busted by U.S. marshals and stripped of $50,000 he'd just managed to raise at a black-tie dinner. It was one of those routine crack-back blocks you have to get used to in bigtime politics, but Gary took it personally and spent the next 10 days explaining his finances in headlines from coast to coast.

That crisis had no sooner passed when he found himself on the evening news again—this time in a sinister sex story. The *Miami Herald,* in a page 1 exposé on Sunday, accused him of berserk sexual high jinks in his elegant home on Capitol Hill in Washington.

By this morning, *The New York Times* had somehow linked him to a degenerate rock 'n' roll cult in Aspen headed by his old friend Don Henley. . . . The entire Hart organization responded in a frenzy of righteous indignation. Hart's campaign manager, Bill Dixon, denounced the *Herald* for cheap sensationalism. "The system, when reduced to hiding in bushes, peeking in windows, and personal harassment, has clearly run amok," he said. "Those who cover politics have some duty of self-restraint." Well . . . maybe so. But the last politician who said that was Spiro Agnew, who wound up carrying buckets of golf balls around cheap municipal courses for Coors Beer executives while they discussed his future with the company.

Gary will do better than that—if only he gets the help he needs. His old friend George McGovern has suggested that perhaps he should be shot full of the female hormones they use on the chronic rapists in the Arizona State Prison.

May 4, 1987

Caligula and the 7 Dwarfs

Oh! somewhere in this favored land the sun is shining bright;
The band is playing somewhere, and somewhere hearts are light;
And somewhere men are laughing and somewhere children shout,
But there is no joy in Mudville—mighty Casey has struck out.

—Ernest Lawrence Thayer, "Casey at the Bat"

The evil demon, sex-crazed, twisted cowboy preacher is gone now . . . Gary Hart is back in Colorado, and his high-powered 1988 presidential campaign is a smoking ruin, a disaster worse than anything that ever happened in Mudville.

Casey had a bad night. He struck out. He was humiliated. The fans spit on him and even the batboy kicked him in the shins when he came back to the dugout.

So what? The poem was first printed in the *Examiner* on June 3, 1888, but there was no mention of what happened when Casey went to bat the next day and cracked a bases-loaded triple down the right field line. They say he lived happily ever after, and the women followed him everywhere.

That is the difference between baseball and big-time politics. Even the wretched Casey knew he would get another chance. . . . *Many* more, in fact; and his shame would not follow him long. He hit 55 homers that year and led the Negro League in triples.

But when Gary Hart struck out last week, he knew he was doomed forever. He will not come to bat again in our lifetime. There is no second chance on the biggest and fastest and meanest of all the campaign trails.

One half-legal screwball can put you down in the ditch with the skulls and burnt bones of other monstrous failures like George Romney, Herbert Hoover and the fiendish Wilbur Mills.

That is a very ugly league. Adolf Hitler is there, along with Grigori Rasputin, Adm. Tojo and Idi Amin. . . . And now Gary Hart is there, for reasons that are too strange to explain.

Some people called it a sex scandal, and others called it true craziness. The most intelligent Democratic presidential campaign since John F. Kennedy's in 1960 went down in a ball of huge fire like the Hindenburg. . . . And the heaviest winter book favorite since Richard Nixon in '72 was suddenly trapped in a web of foul rumors and stomped to death like a roach.

It happened with a terrible quickness, like a big ship hitting an iceberg and sinking so fast that even the lifeboats went down with it. . . . Most of the crew drowned, along with the captain and many, many passengers. When the sun set over Denver last night, the once-elegant Hart headquarters at 16th and Pine was a lonely abandoned hulk, and there was no joy at all in the national gambling community.

There is not a lot of action in Vegas on presidential futures, but there are clusters of smart boys here and there who take it very seriously. Most of the early betting is on long shots and odd possibilities, but the numbers are high and potential payoffs on odds like 50–1 or even 77–1 on geeks like Lyndon LaRouche and Pierre DuPont tend to keep people interested. . . .

Or whipped like egg-sucking dogs with no warning or reason at all—which is what happened last week to folks who bet heavily on Gary Hart. He was the early-line favorite at 8–1 when he suddenly exploded like the Challenger and disappeared.

The gambling people were left in utter disarray. Hart had been running so far in front of the rest of the Democrats that his demise left the '88 race for the White House in a hellbroth of fear and confusion.

Before Hart got croaked, the *Wall Street Journal* was calling the Democratic race "a rerun of Snow White and the Seven Dwarfs." . . . Gary was running about 55 points ahead of everybody except Jesse Jackson, who was in the process of doing business.

Jackson and Hart formed a loose sort of alliance during the '84 campaign, and this time they were ready to formalize it. Three days before the bomb hit Gary, Jesse and Hart Campaign Manager Bill Dixon had met privately in Santa Fe and agreed to share research, staff talent and maybe even the 15 percent chunk of delegates that Dixon figured Jesse would have locked up by the time of the convention next summer.

That deal is a bad joke now, and the new numbers show Jackson up from 15 percent to 20 percent. "Jesse could win nine states on Super Tuesday." Dixon figures. "Gary was his only real competition in the South."

Only a madman would make numbers on the Democratic race right now. The whole game has changed, and the first caucus in Iowa is still 10 months away.

That is a long time in politics, but the Democratic numbers are not likely to change much between now and Christmas. The Seven Dwarfs were mainly running for vice president, anyway, and now they will probably split the vote seven ways.

Gephardt will probably win Iowa—if only because he has spent 75 weekends there, pressing flesh—and Dukakis is a heavy favorite in New Hampshire, Massachusetts and Maine. . . . But after that, things get hazy. Biden will take a hometown victory in Delaware and Babbitt is a sure thing in Arizona and maybe three other Western states.

Probably nobody will win more than one primary by the time "Super Tuesday" rolls around in the second week of March. . . . That is 11 Southern states, including big ones like Texas, Florida and Georgia.

Gary Hart would have been a prohibitive favorite on Super Tuesday, on the strength of early wins in Iowa and New Hampshire—but times have changed, and right now the best bet to sweep the whole South on Super Tuesday in Sen. Sam Nunn, a Georgia boy who will have a lot of TV exposure by then, from his perch on the Iran/contra hearings.

But the South will not be enough, and nobody will go to Atlanta with a lock on the nomination; 1988 might be the first deadlocked and brokered political convention in America since Ike ambushed Taft in '52.

With Hart and Ted Kennedy out, the only other big hitter around is New York Gov. Mario Cuomo, who might be a genius wild card. Cuomo could lay low for at least the next six months, then jump in late and win New York, New Jersey and California all at once, then stampede the convention.

That is about the only hope the Democrats have right now of beating the crooked wimp, George Bush—who until last week appeared to have no hope at all.

May 11, 1987

Memo from the Queer Desk

Dear David,

Never mind the huge fireball of wisdom that I told you was coming on the Mac. . . . (yeah, good ole Mac; he's been with us for 91 straight weeks now, and I still love the way he feels when we work on him, and the way he always responds. It's like magic. . . . good ole Mac. . . .)

Anyway, cancel the wisdom. We will get to it next week, if I ever get to Washington—which might not be as quick as we thought: The Secret Service is after me on both coasts for something that has to do with a plot to assassinate George Bush. The SS agent in Denver told me on the telephone that my life might become a series of terrible misunderstandings if I even thought about going to Washington without consulting him first.

A personal interview, in fact—*tomorrow,* at the Holiday Inn. He is driving over from Denver in a van with a cage behind the driver's seat, and he may want to take me back with him.

I warned you about Bush. He is evil, far worse than we thought.

George Bush might go down in history as the meanest yuppie who ever lived. He is once again the front-runner in the '88 presidential race.

Bill Casey is dead. Secord is crooked, and McFarlane is crazy. North is doomed, along with Poindexter and probably Dutch.

Why not? Let's get him out of there. He is no longer a part of the solution. Tell that woman to take him back to that place in California, wherever it was that he came from. . . . I never liked him anyway.

George Bush thinks like that, David. He has a very efficient mind, like Albert Speer—and, like Speer, he truly believes that his heart is in the right place.

Indeed . . . but that is another story, and we will deal with it next time around. I have to meet the SS man at the Holiday Inn before noon.

In the meantime, here is a thing I want you to ponder. I found it on the handout desk in the pressroom at the Watergate hearings in the spring of '74. . . . It was a Xeroxed thing, like all the others, but this one had a dark simplicity to it, a clarity that almost glowed.

It is a partial transcript of a phone call between John Ehrlichman—then White House chief for all domestic affairs—and the second-most powerful politician in America—and California-bred Herbert Kalmbach, the president's personal attorney. Read it and weep.

E: Ehrlichman.

K: Kalmbach.

E: Hi, how are you?

K: I'm pretty good. I'm scheduled for two tomorrow afternoon.

E: Where—at the jury or the U.S. attorney?

K: At the jury, and I'm scheduled at 5:30 this afternoon with Silver.

E: Oh, are you?

K: Yeah. I just wanted to run through quickly several things, John, in line with our conversation. I got in here last night, and there was a call from O'Brien.

E: Did he tell you about Dean?

K: Nope.

E: Well, Dean has totally cooperated with the U.S. attorney in hopes of getting immunity.

K: The whole enchilada?

E: He's throwing on Bob and me heavily. . . . taking the position that he was a mere agent. Now on your episode, Dean told me really my transaction with him involving you was virtually my only area of liability in this thing, and I said, well, John, what in the world are you talking about? He said, well I came to you from Mitchell, and I said Mitchell needs money, could we call Herb Kalmbach and ask him to raise some. And I said, and Dean says to me, and you said yes.

K: You know, when you and I talked and it was after John had given me that word, and I came in to ask you, John is this an assignment I have to take on? You said, yes it is period and move forward. Then that was all that I needed to be assured that I wasn't putting my family in jeopardy. . . . And I would just understand that you and I are absolutely together on that.

E: No question about it, Herb, that I would never knowingly have put you in any kind of a spot.

K: Yeah. Well, and when we talked you knew what I was about to do, you know, to go out and get the dough for this purpose; it was humanitarian.

E: It was a defense fund.

K: God, if I can just make it plain that it was humanitarian and nothing else.

E: Yeah, and the point that I undoubtedly never expressed to you that I continually operated on the basis of Dean's representation to me.

K: Yep. It was not improper. . . . And I just couldn't believe that you and Bob and the President, just too good friends to ever put me in the position I would be putting my family on the line.

E: Yeah, I wouldn't haul the President into it if you can help it.

K: Oh, no, I will not.

E: Yeah, well, as far as propriety is concerned I think we both were relying entirely on Dean. I made no independent judgment. And I'm sure Bob didn't either.

K: Nope and I'm just, I just have the feeling, John, that I don't know if this is a weak reed, is it?

E: Who, Dean?

K: No, I mean are they still going to say well Herb you should have known.

E: I don't know how you could have. You didn't make any inquiries.

K: Never. And the only inquiries I made, John, was to you after I talked to John Dean.

E: And you found that I didn't know just a whole helluva lot.

K: You said this is something I have to do and . . .

E: Yeah, and the reason that I said that, as you know, was not from any personal inquiry but was on the basis of what had been represented to me.

K: . . . Can I get in to see you tomorrow before I go in there at two?

E: If you want to. They'll ask you.

K: Will they?

E: Yep.

K: Well, maybe I shouldn't.

E: They'll ask you to whom you've spoken about your testimony and I would appreciate it if you would say you've talked to me in California because at that time I was investigating this thing for the President.

K: And not now?

E: Well, I wouldn't ask you to lie. . . .

May 18, 1987

The Time of the Geek

The Republicans were on the march last week. George Bush paid his taxes, Bob Dole denounced Bush as a sophomore wimp and Jack Kemp cam down to Savannah for a whoop-up with his Super Tuesday people . . . and there was also the tainted evangelical, Pat Robertson.

The GOP had been down in the ditch for so long—whipped day and night for the sins of every half-mad neo-Nazi hustler from Ollie North and Ivan Boesky to Jerry Falwell and the nightmare bullfruit Jim Bakker—that the world was beginning to look like a bat cave somewhere in Antarctica. . . . The Congress was lost, the Generals were crooked, the Preachers had gone crazy, and even the president himself was fighting off threats of prison, disgrace and impeachment.

Dutch called it all nonsense, but some of the smart boys knew better. The Iran/contra hearings were getting nasty, the Japanese were printing dollars in Tennessee, the Bradley fighting vehicle was a $55 billion boondoggle and maybe the worst thing that ever happened to the U.S. Army, the Navy was helpless, Iranian terrorists roamed the halls of the White House at night, and some of the president's closest advisers from the good old days were going to prison for fraud and felony theft.

Ed Meese was being investigated again—this time on charges of bribery, conspiracy and fraud. The U.S. Department of Justice—which Meese *runs,* in his role as attorney general—was once again being forced to assign what they call an "independent counsel" to probe Big Ed's connection to a "major political corruption scandal."

Well . . . how long, O Lord, how long? The last time Meese got investigated, he was working in the White House as a main presidential adviser and allegedly selling low-end government jobs to any rich California Republican who would lend him money for a while.

He was on his way to a seat on the U.S. Supreme Court, at the time—by way of the A.G.'s office—and it took him almost a year to get cleared of those charges. Or at least clear enough to be allowed to take over the whole U.S. Justice Department. His confirmation hearings in the Senate would have shamed Ivan Boesky, but Meese never noticed. All he wanted was rent money, he said, and enough power to lock up his enemies. The Senate eventually confirmed him as U.S. attorney general by three votes, and Big Ed was on his way.

Michael Deaver was still running the White House and Dutch could do no wrong. . . . But those days are gone, along with Deaver and Casey and Nofziger and most of the other Big Boys.

There are no bright spots, no lights at the end of the tunnel. All the standard brand GOP gods—the Army, the Church, and the Banks—were going belly up, in public. The Challenger exploded, Terry Waite disappeared, James Lofton got busted for sodomy, Reaganomics turned out to be the low-rent "voodoo economics" that George Bush had called it back in 1980, and even the sex turned horrible. . . . The president was a fool, the rain was full of acid, and the sweetheart of Sigma Chi had AIDS.

Into this hideous mess wandered the mad cowboy priest, Gary Hart-pence, formerly of the U.S. Senate and the Nazarene Church, and one of the most successful politicians in recent memory.

"Gary was the closest thing to a president-in-waiting that any of us will ever see," said former Hart campaign manager Bill Dixon, on his way out of town in a faded Mercedes 280.

"You want to hear what *really* happened?" he snapped. "Can I tell you a really *good* story?"

"Why not?" I said.

"OK," he said. "Here's how it went. The *Miami Herald* was *nothing*. All they did was print gossip. . . . The *real* horror is what we were looking at from the depositions in the Joe Tydings divorce case.

"Remember Tydings? The senator from Maryland? The guy who tried to bust the NRA, the gun lobby?"

I did, but so what?

"Well," he said, "Joe Tydings was divorcing his wife and he thought Gary was sleeping with her. She wanted $7 million, but he offered her three. . . . But she wouldn't settle, so he hired private eyes to follow her. He also had Gary followed—day and night—everywhere, for months.

"He never caught them together, but his spooks caught Gary with seven other women, and they were all ready to go public. We were looking at something worse than the diaries of the Marquis de Sade, with pictures."

Dixon left the next day, but on the way to the airport we picked up a *National Enquirer* that explained the whole thing with total accuracy. There was one picture of Hart pounding marimba and looking crazier than Jerry Lee Lewis . . . and that was it: There was nothing else to say. He was crazier than six loons.

Meanwhile, all the Republican candidates except Bush went down to Savannah to press flesh, beg for money and swear they were not adulterers like Gary Hart. . . . George seemed to feel he was not vulnerable in that area, or in any other dark venue, for that matter, except in the strange and hazy mind of some dingbat named Col. Dutton, who is scheduled to testify this week at the Iran/contra hearings in Washington.

It sounded ominous, but none of The Boys seemed worried. Dutton was said to be A Company Man, with one or two quirks of his own, but nothing so weird that he might go sideways in public. . . . He was singularly undistinguished in every way, they said; no different from any other retired Air Force lieutenant colonel, except for persistent rumors that he had spent his first year out of uniform as the only living connection between the Iran/contra co-conspirators and the famous yuppie vice president, George Bush. . . . Only Dutton, they said, had stashed enough rocks in his sock to nail Bush up on the same cross with true criminals like North, Gen. Secord, Adm. Poindexter and Marine Sgt. Clayton Lonetree.

Dutton is another one of these speedy rogue colonels who worked, more or less, for the doomed and degraded Lt. Col. Oliver North, who was known in the White House as "Ollie."

Dutton will presumably take a stand this week—under oath and with full immunity—and his testimony, if he lives, will be crucial to the future of Vice President Bush and the entire Republican Party for the next decade.

May 25, 1987

A Wild and Crazy Guy

While preachers preach of evil fates,
teachers teach that knowledge waits,
can lead to hundred-dollar plates,
goodness hides behind its gates,
but even the president of the United States
sometimes must have to stand naked.

—Bob Dylan

They were whooping it up in the Admiral's House last week. The neighbors on Embassy Row tried to ignore the wild cries and harsh drum music for as long as they could stand it, they said—but finally they had to call a Secret Service patrol car to investigate the uproar. . . .

It was, after all, the official residence of Vice President Bush, who is not normally given to orgies and big-decibel, dopey-sounding boogie displays after midnight.

"I thought he was dead," said the wife of a Middle European diplomat who lives across the street. "They were always quiet people," she said. "I saw the woman roaming around the yard now and then, but she never did anything weird. . . . Mr. Bush used a lot of helicoptors and there were always strange men on the property, but you get used to that in Washington."

"The noise was intolerable," said a Swedish neighbor. "They were screaming and setting fires on the lawn. Some of the women were naked. The noise was horrible. They were all drunk."

The party went on all night. The driveway was full of limousines and trucks from the *National Enquirer,* delivering bales of the June 2 issue with former Democratic front-runner Gary Hart on the cover.

Hart had already withdrawn from the race in a nightmare sex and whiskey scandal, which destroyed his candidacy and left the Democratic party in chaos. Hart had been a confident front-runner, leading all candidates in both parties. Presidential preference polls out of Washington showed him leading Bush by margins of up to 20 points. The smart money had already conceded the '88 race to him. "And then he went totally nuts," said one political pro.

Which was true. In a matter of five or six strange hours, Hart got himself pegged as a dingbat and a sex fiend on every front page in the country. Even the *National Enquirer* had a color photo spread on him, staggering around in Bimini with two bimbos from Miami, with the eyes of a dangerous sot.

The whole nation cringed, and the winter book numbers for the '88 race went up in smoke. . . . It was a disaster for the Democrats, and a whole new life for George Bush.

The Democrats had done it again. They are still the majority party, in terms of national voter registration and issues, but for the last 20 years they have wandered from one frantic disaster to another and lost four out of the last five presidential elections. "It was the Vietnam War that destroyed the Democrats," said former White House Pollster Patrick Cadell. "The last legitimate winner we had was John F. Kennedy in 1960. Johnson was an accident and Carter was a fluke."

I found Caddell hunkered down on a cliff on the edge of the sea in Santa Barbara, in the shadow of Ronald Reagan's "Sky Ranch" high up in the coastal mountain range. He was brooding over a spool of computer printouts and arcane voter data, spitting out of an Apple computer. He was in a deep funk.

His eyes were like slits in a grapefruit and his voice came out in a hiss. "Never mind this craziness about Gary," he said. "He could never have won anyway . . . according to my figures, we won't win another election for 66 years. We'd be lucky to win if Thomas Jefferson was on the ticket. I'd rather go to work for the Whigs."

He rolled sideways into a palm tree and tossed me a heavy document full of numbers. "Here," he said. "Read this thing. The numbers are worse than we thought. We were fools to ever get into this business. We should have gone to work for Ivan Boesky."

It was a monstrous volume, 75 pages of gloom and broken dreams:
- Starting with 1968, the Republicans have won four of five presidential elections, three by a landslide.
- There are 23 states with 202 of the 270 electoral votes needed to win that have voted Republican in all five elections.
- By contrast, the Democrats have won *zero* states five straight times, carrying only the heavily black District of Columbia—with a grand total of three electoral votes—in all five elections.
- Considering states won in four elections out of five, the Republican electoral base rises to 36 states with 354 electoral votes—84 more than needed to win.
- By contrast, the Democrats add only Minnesota to the District of

Columbia for a base of 13 electoral votes. Indeed, the only time a Minnesotan was not on the ticket (1972) the state voted Republican.

- If you add together the popular vote from all five elections, the Republicans defeat the Democrats by a margin of 53 to 42 percent—or by a total of over 40 million votes.
- The Republicans have averaged over 50 percent of the vote in each of the five elections in 40 states.
- Only three states have given the Democrats over 50 percent—indeed, there are only nine states that have given the Democrats 45 percent or more of the vote.
- Put another way, the 25th most Republican state in average popular vote, Indiana, has given the Republican candidates an average vote that is higher than that given by any state to the Democratic candidates.
- The Democrats' 10th best state in average vote, Wisconsin, has been carried only once in five elections by the Democratic nominee—and then by an average of less than 2 percent.
- The 11th—and 12th—most Democratic states, Maine and Michigan, have been lost in the last four straight elections. The 13th most Democratic state, Illinois, has been lost by the Democrats in all five elections.
- Until 1980, the two major demographic subgroups, besides blacks, that the Democrats could depend on were men and younger voters. In 1980, Reagan won men by three times the margin that he carried women. In 1984, younger voters went from being the Democrats' best age group to their worst. Indeed, in 1984, Reagan received the vote of 71 percent of white males under the age of 30.

The hideous figures went on and on, proving only that George Bush had been right from the start and would rule until the year 2000. . . .

June 1, 1987

Ollie's Choice

"It's not a question of doing the heroic thing and passing an acid test; it's a business situation and should be treated as such."

—Albert Hakim, U.S. arms dealer

"If I got 52 years for what I shipped, Ollie North ought to get 300 years."

—Edwin P. Wilson, former CIA agent

The first phase of the Iran/contra hearings is over now. It has been five weeks in the slow lane, with not much wisdom to show for it and no coonskins on the wall. Lyndon Johnson would have had at least half of these venal dingbats hanging from telephone poles on Pennsylvania Avenue by now, if only for making him look bad.

Johnson would rather have gone to Parchman Prison Farm than beat a felony rap by pleading dumbness and giggling in public like some batty old woman. . . . And Richard Nixon tried to crush every human being who even smiled at him the wrong way. The last president who didn't mind being mocked in the public prints like some dolt worse than Alfred E. Neuman was the hapless Warren Harding, who cared about nothing except stud poker, rye whiskey and bimbos.

And before Harding there was Ulysses S. Grant, who was plagued by a cross-eyed wife with the brains of Tammy Bakker and a fearful lust for publicity. Mrs. Grant wanted photographers around her at all times, but she refused to show her face while posing for them. . . . Ulysses grinned and drank heavily, while his henchman looted the Treasury and called him a drunken fool.

These things are instructive. The Iran/contra hearings will pick up again next week, and Ronald Reagan will no doubt be portrayed once again as a blundering stooge who signed everything they put in front of him. . . . But there will be a difference this time: At least somebody in the Oval Office will be watching the hearings on TV, for a change.

The testimony will be slow and ugly, as usual, but it will not be entirely irrelevant. These are big-time hearings, featuring major political players with major ambitions and very keen memories of Watergate, when the whole world waited for their judgments.

That has not been the nature, thus far, of the Iran-contra hearings.

The press is already rumbling with talk about "show trials" and "white-wash." It is not a happy posture for Watergate heroes, like Rep. Peter Rodino and Sen. Daniel Inouye, who went up on the ramparts and brought down a crooked government.

Richard Nixon was "not a crook," he said, and Spiro Agnew swore he would "never plead guilty." But they were both run out of Washington like poison rats, and many of those who called them "Boss" went to prison.

The current investigation has not yet reached that stage, but it will. The charges are too serious and too much big artillery has been wheeled into place to let the whole thing die with a whimper. . . . No, there *must* be a bang; heads *shall* roll, and if the tumbrels stand empty today, they will not be empty for long. The guilty will soon be seized and carried off like stinking animals.

USMC Lt. Col. Oliver North will probably not get 300 years—even if Ed Wilson is right—but he is too guilty and too obvious and too easy, in fact, to get off with anything less than 25 or 30 concurrent, which means he will do about three—unless he can come up with a better idea, like turning in somebody bigger.

Well . . . Ollie has a nasty problem here: He can be either the John Dean of this scandal, or the G. Gordon Liddy. . . . But either way, he will be rich and famous very soon: He will be seen with Donna Rice, and Robin Leach will whine over him. The only people who get seriously burned in these things are the bit players, the poor dupes like Fawn Hall and flaky "Bud" McFarlane, who thought they were "serving the president."

Indeed. They were all serving the president, and they recognized Ollie North as his mouthpiece, the "dream boss" who worked all night and spent a million dollars a day and carried a top-secret "KL-43" communications device in his hip pocket.

Hell yes! They all loved working for Ollie. Who wouldn't? He would kick the nuts off a palm tree now and then, just for practice, and then sell the nuts to the Ayatollah. . . . Ollie was a class act, they said, a true patriot.

And he was also honest, they said. Incredible! The man never stole—except for the $200 he grabbed one night, to buy himself four snow tires at a gas station south of Arlington.

That is why Oliver North will go to prison. Not because he loved his country too well, but because he put $50 snow tires on his car. . . . Only a fool would do that. Here was a man who could swagger like James Bond through the lobbies of every Swiss bank and Merrill-Lynch office between London and Hong Kong, and he was buying cheap retreads for his own car in Washington.

North will go: 30 years for conspiracy and obstruction of justice.

Fawn Hall is guilty of these same felony crimes, but she has been given immunity and will not be locked up for anything she has said on TV—even the orgy of shredding she and Ollie went through when Ed Meese called to say the jig was about to be up. She will wind up as a well-paid advance woman in the Bush '88 campaign.

Both Richard Secord and Hakim will go—probably for 15 or 16 years each, and they will both be out in two, eager to split that $8 million in pure profit they still have in their Swiss bank account.

McFarlane will not go. He remains under psychiatric observation and will never understand the real horror of the crimes he committed routinely, in a fog of booze and Valium.

Casey will get 600 years, in absentia. Casey will never testify against anybody, and he went to his grave knowing more about these crimes than anybody except perhaps Ollie North.

Meese will go. He has been the subject of too many federal investigations for too many cheap reasons. Only Reagan and Bush are left now, and Ollie North will have to sell one of them, if he means to stay out of prison. Reagan can get sick and quit, but Bush can't. He is the future of the Party, while Reagan is the past. That is the choice that the boys at Duke Ziebert's are saying that Oliver North will have to make.

June 16, 1987

The Trickle-Down Theory

Ronald Reagan will be gone soon, another classic victim of the Peter Principle and the curse that hangs on the White House. It has been a long time since anybody came out of that place alive—or at least alive enough for anything except top-dollar speaking engagements and occasional photo opportunities.

There is a very rare photograph, taken at the funeral of assassinated Egyptian President Anwar Sadat, showing four living American presidents standing in the tight focus of one 35mm frame: Richard Nixon, Jimmy Carter, Gerald Ford and Ronald Reagan.

Three of the four had already been chased out of the White House in defeat or disgrace, or both, and the fourth is about ready to go. The odds against Reagan hanging on for the remaining 19 months of his second term are up to something like 13–1, and rising. . . .

The ominous drone of the Iran/contra hearings will be back on the national airwaves this week, and the bad word in Washington is that investigators for the select congressional committee have already come up with the long-sought "smoking gun" memo that will nail Ronald Reagan with evidence that will lead to *impeachment.*

It gets back, as usual, to USMC Lt. Col. Oliver North, who ran the whole operation. North sent many confidential memos to many people in the White House, but he tried to shred and destroy most of them when he was warned by increasingly tainted Attorney General Ed Meese that the Big Balloon was about to go up. . . .

Meese in his wisdom somehow managed to give North almost 48 hours to destroy the evidence—but, even then, there was not enough time, and North didn't understand the *destructo* function of his computer well enough to make it eat everything he'd put into it. . . . And when smarter people punched a different mix of recall buttons, all manner of dark plots and criminal gibberish came spitting out on the printer, dredged up from some seldom-used memory chip, deep in the bowels of the mainframe.

Many of these turned up in the published report of the Tower Commission, a sort of in-house investigation put together in haste by the White House. They ranged from constant complaints by North about his lack of sleep, to former National Security Adviser "Bud" Mc-

Farlane's memo to North, saying that "if the American people knew what a hero you are, they would make you secretary of State."

North believed it, and that was the root of the problem. He had also been called "a great American hero" by President Reagan and former White House Communications Director Patrick Buchanan, a relentless right-wing zealot who resigned abruptly, just after the story broke, in order to run for president in 1988 with either Alexander Haig or Lyndon LaRouche.

The legacy of Ronald Reagan will be different from those of the other three gents in that famous Egyptian photograph. . . . Richard Nixon was a crook, Gerald Ford was a shameless fixer and Jimmy Carter was an awesome bungler who gave once-proud political values like "decency" and "honesty" a bad name.

But these things are small compared to the horrible stains and half-blotted failures that Ronald Reagan is going to leave on the lives and memories of this sad generation of the 1980s that he once presumed to lead and inspire, while at the same time telling a reporter from *People* magazine, "This generation may be the one that sees the end of the world."

In times of stress, Dutch has always fallen back on his well-known faith in the Bible—and especially in the Book of Revelation, which he quotes with the same brainless zeal that used to grip Jimmy Carter when he quoted Bob Dylan, or spark Richard Nixon's worship of Vince Lombardi.

The Book of Revelation, however, is a very different thing. It is perhaps the bleakest document ever written by human hand:

Then I saw coming out of the mouth of the dragon and from the mouth of the beast and from the mouth of the false prophet, three unclean spirits like frogs. For they are spirits of demons that work miracles. They go out to the kings of the whole world to muster them for the war of the sovereign God's great Day.

What other American president—from the corruption of Grant and Harding to the harsh wartime judgments of Roosevelt and Truman—will ever be nailed by biographers with anything even vaguely approaching the charge that he left a whole generation grappling with the idea that the only thing in nature more poison than The Rain is the possibility of coming in contact with human blood, for any reason at all.

Between AIDS and acid rain, there is not much left of what Scott

Fitzgerald called "a fresh green breast of the new world." That was in the last lines of *The Great Gatsby,* some of the highest and purest and cleanest words ever written about the real beauty of what they were just beginning to call, back then, *The American Dream,* and all its magic possibilities. . . .

So let's have a look at how the big boys write. Stand back.

As the moon rose higher the inessential houses began to melt away until gradually I became aware of the old island here that flowered once for Dutch Sailor's eyes—a fresh green breast of the new world. Its vanished trees, the trees that had made way for Gatsby's house, had once pandered in whispers to the last and greatest of all human drama; for a transitory enchanted moment man must have held his breath in the presence of this continent, compelled into an aesthetic contemplation he neither understood nor desired, face to face for the last time in history with something commensurate to his capacity for wonder.

Those lines would never have been written if Daisy had been a carrier of AIDS, or if Gatsby's lonely swimming pool took on a crust of poison water every time it rained.

Reagan's children must be proud of him. With AIDS and acid rain, there is not much left in the way of life and love and possibilities for these shortchanged children of the '80s. In addition to a huge and terminally crippling national debt, and a shocking realization that your country has slipped to the status of a second-rate power, and that five American dollars will barely buy a cup of coffee in Tokyo, these poor buggers are being flogged every day of their lives with the knowledge that sex is death and rain kills fish and any politician they see on TV is a liar and a fool.

June 22, 1987

Four More Years

"Now it was there. Now it grew out of me like a tumor, like a second head and it was part of me, though it could not belong to me at all, because it was so big. It was there like a huge, dead beast, that had once, when it was still alive, been my hand or my arm. And my blood flowed both through me and through it, as if through one and the same body. And my heart had to make a great effort to drive the blood into the Big Thing; there was hardly enough blood. And the blood entered the Big Thing unwillingly and came back sick and tainted. But the Big Thing swelled and grew over my face like a warm bluish boil and grew over my mouth, and already the shadow of its edge lay upon my remaining eye.

—Rainer Maria Rilke
from *Surviving Schizophrenia: A Family Manual*

According to a 1978 report by the now-defunct Presidential Commission on Mental Health, which was put on bookstore remainder lists immediately after it was published—"there are as many schizophrenics in America as there are people in Oregon, Mississippi and Kansas, or in Wyoming, Vermont, Delaware and Hawaii combined."

That was 10 years ago, more or less, and the numbers are still rising. There has not been a lot of talk about mental health in the White House since Reagan took over, but studies by the Democratic National Committee indicate that there are now more functioning, street-level schizophrenics loose in the nation than the combined populations of Florida, Ohio and Texas.

None of these are "Democratic states," according to DNC figures—with the possible exception of Hawaii, and that will presumably end in 1988 if the party nominates its current front-runner, the Rev. Jesse Jackson, of Chicago and Greenville, S.C.

Jackson is a black man, and the country is not ready for that. Not even in Hilo . . . It is a problem for The Party, which has not been doing well lately. In the last five presidential elections the Democrats have lost the cumulative electoral vote by a hideous margin of 77 percent to 21 percent . . . and that was when they had white people on the ballot.

American politics is a profoundly atavistic sport, and the odds are that a black man will not be president of the United States until long after

Oral Roberts dies and "comes back," like he swears he will, "to rule the world, with Jesus."

TV has changed our perceptions, but not much else. If Warren Harding "came back" today, with a high-tech organization, he would probably carry 44 states and appoint four justices to the U.S. Supreme Court.

Nixon did four, and now Reagan will have done four more before he gets carried off by polyps, and that will define the nature of the court for the rest of our generation.

Jimmy Carter, as it happened, made no Supreme Court appointments. He was saving that move for his second term, according to people who worked with him.

Jimmy is gone now, and so is Gary Hart. . . . Lust and craziness croaked both of them. Hart, the Democratic front-runner until six weeks ago, was a known sex fiend who drank beer in the morning and wanted to scrap the whole U.S. Navy—but he was doing well enough in the polls until his picture turned up on the front page of the *National Enquirer* wearing a rayon jock strap and eyes like squashed grapes.

That was too much for the electorate, apparently—although nobody ever really checked it out—and Hart dropped out of the race in a blaze of shame, for reasons that wouldn't have raised eyebrows in a Rotary Club between Pittsburgh and Harlingen, Texas

The schizophrenia vote was not polled, despite its mushrooming numbers. Hart was an odds-on favorite to win both the Democratic nomination and the presidency before he got his picture in the papers with a bimbo from Miami—and even after the scandal broke and the dust settled he was running ahead of every Democrat in Iowa except Jesse Jackson.

The schizoid vote is about all that is left to the Democrats these days. They are about to self-destruct again, almost a year ahead of schedule.

Two months ago they had a nationally popular front-runner who was running 16 to 20 points ahead of George Bush—and now on this bottomless Fourth of July they are scrambling around like unborn rats and confronting the voters with a cage-full of nondescript presidential candidates called "The Seven Dwarfs."

The Republican Party is on trial on TV for crimes worse than anything Richard Nixon or Boss Tweed ever committed. The president is about to be impeached, and his closest advisers from the glory days of his first term are going to jail for greed and corruption. . . . The attorney general and the vice president are too dirty to appear in public unless they're subpoenaed.

Despite all this, current GOP vice president and former CIA Chief George Bush is currently a three-to-one favorite among professional gamblers to be the next president of the United States, adding another four years of rampant greed and blundering to the seven that Ronald Reagan has already racked up.

Oliver North and Adm. Poindexter will end up taking the rap for most of Reagan's crimes, but it will not be a long-term problem for either Bush or the future of the beleaguered GOP.

The party of Grant, Harding, Hoover and Richard Nixon will open the 1988 campaign knowing that 23 states have voted Republican in all five presidential elections since 1968 and 13 others have gone GOP in four of the five. That is 36 states out of 50, with a massive, overripe nut of 354 electoral votes.

Only 270 are needed to win.

The Democratic Party, on the other hand, can count on a power base of no states at all. Only the District of Columbia, with three electoral votes, has voted consistently Democratic in the last five presidential elections.

The Whig party abandoned all hopes and disappeared from the face of the earth in 1852 on the basis of better numbers than the Democrats can muster today. . . . The Whigs actually elected a president, the ill-fated Zachary Taylor in 1848, only four years before they went belly up and quit politics forever.

The real miracle of American politics in the '80s is that the Democratic Party still exists. It is the "majority party" numerically—but in truth the Democrats have not done anything except bitch and whine and fight savagely among themselves since Franklin Roosevelt was elected to a fourth term in 1944.

June 29, 1987

Dance of the Seven Dwarfs

Every time I come to town
The boys keep kickin' my dawg around;
Makes no difference if he is a hound,
They've got to quit kickin' my dawg around.

—Champ Clark's campaign song 1912

Music was a big thing in politics, back then. Every candidate had a battle hymn, or at least a marching song, and Clark's vulgar little ditty was not much worse than the others. But it didn't do him much good. He was speaker of the House at the time, a famous congressman from Missouri and a powerful man in Washington. He was also a Democrat, lusting after his party's nomination.

But his song was not right for the times, apparently: The Society for the Prevention of Cruelty to Animals was not a real factor in the presidential politics of 1912—and when the votes were finally counted, Champ Clark took a beating worse than anything the boys ever did to his dawg.

That was the year Teddy Roosevelt ran on the Bull Moose ticket, splitting the GOP vote with "Dead Bill" Taft and electing Woodrow Wilson—the first of only five Democratic presidents elected in this century.

Only six Democrats were elected in the previous century, for that matter—most of them refugees from the Bum of the Month Club—and the real odds of another Democrat moving into the White House between now and the year 2000 are no better than 50–50.

That would be the long-awaited Third Coming of the Kennedys— young Joe, who is only 34 and just won his first election last year. . . . Or maybe the Fourth Coming, according to the very few and very nervous Party Wizards who still think Teddy might emerge like Caligula and make one final crazed charge in 1988.

I started off as a small-town newspaper publisher. Because we had
some underworld characters who were trying to dominate our area of the
state, next thing I knew, I found myself in politics.

—Paul Simon

The candidates came together in Houston Wednesday, courtesy of PBS, along with the legendary, rheumy-eyed, right-wing, Yalie yahoo, William Buckley, who asked most of the questions.

Buckley would have been a clear winner if the show had been "Entertainment Tonight" or "Donahue" and a normal white-trash audience . . . but in this case, nobody won; not even George Bush, who might have been bored by the show, but only because all of the once-mocked "Seven Dwarfs" were obviously a lot smarter than he is.

The Seven Dwarfs just won't work anymore. These were not bad people. Not one of them would have allowed a thug like Oliver North or weak reeds like McFarlane or Poindexter come anywhere near them in a decent public place, except to serve the drinks. . . . For the first time in a long while, the true face of the punks and thieves and fixers who actually run the machinery and do the real business of the Republican Party was put on public display, and it was a horrible thing to see.

There were a lot of small changes in the wake of the debate, but the only big one was the emergence of Sen. Paul Simon of Illinois as a genuine contender.

Simon is small and ugly and weird and he almost never smiles. He has lips like Mick Jagger and the ears of a young baboon.

But none of these things really matters. Simon could be as ugly as the Elephant Man and as small as "the other Paul Simon" who wrote "Sounds of Silence" and "Bridge Over Troubled Water" and he would still stand alone among the Democratic hopefuls. The Senator is an old-timey politician, a throwback to the times of Harry Truman and Clarence Darrow, *before the days of television*. He projects that rarest of things in politics—an awesome sense of integrity and commitment and utter conviction. That is pure magic in politics.

Which was recognized with stunning clarity, according to polls of Iowa voters taken immediately after the Houston debate. In what was virtually his first appearance on the '88 campaign trail, and without ever smiling, Simon leapfrogged all the other candidates and shocked most political pros by emerging as a real candidate *and* a possible front-runner. He went into Houston as a cranky no-name darkhorse with no chance to win anything and left Friday morning with his name suddenly in the headlines and jumped up to the top of the leaderboard in Iowa and even New Hampshire; in 24 hours his numbers went from 70–1 to 7–1, almost even with Gephardt and Jackson, the current front-runners.

It had the look of a major development in the race for the Democratic nomination—easily the biggest thing since the Gary Hart disaster—and many wizards were seen crawling back to their drawing boards on Friday morning. Paul Simon had stomped on the terra.

The only other real shift in the Demo numbers, after Houston, was a very visible jump by Massachusetts Gov. Michael Dukakis. It was minor, compared with Simon's great leap, but it jumped Dukakis up from nowhere to the position of a real contender: Down from 20–1 to about half that on Friday.

Dukakis is a feisty little bugger with impressive credentials and the style of a mean counterpuncher. He was not in a mood, that night, to be poked and goaded by host/moderator William Buckley, who tried to make Dukakis the butt of his neo-Nazi jokes and left Houston with a rash of fresh teeth marks. . . . Buckley has lost speed, in his dotage, but Dukakis is faster and meaner than a bull mongoose. He picked up some of the best pros from Hart's staff and he will be hard to beat in New Hampshire or anywhere else east of the Mississippi and north of the Mason-Dixon line. . . . But his chances of getting anything except a purple heart out of the 11 Southern states that will vote on "Super Tuesday" next March are not ripe. The good ole boys will beat him like a gong, and after that he will be little more than a stalking horse for New York Gov. Mario Cuomo, who still insists he's not running.

The Houston debate was not a big hit in the Nielsen ratings. Not even hardline Democrats made much of an effort to watch it, and the yuppies called it dull.

That is the problem with this rich and anguished generation. Somewhere a long time ago they fell in love with the idea that politicians—even the slickest and brightest presidential candidates—were real heroes and truly exciting people.

That is wrong on its face. They are mainly dull people with corrupt instincts and criminal children.

July 6, 1987

It Was You, Charlie

Some time around noon on Thursday, last week, I took a break from the Ollie North show on TV and drove down to Woody Creek Tavern for lunch. It was one of those fine, bright mornings that can make the idea of living 8,000 feet up in the mountains on a half-paved dead-end road seem very wise and elegant, instead of that crazy dumb feeling that you get on some days in the winter.

The tavern was not crowded at that hour, except for a few stools at the far end of the bar, where a small crowd of cowboys and beer hippies were nursing long-necked Budweisers and staring balefully at a "pro wrestling" rerun on ESPN.

Nobody spoke when I sat down and dumped my brown bag full of mail and newspapers on the bar and rifled through the pile for anything that looked like a check. But there was nothing except two bills from *Time* magazine and a handwritten note from the garbage man, saying that my cans were no longer serviceable and he was cutting me off until I got new ones.

I tossed it away and asked Crazy Bob, sitting next to me, if the Meat Loaf Special was any good.

"Nothing is good," he replied. "Tonight is the full moon. Terrible things are happening. Al got kicked by a horse and Terry lost one of his eyes when he got in a fight with a stranger. The whole valley smells like death."

I noticed that it was time for the Ollie North Show to start up again on TV—so I grabbed the remote-control unit and punched the channel over to CNN, where Bernard Shaw was saying, "Col. North is about to undergo another round of tough interrogation this afternoon."

"Hot damn!" said Crazy Bob. "This should be *good*. He's been beating the crap out of those wimps all morning."

The man next to him laughed and shifted his stool for a better view of the TV set. Somebody behind us at a table yelled, "Turn up the goddamn volume! I want to *hear* this."

I was surprised. The tavern is not normally a hotbed of big-time political discourse. On most days I like to have a firm grip on a fork before switching the tube over to a news channel. . . . But not today. These boys were definitely *hooked* on Oliver North. They had *adopted* him, for some reason; it was like a gang of teen-agers seeing "Rocky" for the first time.

The proceedings opened, as usual, with another lecture on duty, honor and patriotism by Oliver North—in response, once again, to some waterwit question by the committee's main mouthpiece, John Nields, a wretched little jellyfish who somehow got himself appointed as chief counsel for the House of Representatives' side and had been doing most of the questioning for three days.

Crazy Bob was getting so many laughs from listening to Nields that he said his ribs were starting to hurt. "Jesus!" he said. "If I ever go to court I hope they give me this guy for a prosecutor. He probably cuts grass for Ed Meese."

Nields was clearly a hired fool of some kind. Every question he served up to North was like tossing meat to a wolf. By the end of the Thursday session, North had been fed so many home-run balls that he and his lawyer were laughing out loud and slapping each other on the back every time Nields asked a question—and then North would give another 20-minute speech about how much he loved his wife and his children and his uniform and, above all, his commander-in-chief, The President.

By midnight on Thursday, Oliver North was a national hero and his "Legal Defense Fund" was so swollen with contributions that even George Bush was saying that he might be the next president of the United States, or even head of the PTL Club.

Bush came out of hiding for the first time in many months and laid claim to North like he'd just found a long-lost son, calling him a great American hero with the heart of Charles Lindbergh and the gonads of Gen. Patton.

One public opinion poll on Friday had North with a truly awesome "approval rating" of 96 to 4 percent, much higher than Ronald Reagan, Jesus or even pure cocaine. The Iran-contra scandal that once looked deeper and dirtier than Watergate was suddenly transformed by North's performance on network TV into something on the scale of American heroism like Valley Forge or MacArthur's return to the Philippines. . . . The shameful saga of Oliver North was so heavy and strong that it caused rich men on Wall Street to weep openly and small children in Hollywood to dance and jabber with joy.

It even brought tears to the eyes of Crazy Bob. "This guy is the real thing," he said when North went off the air on Thursday. "I want to send him a check."

I stared at him for a long moment, then I whacked him on the side of his head. "You fool!" I said. "I'm tired of your lame Nazi gibberish."

He leaped off is stool and went into a fighting stance, but I quickly jumped back and hissed at him: "Semper Fi! Semper Fi! 269 dead boys at the Beirut Airport! *Two hundred and sixty-nine dead U.S. Marines, Bobby!*"

He stiffened, then dropped his hands.

"Yes!" I shouted. "And we know who *did* it, don't we?"

"Iranians," he muttered. "That stinking Ayatollah."

I knew he had been in the Navy—nine or ten years in one of the super-elite SEAL units . . . the Marines get a lot of publicity and they look good on TV commercials, but even drill sergeants at Parris Island will admit that 99 out of 100 Marine recruits would be routinely rejected if they ever tried to qualify for the SEALS. A pencil-necked weekend warrior like Oliver North couldn't get hired as a male nurse in a SEAL unit.

I put my arm around Crazy Bob's shoulders and sat him back down on his stool. "And who was it, Bobby, that sold all those bombs and missiles and rockets to the Iranians?"

"Jesus Christ," he said. "It was Oliver North, wasn't it?"

"Yeah, Charlie," I said. "It was him—and he was well paid for it, too. Ronald Reagan called him a great American hero, and George Shultz put his arm around him and thanked him for doing good work."

So much for Ollie mania.

July 13, 1987

Fat Men on Horseback

Last week was a slow one for news, but for big-time politicians it was like being put out naked and alone in the jungle and being forced to watch a python swallow a pig.

There was no joy in Mudville, but so what? Ronald Reagan slipped the noose, George Bush walked, and Jessica Hahn was pictured on the front page of the *New York Post* while on a "shopping spree" in downtown Manhattan, accompanied by "a bodyguard with a pistol tucked in his belt."

"That goes with the contract," said her lawyer. "We just sold her story to a men's magazine for $2.5 million." The details were hazy, but the lawyer said Ms. Hahn was grappling with offers "in the multimillion-dollar range" from *Playboy, Penthouse* and *Esquire* for her own personal version of that famous afternoon in Florida when she was flogged and sexually brutalized by Jim Bakker and at least two other born-again TV preachers. "They had no right to tell all those stories about how I 'knew all the tricks of the trade,' " she said. "So I decided to tell the real truth about that day. It was horrible. My life was ruined forever."

Sex and violence has become an everyday thing for the 1980s generation that once embraced the Reagan Revolution. We live in savage times. Oliver North is a hero, Ed Meese is rich, and a monstrous film called "Blue Velvet" is nominated for three Academy Awards.

Two months ago, Gary Hart was running 16 points ahead of George Bush in "presidential preference" polls for 1988, and syndicated columnists were saying that U.S. Marine Lt. Col. Oliver North was so crooked that he should be stripped of his uniform before he could go on national TV and give testimony in the U.S. Congress. . . . But things have changed.

Hart was exposed by the *Miami Herald* for lying about his secret life as one of the dumbest townhouse johns who ever lived and was forced to quit the presidential race and slink off to the hills like a child-raper. . . . And Oliver North went on TV last week with a sloe-eyed story of lies, dumbness and treachery in the very bowels of Reagan's White House that made him a national hero like Audie Murphy and Daniel Boone, or even Willie Sutton.

In the quick crazy window of 66 days and two moons, Hart and North reversed roles in a way that only Hollywood could take seriously—and Bush came out the big winner. Six weeks ago he was looking at the very real possibility of getting jerked out of the White House by federal marshals before he ever had a chance to hit the bricks in Iowa City and get his picture taken on Election Day with his arm around the shoulders of the legendary local sportsman and political wizard, Marcos Melendez, who can deliver more votes than the stork.

When the buck stopped with John Poindexter, it was not only Reagan who beat the rap. Bush, long known in Washington as the guiltiest man in American politics, did a trick that made every camel that ever crawled through the eye of a needle seem like an amateur. If there were any real justice in the world, George would be working with Spiro Agnew on the wrong end of some driving range in Baltimore, for $2 a bucket.

Also in the weekend news, CIA Director William Webster has dismissed two high-ranking agents for "the roles they played" in the Iran/contra affair.

Webster was planning to retire after 10 scandal-free years as director of the FBI when the Iran/contra story broke last November, but when he learned that his nominal boss Ed Meese had known about it all along and never bothered to tell him, he got so angry that he canceled his retirement plans and announced he was going to stay on a little longer, or at least for the duration of the scandal.

Big Bill Casey didn't mind. He was dead. And so Webster took over the CIA and postponed his retirement back home to St. Louis for "at least the indefinite future."

That is what T.S. Eliot said, and also William Burroughs. But that was a long time ago, and neither one of them ever went back to their roots, as it were, in St. Louis. It is a nice town to be from, but that bridge under the great golden arch on the west side of the Mississippi is a one-way street for the big boys. The only St. Louis native who ever went back home after getting famous was Hadley Richardson, Ernest Hemingway's first wife, and they say she didn't stay long.

People like to talk about the difference between the '60s and the '80s, and also about the difference between Watergate and this monstrous Iran/contra mess. . . . Well, I'll tell you the difference: The criminals in Watergate knew they were guilty and so did everybody else; and when the dust cleared the crooked president was gone and so were all the others. They were criminals and they had the same contempt for the whole concept of democracy that these cheap punks have been strutting every day for the past two months of truly disgraceful testimony.

The whole Iran/contra investigation was a farce and a scam that benefited nobody except Washington lawyers who charge $1,000 an hour for courtroom time. North's bill for legal fees will be a million dollars, which has already been covered by the private donations.

If this low-rent scandal is the best this generation can do, they deserve what they're getting and they are going to have to live with it. They deserve to be called A Generation of Swine.

Not even Tex Colson sold bombs and rockets to crazed Persian maniacs who used them to kill his own kind—and not even Kissinger would have put his arm around him and said, "Well done."

And where was the press, in this one? Where are the sons of Woodward & Bernstein, that great new wave of investigative journalists that was going to spring out of Watergate?

Kissinger was a monster, an arrogant elitist with a harsh German accent and a mean intellectual's contempt for the politicians he had worked for all his life. Kissinger was the man who hung around the White House at night, drinking Perrier water and taking notes while Richard Nixon drank gin and raved crazily at the portrait of Abraham Lincoln.

But Henry Kissinger, for all his nasty faults, was a true prince among men, compared with the half-bright rejects, Marine vets and born-again Annapolis grads that Ronald Reagan hired to work in the White House basement and run the National Security apparatus like a gang of demented Hell's Angels.

July 20, 1987

Cowboys at Sea

"Kuwait—The supertanker Bridgeton *hit an underwater mine early Friday as it and another Kuwaiti oil tanker flying the American flag were being escorted in the Persian Gulf by* three U.S. Navy warships. . . . *Saudi Arabia, U.S. and Kuwaiti (naval defense) teams last week reported they had cleared mines in the al-Ahmadi shipping channels, where ships previously have hit mines. . . . The* Bridgeton *was hit* 40 miles south of that area. *In Tehran, Iranian Prime Minister Hussein Musavi called the incident an "irreparable blow to American's political and military prestige." He said the mine had been planted by* "invisible hands."*

—Examiner News Services

The news comes in bursts out here in the mountains. On some nights, when it all comes together, I get 200 crystal-clear channels on TV and all three of my telephones ring constantly with calls from rich publishers, famous gurus and presidential candidates on both coasts. . . . But not always: Last week my dish got blasted by lightning and the phones went dead for three days. There was no information, no news at all—except what Ed Bradley could pick up on his personal satellite with New York.

Which hardly mattered. The news went into a lull that allowed us to concentrate on local matters. We spent some time on the driving range, Ed got good with the Luger, Doug put in two new windows, P.J. O'Rourke did the whole porch with Watco Oil and a CBS correspondent came out to mow the lawn. . . . The Iran/contra hearings went into recess, Rear Adm. John Poindexter slithered off to whatever stylish rock in suburban Washington that he lives under when he's not testifying or bamboozling the president.

While Poindexter sucked on his dead pipe and stonewalled the committee with an arrogance in the style of the late Roy Cohn, Oliver North dolls were selling like hotcakes from coast to coast and Ronald Reagan was still sunk in a terminal memory lapse.

But Congress got a new hero last week, an amiable dunce named George Shultz. Shultz has been around for a while—"been around the block a few times," as they say: he was Secretary of the Treasury under Nixon, at the time of the Watergate scandal, and he wallked away from that one by swearing he knew nothing at all about anything. . . . And now he is Secretary of State under Reagan, neck-deep in the Iran/contra scandal, and once again he is swearing that he was "cut out of the loop" by yet another perfidious president, and once again he is flashing those corrupt beagle-hound eyes at the TV cameras and claiming to be as pure as the driven snow.

"The President has excellent judgment," he said, "but only when he's given the facts." And when George tried to give him "the facts," he was cut off at the knees by culprits like Oliver North and the swinish Poindexter. They had somehow seized the reins of U.S. foreign policy, he told the congresssmen on TV, and when George tried desperately to tell his own truth to the hopelessly isolated president, they called him a fool and made him a public dunce.

Which is true—and it may be the only main point on which the thug-team of North and Poindexter will prove out to be utterly right. Neither one of them could get a job with Ivan Boesky today, but in the matter of their judgment on the erstwhile Shultz, they saw him for what he is and always has been, and they treated him like a natural punk.

Meanwhile, the "Oliver North Defense Fund" had collected over $1.5 million in public contributions, as of last Friday—despite frequent emphasis by the press and TV news reports on the grim fact that all $2 million of Ollie North's legal expenses, along with all the other "witnesses," will be picked up and paid in full by The Taxpayers.

That's you and me, Charley. The next time the IRS man comes calling, ask him how much of your bill will go to pay North's lawyer and the million dollars a day of normal operating expenses that it costs the U.S. Navy to escort "reflagged" Kuwaiti oil tankers up and down the Persian Gulf in the war zone between Iran and Iraq.

That was a fraud on its face, even before the first convoy set sail— but when the first bogus "U.S. supertanker" to run the gauntlet with an escort of U.S. gunships was almost sunk by a floating mine, the joke was over. Navy Capt. David Yonkers, commander of the U.S. task force, had warned the fiendish Ayatollah that his ships were so loaded with firepower and so cranked-up and combat-ready that "any missile attack [by Iran] would probably be the last one." There would be no more careless blunders like the one that killed 37 sailors on the *USS Stark* a few weeks ago; this time his boys would be alert like a pack of trained sharks. All attackers would be blown to smithereens.

The doomed and disloyal Shultz was just winding up his final lecture to the hapless select committees when his "testimony" was interrupted by a news bulletin, saying that the giant 401,000-ton *Bridgeton*, 1,200 feet long, had plowed into a floating mine while cruising 40 miles south of the well-marked al-Ahmadi shipping channel, which was carefully cleared last week by U.S. minesweepers and hundreds of highly trained frogmen.

What the *Bridgeton* was doing 40 miles off course was not explained, at the time, by gung-ho Capt. Yonkers when his ship was taking on water and threatening to sink like a huge punctured beer can, as long as four football fields, in 90 feet of water at the mouth of the channel leading into the main Kuwaiti oil-loading terminal.

As of Sunday night, the *Bridgeton* was still afloat. And so was Shultz, but they were both described by experts as "just limping along and aimed for the nearest safe harbor."

Shultz completed his shameful testimony on Friday afternoon—clearing the decks, as it were, for the long-awaited appearance of the main monster in this saga, Attorney General Ed Meese.

Meese is so crooked that he is said by Washington gossips to require the help of three legal assistants to screw his pants on every morning. If he was looking down the barrel of a real interrogation by anybody except yoyos like Nields and Liman, he would be in serious trouble. Alphonse Karr was right.

July 27, 1987

Blame it on Dead Bill

Ed Meese's hair appears to be turning white. He needs a quick wash of that Grecian Urn stuff—or a blast of fat black Rustoleum, which will turn anything it touches stone black in a matter of two or three seconds. Permanently. Never mind the weather, or even fire. Rustoleum is the .44 Magnum of spray cans. One $5 tank can make a whole car look like black lava rock in less than two minutes. Including the windows. Heavy flat black.

Big Ed was back on the tube last week, and for a few juiced-up moments on Wednesday, as the dreary cavalcade of whiners and wimps and pimps and shysters that has been the Iran/contra hearings began to trail off, we had a little fun.

As the CBS feed comes bouncing in from Washington, I can hear that somebody is *after him.* I am 50 feet away on the porch, two walls and two doors away from the TV set—but I can tell immediately that it is not John Nields, the human puffball. . . . Meese ate him alive, along with Peter Rodino, with a blizzard of jurisdictional gibberish that stymied everything.

But now it's different, apparently. Who *is* this, talking to Meese in the tones of a mean parole officer?

It is Sen. Warren Rudman, an ex-prosecutor of some kind from up in New England. A New Hampshire Republican: Live free or die. Rudman is a pugnacious bugger, and Meese is clearly nervous with the tone of this questioning. Rudman wants a piece of his ass, or at least that's what it sounds and looks like. . . . Maybe not; these people are all lawyers and politicians.

But Meese has been forced to fall back on *The Honor of Dead Bill*— "who can't be here to defend himself."

Well, Ed—that ain't the question. This time we were talking about the "Evans case," the huge arms-smuggling case that was happening in New York just before the Iran/contra scandal blew . . . It was something like $17 billion, or maybe it was 17 people-individuals-defendants and the money was $200 billion . . . We can check those numbers. Let's listen in . . .

Rudman is saying, "You certainly had evidence that some strange things were going on (the Evans case)." Now Rudman *seems* to be flogging Meese with direct accusations of fraud, negligence or dark malfeasance of some kind . . . and Meese is *off balance*. His bitchy little points of order are not working today.

Rud: *"The single most important question we can ask you:* How is it that either you or the president didn't get these people into a room and find out, *right then,* what was going on and who was doing what to whom, and why, and where all this money was going?

EM: Admits meekly to Rudman's charge that "The president was not well served by his people on this." *"Yes, that is true."*

Rud: Like Hulk Hogan in a tag-team match, suddenly quits and yields the balance of his time to Sen. William Cohen, R-Maine . . . who comes in swinging.

EM: Suddenly begins addressing Cohen as *"Yessir."*

Yes . . . and now it is Judge Mitchell: "Doesn't it bother you that you were told things that were untrue, and that because of that you then made statements to the American people which were also untrue? Doesn't that bother you?"

EM: Yeah, it bothers him, but not much . . .

MITCH: Wants to know how he can be expected to believe that Meese spoke (alone) on the weekend prior to the Nov. 25 press conference . . . with the president, the vice president, Adm. Poindexter, Dead Bill. . . . *AND TOOK NO NOTES.*

"Is there a reason why you took no notes in these critical conversations with all the principals? *When you always took notes before?"*

Meese goes back to flyspecking, frantically treading water—and his hair is now cotton-white.

MITCH: "Well, giving you every benefit of the doubt, that is very hard to accept."

EM: Says that truth is sometimes stranger than fiction, and wants to clear up with Mitchell, this question about *why it is hard to accept.*

Mitch does not smile. He could run for president tomorrow and chop both Bush and Dole.

These Downeaster boys are tough, and *they don't like Ed Messe.*

And now Mitch introduces a deposition by Lt. Col. Robert Earle, North's deputy at NSC—

MITCH: "DID YOU TALK WITH COL. NORTH ON THE AFTERNOON OF NOV. 21?"

EM: *"No—to the best of my recollection, I did not."*

Mitch frowns: The specter of perjury looms.

"It's page 15 of the notes, Exhibit 47—you may wish to refer to those. . . ."

Mitch is asking, in tones of the Grim Reaper, if Meese is aware that Col. North was shredding crucial documents in the vital 72 hours before Meese's press conference on Nov. 25, '86.

Mitchell is bearing down. No smiles, no filigree: *This is a New England judge, interrogating a man he knows has been lying to the committee.* . . .

AND NOW DANNY INOUYE COMES ON. . . . GRIM EYES BEHIND COKE-BOTTLE LENSES. . . . AN ANGRY MAN, FRUS-TRATED AND INSULTED. . . . and he says to Ed Meese: *"Isn't it a fact, Mr. Attorney General, that it makes no difference what kind of immunity you might or might not have (Meese has none)—if you lie to Congress it's still a federal crime, isn't it?"*

Meese agrees, very nervously. (Where is my goddamn lawyer? What kind of fool advised me to come in here without one?)

"Let me look at my notes, if I may—or Mr. Richardson's notes," now he gabbles around on the table like a lizard on a hot rock.

DI: "So you were dealing with a good friend [Dead Bill], not a stranger—why were you so shy about asking him the $64,000 question?"

Meese retreats into procedure again. Nothing he says now will be accepted as truth. He has become a public liability to Dutch, and perhaps is also looking at a perjury charge—another felony, to go along with his Wedtech deal. *Meese is going to have a hard time just getting a job when he goes back to Oakland.*

"There is no there, there."

—Gertrude Stein

August 3, 1987

The Last Taxi to Scotland

It was sometime after midnight when we finally got organized and ready to take off for Scotland. The first leg of the trip would be over the mountains to Denver, by long-range taxicab, then a straight flight to New York to pick up the passports and finally across the water. The plan was to arrive in Edinburgh just in time to make a speech of some kind to a huge crowd of British motorcyclists at the Edinburgh Book Fair.

It was a big event. My old friend Ralph Steadman, the famous English artist, had put it together and he was very excited. But he was getting edgy: It was midnight on Thursday and I was still in Colorado, with the Continental Divide, four airports and the Atlantic Ocean between us. Our show was scheduled for noon on Saturday and the crowd had been waiting for several days.

"They're drinking whiskey and getting very rowdy," he said on the telephone. "I've never seen such a terrible mob. They'll likely tear me to pieces if you don't get here on time."

"Don't worry," I told him. "Everything is under control. Our driver will be here in 20 minutes. He's a very reliable person. I've known him for years."

Which was true—or at least I believed it was true. The trip to Denver was about four hours, but when I'd spoken with our driver earlier in the day he said we could make it in 3½ at that time of night. Maria was worried about roaring over Independence Pass at top speed with a stranger at the wheel, but I told her to relax. "Dilly's an excellent driver," I said. "We can sleep all the way to the airport."

Those were the last calm words I uttered for the next 10 hours. The trip turned weird even before we left the house. It was not quite 1 A.M. when I heard a big car in the driveway and then a knock on the door. "Come on in, Dilly," I yelled. "We're just about ready to go."

An odd laugh crackled in the darkness outside, then the screen door slammed open and a gaunt-looking man with wild eyes came loping into the kitchen. "Hi there," he said. "My name's Earl. Dilly couldn't make it. He had to go over to Telluride for the Dead concert, so he loaned me his cab."

There was a crazy grin on his face as he extended his hand, then he put his arm around Maria and kissed her on the forehead. "Wonderful,

wonderful," he said. "Dilly said you were good people. We'll get along just fine."

Ye gods, I thought. He was wearing a black Harley-Davidson T-shirt and heavy motorcycle boots—not the right kind of footwear for any sensitive heel-and-toe work on the narrow winding road across the pass, which climbs up to 12,000 feet at the top and is always crusted with snow.

But we had no choice. Our plane for New York left at 6:30, and there was no time to find another driver. When I offered Earl a beer, he said he'd rather have vodka. "It's better for driving," he said. "They can't smell it on your breath."

It was almost 1:30 when we finally left the house, but Earl was optimistic. He drove with a heavy foot, screeching back and forth around the turns, and we made it to the top of the pass without incident—but that was where the trouble started.

Earl wanted to stop for a moment and he pulled off in a darkened rest area. "Don't worry about me," he assured us. "I'm wide awake. I ate 12 Vivarins just before we left. I'm feeling better and better."

I was feeling worse. Earl had been drinking heavily out of a quart bottle of vodka that he kept under the front seat. His eyes were like black holes in space and he was jabbering constantly while he drove, turning around to look at us with every new idea.

"I was the first person ever arrested in Arizona for possession of LSD," he'd said earlier. "The judge was a friend of my family, so he put me in the insane asylum instead of sending me to prison."

And now, on the top of this dark and lonely pass, he suddenly jammed the car into reverse and backed it over the edge, into a sea of mud. "Mother of God!" he shouted. "I never drove this thing before: How the hell did it get into reverse?"

The wheels spun helplessly, sinking deeper and deeper into the lichen-covered mud. It was after three when we finally flagged down a charter bus full of tourists from Texas and gave the driver $100 to haul us out of the mud. . . . I looked at my watch and saw there was no hope of making the 6:30 plane, but Earl said it was no problem. "There's all kind of flights to New York in the morning," he said cheerfully, "All I need to do now is to fly like a bat out of hell."

Which he did—nipping frequently out of the tall vodka bottle between his thighs, and also from a small black jar that he had on a chain around his neck.

• • •

We stopped once for gas, in Leadville, where Earl had to rip the cap off the gas pipe with a claw-hammer, because Dilly hadn't given him a key. Then he had to open the hood with the hammer, to check the oil. The woman in the Quick Mart threatened to call the police on us, but she calmed down when I gave her a $100 bill.

It was 7:15 when we finally screeched up the departure ramp at the airport. Maria rushed inside to find another flight to New York, while I unloaded the bags and Earl got in a nasty little fight with the curbside baggage attendant. "The man got snide with me," he explained later. "I had to slap him around."

He was seized in a hammerlock by airport security guards, just as Maria returned in tears to report that all flights to New York were full until six or seven. "This is Friday," she said. "Even the stand-by lists are filled up."

It was hopeless. No flights to New York or even Newark, no passports and no flight to Scotland. Ralph would be stomped like a frog by drunken bikers, just as he'd feared—and there were not even any seats on a plane back to Aspen. . . . We were stuck at the Denver airport with Earl, who would have been taken to jail if I hadn't peeled off another three $100 bills for the security guards.

"Thanks a lot, man," he said. "I can't stand another parole violation. Let's get out of this hellhole. We can be back home by noon—but I have to make a stop at Roberto's house and pick up some business."

"What?" I screamed. "You dope-sucking swine!" He grinned sheepishly and staggered back to the car with our luggage. The jig was up. We had no choice. Earl jabbered frantically as we crawled back into the wretched cab—and then he jammed the thing into gear and we roared away, headed for Roberto's place.

August 17, 1987

Swine of the Week

"A thousand thousand slimy things lived on, and so did I."

—Sam Coleridge, "The Rime of the Ancient Mariner"

The political situation slipped another few notches last week, a hideous clicking and screeching of loose pig iron out of control—bad slippage, cheap teeth with bent edges that won't mesh or grip or hold on to anything, much less on the Great Pole of Weirdness. That is the one that politicians cling to, the black one that goes all the way down—not polished brass like the ones the firemen used to slide down whenever the main bell rang.

No, this pole is different. It is dark like a stovepipe and slick with human grease, criss-crossed with long scars and teeth marks that will give you a queasy feeling if you stare at them too long. Desperate men have struggled and slid down this pole, and only a few have gone up. It is like Jack's beanstalk, with a long root on the bottom end.

La Bas. Down there. Where the beasts are all blind and the doomed scream all night in the darkness. Spiro Agnew is down there, and Richard Nixon will join him soon enough. . . . There is also Lyndon LaRouche, Jim and Tammy, Michael Deaver, Patrick Gray and maybe Gary Hart. . . .

And there are also the old-timers, the vets: Boss Tweed, Phillip Nolan, Joe McCarthy, Martin Bormann, Caligula, Marshal Tojo, James Hoffa and a whole crowd of mutants and zombies like Papa Doc, Hubert Humphrey and the ineffable Ulysses S. Grant.

It is a special kind of hell for utterly failed politicians. They are a special breed—the Shameless Ones, those rare and rotten talents who don't come along very often, the boys who can crawl so low for so long that not even Thomas Edison could figure it out.

It is difficult for the ordinary voter to come to grips with the notion that a truly *evil* man, a truthless monster with the brains of a king rat and the soul of a cockroach, is about to be sworn is as president of the United States for the next four years. . . . And he will bring his *gang* in with him, a mean network of lawyers and salesmen and pimps who will loot the national treasury, warp the laws, mock the rules and stay awake 22 hours a day looking for at least one reason to declare war, officially, on some hapless tribe in the Sahara or heathen fanatic like the Ayatollah Khomeini.

• • •

So—with the gambling market gone flat and only Gary Hart to stare at until Iowa rolls around—we should seek a whole new idea, something just a little bit strange, perhaps cruel, or even twisted, to get us through this low period.

The answer came suddenly, as always, from the strange side of life. It was from my genuinely troubled agent, a nervous man named Stanky whose life was getting more and more miserable at the office, because people were calling him a "swine."

"And they're not kidding," he said. "They really despise me now. I'm worried. It's some kind of dirty mob psychology that feeds on itself. There's a lot of hate building up all around me."

They had just voted him "Swine of the Week" at the Friday office party. . . . "I can't stand it much longer," he said. "Some of these people are dope fiends and they wouldn't think twice about hurting me. I'm afraid."

"So what?" I said. "It's a good idea."

Which was true. Hardly a day goes by without some kind of geniunely swinish behavior popping up in the newspapers, or some late-night TV show.

TEXAN EXPOSED TO AIDS HAD
SEX WITH 54 CHILDREN

That was the headline recently on a wire-service story out of some-where deep in Texas:

"It was pretty shocking," said Debra Coca, chief juvenile probation officer in Falls County. The story went on to say that Jimmy Etheridge, a relentless degenerate "deliberately infected at least 54 children—maybe even hundreds, all over south Texas and the northern states of Mexico— with the deadly AIDS virus, which leads to a disease with a 100 percent fatality rate."

Stanky wept as he read me the story. "Why not *him* for Swine of the Week?" he yelled. "Why me? I never raped any children. I'm not sick."

"You're right," I said. "That man Etheridge is definitely the Swine of the Week."

Or maybe not, I thought, after I'd finally gotten rid of Stanky and his whimpering. . . . Etheridge was horrible, but there a few others running neck and neck.

There was a baseball player named Hatcher, leadoff hitter for the

Houston Astros, who got caught with a bat so full of pure cork down the middle that he could toss up a normal baseball and whack it about 600 feet every time—until he whipped it around on a high fastball and watched it explode like a Silkworm missile.

He was suspended for 10 days, an object of public shame. . . . But he was still insisting, even as they led him away, that he was technically innocent because the bat was not his; it belonged to his teammate Dave Smith, he said, and he had picked it up by accident.

Indeed. Hatcher deliberately poisoned Smith, for no good reason. He became a classic example of what many are calling these days: The Generation of Swine. . . . It is an ugly concept, a wretched kind of identity somewhere between Ed Meese and Ivan Boesky.

No two men between Wall Street and Tijuana have been accused of more fraud, corruption and flagrant swindling than Meese and Boesky—yet they are heroes to a whole generation: The Cruel and Loveless '80s, the Generation of Swine.

Both of these gents would be heavy favorites to win the Swine of the Week Award in any normal week. They would rank right up there with Al Davis, formerly of Oakland and a *perpetual* nominee for the Swine Award.

But none of these rotten dirtbags will go home with the Swine of the Week Award, this time. . . . That honor belongs to former Georgia State Sen. Julian Bond, who walked very smoothly away from a bad lot of felony cocaine charges in Atlanta, then stood back and watched as his alleged longtime lover and good friend, Carmen Lopez Butler, was sentenced to 22 years in the Georgia state prison.

Twenty-two years. For getting mixed up with Julian Bond and his high-powered political friends, including the mayor of Atlanta. It was a shame on us all, and if there was ever a sure-fire winner for the Swine of the Week award, it has to be Julian Bond.

September 14, 1987

Here Come de Judge

We are the hollow men
We are the stuffed men
Leaning together
Headpiece filled with straw. Alas!
Our dried voices, when
We whisper together
Are quiet and meaningless
As wind in dry grass
Or rats' feet over broken glass
In our dry cellar

—T.S. Eliot, "The Hollow Men"

The fat man walked last week.

It was "a question of supply and demand conditions," like he said. It was a purely mathematical situation, as usual. A free market gig. There was in fact a *demand* for a new justice on the U.S. Supreme Court and Judge Bork figured he was the supply.

Why not? The president had appointed him, and the president is on a roll these days. He has won just about everything he could get his hands on since losing the midterm elections in '86.

That was the one that whacked eight GOP senators and 12 representatives and turned the whole Congress into a Democratic fortress for the first time since 1980.

So much for big victories. . . .

Judge Bork, a certified hair-shirt punishment freak out of the Mussolini/Torquemada school, was one of the easiest and fattest targets since that wretched Bum-of-the-Month gang that Nixon tried to ram through, in the last crazed months of his reign. . . .

They were geeks and losers and the Senate rejected them all.

But Judge Bork was a different creature. He was smart, with fat little hands and a cheap-looking beard and a relentless ultra-conservative legal philosophy that sounded like a mix of Herbert Hoover, Joe McCarthy and the pope.

And by the end of the week he looked like a big winner, with a solid 8–6 plurality that stonewalled Ted Kennedy, embarrassed the Democratic majority and left Joe Biden's '88 presidential campaign in a pile of smoking ruins.

Biden went into the hearings on Tuesday as a real contender for the presidency of the United States in 1988. He was the junior senator from Delaware who had paid all his dues, thought fast on his feet, hired a blue-chip staff and had what the polls called "Kennedy-style charisma."

He would be a stretch-runner, they said. Maybe third in Iowa, then a close second in New Hampshire—and after that, a killer sweep on Super Tuesday in the South. With Hart gone and Nunn out, the big states like Florida and Texas were like huge ripe cherries, almost eager to fall in his fingers.

That was the scenario last week, but not now. Ted Koppel and Pat Buchanan burned 33 minutes of "Nightline" on Thursday discussing the Biden candidacy, and when they finished, Joe Biden was down in the ditch with all the other failed dumbos who faltered and then had to go on national TV like Richard and his faithful dog, Checkers.

Sen. Biden, with no front-warning at all, was suddenly exposed as a liar, a plagiarist and a dupe who'd spent most of his life as a whimpering, cheating fool. He was stealing his best lines from old Bobby Kennedy speeches, they said, and he also cheated one time about 20 years ago on a law school paper at Syracuse.

Biden immediately called a 9 A.M. press conference in Washington to flog himself on network TV and wallow publicly in his own guilt.

I spoke to a man in Washington the other day who said, "ONLY THE DOOMED ARGUE WITH PATRICK BUCHANAN."

He spoke only on the condition that his name not be used.

"Rest easy," I told him. "I won't tell on you. If the judge gets your name, it sure as hell won't be from me."

"Please," he said. "They'll run me down like some kind of crippled animal—you *know* who we're dealing with, don't you?"

"Of course," I said. "I've known him for years—he's a murderous swine but he may be the best in the business."

"Or the worst," he muttered. "That horrible thing he did to Joe Biden was really *over the line*."

"It was politics," I said. "Politics in the '80s."

Which was true. I was not talking to Peter Pan. This man was a lawyer, a well-paid *political consultant*. He lived in a townhouse on Capitol Hill, near Gary Hart's old place. There was no excuse for his whining and knee-crawling weeping about what the mean boys had done to Joe Biden. That was the business he had chosen.

It was the ugliest thing in politics since Hart dared the press to follow him around and see for themselves what he did in his spare time.

That one bombed. He went from a 2–1 favorite for the White House in '88 to a one-room cabin in Ireland, which he fled without paying the rent when his hare-brained ex-campaign manager, Bill Dixon, went on the radio somewhere up in Wisconsin and said Gary would "soon be back in the race."

It was a bad idea. One of Hart's former speech writers said, "If this is a trial balloon, it's the worst one since the Hindenburg."

Joe Biden had a different problem. He was not a front-runner, like Hart; he was more like Hart in '84, a genuine darkhorse with a hot-rod staff and more money in his bank than anybody else except Mario Cuomo, who dropped out of the race this year.

But Biden had to *cheat* to get through law school at Syracuse, and now he's denying that he steals all his speeches from old Bobby Kennedy transcripts.

What kind of fool would *deny* a thing like that?

Hell, I was *proud* to steal one of those high white notes from Bobby, now and then.

THE SWINE OF THE WEEK AWARD, however, was not in the reach of these people, these gimps and flakes and frauds that . . . well, never mind all that. The Swine of the Week, this time, will have to be the creep who turned in Joe Biden for cheating in law school.

Nobody knows who it was. But my own guess is Patrick Buchanan, who has done these things more than once—but not in the guise of the swine. He is a hit man, and he does pretty well at it. Res Ipsa Loquitor.

September 21, 1987

Wooing the Degenerate Vote

I got a new white cotton shirt last week. it was one of those long-tail, wet-weave XL *Fruit of the Loom* jobs that will shrink down to fit tight on a young greyhound dog the first time it touches hot water. But so what? It looks good tonight and people back off when they see it. The main logo is on the front, very large and stark and clean. . . . And right there in the middle of the message, like one of those screaming eagles on the old silver dollar, is the handsome smiling head of Richard Nixon.

"HE'S TAN, RESTED AND READY!" it says. *"NIXON IN '88."*

Why not? The moon is in Scorpio this week, and The Man is back among us. None of the standard-brand voter-preference polls have listed him yet, but that is mainly a matter of protocol. . . . In the *real* polls, the *dark lists* where the street people speak, *He Has Returned*. . . .

He has risen. There is no doubt about it. Recent backroom charts in Vegas show Nixon running third (with a bullet) just behind Vice President Bush and Senate Minority Leader Bob Dole.

None of the others are even in double figures. There is Howard Baker from the White House, Plastic Jack from Buffalo, the Preacher Robertson and that dingbat du Pont, who is playing a sort of Judas Goat role.

The only wild card in that crowd is . . . yes . . . The General, Big Al, who did his own stint in the White House and almost seized control, one time, but was beaten back by George Bush and squeezed totally out of power.

That was in the good old days, when men were men and crooks were whipped like dogs.

They walked tall, back then. Not like today, with these cheapjack hoods in control. Where are the heavy hitters? Spiro Agnew's people, the Vesco crowd, the boys from Key Biscayne and Norman's Key?

Where indeed? The smart money said they were gone, like the snows of yesteryear. . . . But the smart money was wrong: They were so baffled by Al Haig's candidacy that they took him completely *off the board* in Las Vegas. No odds at all. He was a ringer of some kind, they said. Big Al had no money, no staff, no allies, no power base, and he also appeared to be crazy.

It was a bad mix for sure. They called him a creep and a fixer, just another old soldier with the soul of an eel and the brains of a Trojan Horse.

Ho, ho. . . . They laughed at Thomas Edison, and strong men wept when Russell Chatham ate half of the Jackson Hole elk herd in six days and then went north for more.

They called him a degenerate, but even bankers bought his paintings, and when the Meat Sickness finally ended, Russell was a rich man. Maybe the richest man in the West. . . . That was a long time ago, but the lesson is still clear, and the General has learned it and put it to work with the same hungry vengeance that he brought to all his other jobs.

A Nixon-Haig parlay for '88 looks like a very strong bet right now—especially at 11–1. The numbers will run a bit higher in places like Ely and Jackpot (up to 20 or even 24–1), but in London it is down to single digits.

They don't have a lot of faith in us, over there. A recent editorial in *The Economist,* a profoundly wise and conservative British weekly, went so far as to worry out loud about the death of the American sense of humor. "Whatever happened to America's smile?" they asked. Why are the Yanks wallowing so horribly in "sulkiness, defensiveness and pessimism?"

Well . . . let them wonder. They will get their answer soon enough, when the new degenerate backlash hits home. The final irony of the 1988 presidential race, which has already destroyed and humiliated two of its genuinely best and brightest talents in a frenzy of public moralism, is that the eventual winner in November of '88 will almost certainly be a degenerate rake worse than anything that moved into the White House since Warren Harding, or even Ulysses S. Grant.

There is another whole year to go, before election day, and the conventional wisdom says more and more of these hapless presidential candidates will be fed unto the meat grinder of moralism. . . .

(Whacko! Uncle Pat will be proud of me for that one. It ain't quite up to the "nattering nabobs of negativism" but what the hell? I never worked for criminal swine like Spiro Agnew.)

Joe Biden is gone now—or at least gone from the '88 presidential campaign—and we are all a bit poorer for it. He was a *player,* and we need those people in politics. They are the ones who have defined us to ourselves as a nation of leapers and dreamers and risk-takers, an awesome world power with a lover's sense of adventure.

If Ben Franklin and Tom Jefferson had been nickeled and dimed to death by lawyers and bimbos and preachers, we might still be some kind of rich and stolid British colony like Canada—or just another continuous new-world experiment in mutated democratic giantism like Brazil. Ben's lechery made even the French nervous, and Jefferson was known to have an overweening affection for his slaves. But the French are still our allies, and the Louisiana Purchase still looks like a decent investment.

If "the business of America is business," like Calvin Coolidge said, then Franklin and Jefferson still qualify as Good Americans.

Biden went down so quick and so easy that even Gary Hart was shocked. Six months ago they were both champions—the front-runner and his shadow, two sharp young studs running for daylight and victory and the most powerful job in the world.

The conventional wisdom says the voters want more and more heads to roll; they got Hart, then Biden, and soon they'll have Gephardt and Gore. One of Washington's cheapest and scurviest big-time political consultants says the Democrats can't stand another one of those hideous exposures—that the whole party will turn into a late-night TV joke.

But he is wrong. The voters are fed up with this orgy of dumbness and punishment. The electorate will *demand* a degenerate in the White House.

September 28, 1987

The Weak and the Weird

The years creep slowly by, Lorena,
the snow is on the grass again.

—Henry de Lafayette Webster, "Lorena"

The road to the White House has always been tricky and dangerous, but this year a truly awesome new hazard was added: The Guillotine, and last week it was still working overtime. The Fast Lane, such as it is, was still cluttered with rolling heads and new lumps of clotting blood.

Most of it came from doomed Democrats, but there was also a touch of that thinner, bluer strain that could only have leaked from George Bush, the current GOP front-runner and huge odds-on favorite to win in '88.

After dodging more bullets than Rambo while he ran the long gauntlet of the Iran-contra hearings, George felt a powerful surge of new hubris in his veins and went off on a long-postponed European tour that his advisers said would yield maximum *presidential publicity*. In nine days, he was pictured all over the world with the leaders of Italy, Poland, West Germany, France, Belgium and Britian.

"Throughout his stay in Poland," said a *USA Today* dispatch, "a two-man video crew—hired by his presidential campaign—shot Bush's activities for later use in his run for the GOP presidential nomination. In London, the crew captured Bush together with British Prime Minister Margaret Thatcher.

" 'I hope those pictures will be very good—when I get into politics,' said Bush, standing in front of 10 Downing Street."

It was shrewd thinking, for a company man, and it might have worked out and even translated into a few votes—but then George came back home to meet the TV cameras and blew himself right out of the race in Michigan, a key primary state, by saying that maybe the Soviet Union could spare a few of its skilled tank mechanics. "Send them to Detroit," he said. "We could use that kind of ability."

Indeed. It was utterly logical. If the U.S. auto industry can't get the job done, bring Russians into Detroit and put them to work on Pinto production lines, so there won't be any more of these nasty recalls and embarrassing failures.

Who knows why he said it? Michigan is lost to him now. Jack Kemp is more fun and Pat Robertson is better organized. Why would George himself provide the final coffin nail?

Well. . . . Bush is genuine 1980s-style Republican, a quintessential type, and he actually *thinks that way*. . . . High labor costs? Uppity workers? Pintos exploding and a whole line of new vans catching fire whenever you turn on the radio. . . .

Who needs it? Get rid of those lazy buggers. Fire them and bring in Russian scabs. At least they're honest about being Communists.

Bush is still the front-runner in most polls, but not in the ones where it matters. A recent ABC/*Washington Post* poll and both Bush and Dole waltzing into the White House in '88 by margins of 2–1 over current "top Democrat" contenders Jesse Jackson and Massachusetts Gov. Michael Dukakis.

Which is probably true—or at least it was true *last week,* more or less—but the only people in politics who claimed to believe it were the poor dupes at ABC and the *Washington Post* who had to pay for the poll.

There are still two Halloweens between now and November 1988, and a lot of smart people are going to have their brains beaten loose between now and then. It is a 50–50 bet that none of the names on the top of the charts today will even *be listed* when Halloween of '88 rolls around. All the Democrat front-runners have been mowed down, more or less in order, in less time than it used to take to get rich on the Singapore Metals Exchange.

Many heads have rolled. Hart collapsed in a frenzy of mundane sex rumors, Joe Biden ran like a rat when one of his old "law school buddies" turned him in for maybe cribbing a few lines on some kind of obscure exam in Syracuse 20 years ago, and last week the blade fell on Dukakis and feminist favorite Pat Schroeder, along with most of their once-proud staff people.

Loose lips, old grudges, and ugly personal infighting have reduced the smartest and best-qualified group of presidential candidates that the Democratic Party has come up with since 1960 to a gang of demoralized drifters who quarrel constantly about whether they should be called "The Seven Dwarfs" or The Six . . . or maybe only five.

The Loyal Opposition has apparently collapsed, with a whole year to go into the game time. . . . And the only man in America who seems to understand the situation is Richard Milhous Nixon, the 74-year-old ex-president from New Jersey. Three or four months ago, just after Gary Hart's disaster, Nixon put together a lengthy analysis of how he saw the 1988 election year unfolding, and how things looked at the time.

"The best thing going for the Republicans in this election," he wrote (in one of his frequent "confidential memos" to Ronald Reagan and the other new boys in the White House) "is the weakness of the Democrats. There has never been such a motley collection," he said, "of what former Ambassador William Bullitt used to call 'first-rate second-rate men.' "

There was nothing really special or original about it: just another cheap shot, considering the source—but what we tend to forget about Nixon is that, for all his kinks and crimes and even his weird drinking problem, he possesses a truly awesome, bedrock shrewdness that made him perhaps the most successful political mechanic of his generation. He was elected to every public office on the whole spectrum of national politics except the governorship of California, and he came so close to that one that he ran publicly amok when he lost. That was when he called the press a gang of rotten bastards who had ruined his life and who "won't have Richard Nixon to kick around anymore."

People laughed, at the time—but six years later Richard Nixon was elected president of the United States, in a savage national street fight that the Democratic Party has never recovered from. Nixon won again, four years later—and then he got busted, chased out of Washington like some kind of diseased animal.

But it does not matter. George Herbert Walker Bush will not be with us much longer. By next Halloween, he will be living somewhere in New Jersey not far from the Nixon homestead.

October 5, 1987

The Time Has Come

More than half the Americans interviewed in a new poll said they are at least "fairly likely" to vote for Vice President George Bush if he becomes the Republican candidate for president.

—Associated Press, October 10, 1987

The national wire is full of strange items on most days, and it takes a real news junkie to make sense of them—which is usually impossible and usually for obvious reasons.

This "Big Win Seen for Bush" poll, for instance, had no attribution at all. At least not in the *Denver Post,* where it turned up as a two-inch filler on page eight of the Final Edition on Sunday.

Nobody knew where it came from. Probably from Bush, I figured, and it looked like an interesting bet—at least to those of us in the business.

The numbers were impressive, and the answers seemed to come from the heart. "Asked how likely they would be to vote for Bush for president if he were nominated" (presumably in 1988, although the year was never mentioned) "14 percent of the total sample answered 'extremely likely,' 16 percent said 'very likely' and 24 percent 'fairly likely.' "

There was another 44 percent who said "not too likely" or "not likely at all," but the *Post* headline writer dismissed these negative figures as gibberish, compared with what looked like a 54 percent majority—and put a headline on the item that said, "Half in Poll Give Bush Likely Vote."

Well, I thought . . . maybe so. Maybe George is already locked in for '88, and now he is just rolling up numbers. Another poll, on TV, showed him running almost 15 points ahead of Bob Dole and at least 2–1 over current Demo front-runner Jesse Jackson.

Who is making these numbers? I wondered, and how do I get in touch with them? It had the look of a sporting proposition, and I wanted to get a piece of it. There is no better bet in American politics, these days, than getting down at two or three to one against George Bush, or even 3–2. . . . Tell those people to get in touch with me; I can spread that money around.

• • •

The real odds on Bush in '88 are about 4–1 and rising, never mind what these "new polls" say. The word on Bush comes from The Man himself, Richard Nixon, who is one of the better handicappers.

In a June '87 memo, titled "The 1988 PRESIDENTIAL ELECTION," Nixon scanned the whole field of candidates and had this to say about George:

"Bush continues to have a substantial lead in the polls. His major assets are that he has the broadest experience of any of the candidates, by far the best organization, the most money, and most important— can campaign as the Vice President."

Nixon understands these advantages. He had all of them when he ran back in 1960, and he got his head handed to him by a gang of young upstarts who worked for Jack Kennedy—and that name has given him nightmares ever since. He knows what it feels like to be the rich boy at the wedding in "The Graduate."

As for Bush, he continues, "He is a loyal Vice President and does not come through as a strong independent candidate in his own right. His popularity will be directly tied to Reagan's. If Reagan's goes up, *his* will go up. If Reagan's goes down, *his* will go down."

This was written, incidentally, before the vaunted Bush organization got trounced in both Michigan and Iowa by the Preacher Robertson's crowd—and also before Ronald Reagan decided to put the whole weight of the White House behind the nomination of Judge Robert Bork to the U.S. Supreme Court.

It was a horrible mistake—one of those great leaps of hubris into what Gen. MacArthur used to call "The Pitfalls of Unrealism." Bork came and went like a pit bull, snapping and snarling on national TV in his own unique style—which disturbed even elderly GOP senators and left a whole generation of teenagers to feel queasy for the rest of their lives every time they hear the word "judge."

The White House was stunned, and the president's "popularity" went down like a stone in a peat bog.

A few weeks earlier, Judge Bork had come into the hearings with chips on both shoulders, a cheap-looking beard and the beady eyes of a zealot with friends in high places . . . and he had *his own* reputation to protect: He was, after all, a famous political hit man, like "The dirty little coward who shot Mister Howard."

But that is another story, and we don't have time for it now. All we need to know about Judge Bork is that the smart money in Washington had him no less than 7–7 coming out of the 14-member Senate Judiciary

Committee—headed by the now disgraced Democratic presidential candidate, the late Joe Biden from Delaware—and when the vote finally
happened last week, it went 9–5 *against* Bork.

It was one of those rare little wars in politics that neither side could
afford to lose. A Bork confirmation would have "broken the back" of
the Democratic opposition. It would have been one of those things, like
e.e. cummings said, that you can't eat.

It was "Joe Biden's revenge," some said, or maybe "the law of
karma" . . . but Richard Nixon knew what it really was. He has been
elected to almost every office in America except sheriff, and he understands politics as well as almost anybody. He is a *mechanic,* a true
leverage junkie—and what he saw at the end of those Bork hearings
was a gray-haired gent named *Kennedy,* who was sitting to Biden's left
and adding up the votes.

The torch had been passed, once again. And it was Joe Biden's revenge: Not all Democrats are speed freaks, lechers and fools. . . . Nature
abhors a vacuum, and it is the nature of American politics in these times
to have a Kennedy haunting the White House.

A recent survey on the "new realities" of the nation's politics, by the
George Gallup organization and the Times-Mirror Co. of Los Angeles—
"designed to create an extensive political profile of the American electorate"—came up with the "finding" that more people have "favorable
feelings" about Dan Rather (87 percent) than they do about Billy Graham, who was next with 66 percent. . . .

Two notches below Graham was Ronald Reagan, at 62 percent. And
one notch above Reagan was Sen. Ted Kennedy, with 64 percent . . . There was no mention of George Bush or Judge Bork.

The gambling community took notice, along with Richard Nixon, who
was likewise excluded from the top ranks. . . . Indeed, Chappaquiddick
was a long time ago. Enough is enough. The time has come.

October 12, 1987

The Worm Turns

"And I gave her space to repent of her fornication, and she repented not. . . . Behold, I will cast her into a bed, and them that commit adultery with her into great tribulation, except they repent of their deeds. . . . And I will kill her children with death . . ."

—Revelation 2:21–23

Never mind Judge Bork. He was a whimpering knee-jerk liberal, compared to the Book of Revelation. There is language—in the King James version, at least—that will peel the skin off your back. There was no Miranda Rule, back then; *everybody* was guilty, and punishment was swift and terrible.

There was no place to hide, or even run. It was the end of the world, the time of the final judgment: *"And in those days, shall men seek death, and shall not find it; and shall desire to die, and death shall flee from them."*

That is Revelation 9:6—one of the milder and more forgiving verses, and one of Ronald Reagan's favorites. The President is very keen on the Book of Revelation. I love it for the sharp and terrible power of the language, but Dutch really *believes* it.

Some time around Christmas in 1985, he told a reporter from *People* magazine that "this generation may be the one that will face the end of the world."

Indeed. That's you and me, sport. Buried in fire and ripped to shreds like lizards. In 4:8 the realities are made clear:

"And the four beasts had each of them six wings about him; and they were full of eyes within; and they rest not day and night, saying, Holy, holy, holy, Lord God Almighty which was, and is, and is to come."

A lot of acid freaks have been taken away in white jackets with extremely long sleeves for seeing things like that, but the visions normally don't last for more than 72 hours. But Reagan has believed in the coming of these hideous "four beasts with six wings and full of eyes within" for something like 72 years. The Bible is a pillar of his faith, and he is not about to give it up now—especially when it seems to explain why his world is crumbling all around him.

Of course. It must be Armageddon, and never mind what *The New York Times* says. What do they know? It was like Bill Casey's widow dismissing the idea that her husband might have spoken seriously with *Washington Post* editor Bob Woodward. "Why would he talk to a reporter?" she asked. "He was miles above him."

Well . . . maybe so. But if Casey was looking down last week—or even up—on the godless mess of evidence that low-life reporters were putting together, he could not have been happy. *The New York Times* called it "the worst week of Reagan's presidency," and a lot of the damage could be nailed on Casey himself.

He was a Wall Street man, and the market had collapsed. He was a right-wing power lawyer, and the candidate he would have backed for a seat on the Supreme Court was rejected by a huge 16-vote margin in the Senate. He was chief of the CIA, and his pet "secret" project—the scandal-torn Iran/Nicaragua operation—was so out of control that the United States was veering toward accidental war in two hemispheres. He was a big-time political thinker, involved in all the highest and most sensitive maneuvering with the Soviet Union and other world powers, but that too had failed.

At week's end the White House was reeling in disarray from the shock of Soviet leader Mikhail Gorbachev's cancellation of a long-awaited summit in Washington this year, an event that might have saved Reagan's presidency.

The Gorbachev visit was no small thing to Dutch. It was going to be a huge media event, the kind of thing he does best. There was talk of a "national tour" and even a personal visit to the Reagan ranch in the mountains near Santa Barbara, with thousands of journalists kept away by the Secret Service and forced to live on daily spoon-fed tidbits from Marlin Fitzwater.

But all that is gone now. The man with the mark of the beast just pulled the plug on the whole Reaganite wing of the GOP. Reagan is their president, after all, and they are the ones who will be unemployed and unemployable when he is gone.

The tragic events of last week caused one of them to utter a moan of real despair. "It's as if we're alchemists in reverse," said a White House source identified only as a "disheartened Republican politician," "Everything we touch seems to turn to dross."

"If Reagan can stave off an economic recession, the Republicans have a lock on the White House (in '88). But if the administration loses its

*handle on the economy, any jackass the Democrats put up will be elected
president."*

—Richard Nixon, June 1987

Welcome to jackass country. That beast has been the symbol of the
Democratic Party since 1828, when Andrew Jackson seized the White
House in a frenzy of populist power that has characterized the party
ever since. He served for eight years, and his vice president was Martin
Van Buren, who succeeded him in 1836—the last sitting vice president
ever to win the presidency.

Nixon understood this when he said, last June—long before the market collapsed—that if he "had to place a bet right now I would put it
on Bush, but I would certainly not bet the ranch."

Neither would anybody else after last week's events, which led to an
outburst of Bush-bashing in the national press. With the failure of the
Reaganites on all fronts, it suddenly became chic to ridicule the vice
president as a wimp and a loser and a man with no collarbone beneath
his rep tie.

The next president is likely to be a Democrat, and according to the
book of Revelation, he will have his hands full. Chapter 19, Verse 2
says, *"For true and righteous are his judgments: For he hath judged the
great whore, which did corrupt the earth with her fornication, and hath
avenged the blood of his servants at her hand."*

October 26, 1987

The End of an Era

Most smart people tend to feel queasy when the conversation turns to things like "certain death" and "total failure" and the idea of a "doomed generation." But not me. I am comfortable with these themes. There is nothing new about them, except when they come all at once. Any conversation that can make smart people confront a mix of Death, Doom and Failure with a straight face is probably worth listening in on. They don't come around real often, and when they do it almost always means that at least two of the people doing the talking are in very serious trouble.

They have lost their grip, for some reason. Jumped the rails gone mad on whiskey or opium. Who knows? With Nixon it was gin. Mozart was ravaged by syphilis, and Marilyn Monroe was a victim of the "dead bowel" syndrome which cost her millions of dollars.

Today, it is Ronald Reagan, the President, who is wandering out there on the cusp. For seven years, he has lived in the White House and run the country like some kind of cheap imitation of an old John Wayne movie.

But the year coming up is going to be No. 8, and it will be a bad year for Dutch—worse than '87 or even '86, when his world and his life and his final movie began to turn weird on him. Nineteen eighty six was the year when he lost control of the Senate and about 88 percent of the huge and apparently "magic" political leverage that had made him so tough and intimidating and pretty close to invincible ever since he became governor of California in 1966.

That was a long time ago, but to Dutch it must seem like only yesterday. Those were the glory years, when he began thinking he was tougher than John Wayne and meaner than Cato the Elder. Back there in Sacramento, his first official decision was to hire Ed Meese as his main man, and his second was to close the state-run insane asylums and put the loonies out on the street to fend for themselves.

People complained, but so what? The insane don't vote.

And neither will Ed Meese, until sometime around the year 2000, if the special prosecutor decides to lean on him for his role in the Wedtech case. The evidence is about 90 percent there—as it usually is when people begin asking questions about Ed's low-rent money hustles—and if the prosecutor figures that the weather looks just about right for busting the attorney general of the United States and putting him into a federal prison for three or four years, Meese will go. He will do enough push-ups on the hot asphalt of that long black parking lot down at Eglin to get rid of his beer belly and give him the same kind of hard ripples across his gut that Huey Newton had, after two years in solitary.

Meese was an assistant district attorney in Oakland back there in the early '60s, when people like Huey and Ken Kesey and Sonny Barger were running the town, and it had to be a frustrating job . . . he was losing about nine out of ten cases, back then, and it was only the magic hand of Ronald Reagan that rescued him from a shameful obscurity in the alleys of East Oakland and changed him from a toad into the governor's personal assistant in Sacramento.

It was like putting Charlie Manson in charge of the gym at a prison for teenage girls. Meese is dumb and cruel, but he is not stupid; he took all that pig-iron kind of leverage that came with his new job and made himself one of the most powerful men in California politics. Reagan liked his style and gave him all the room he needed—not just for hiring and firing and whipping his enemies with career-crushing "administrative punishments" that permanently destroyed anybody he didn't like; in addition to that, he was given a ranking advisory role that he rode all the way into the White House.

In the first years of the Reagan administration, Meese was one leg of a troika that led the president around like a fruithag and wrote all his personal memos and opinions.

There are thousands of file photos from those boom-boom days in the early '80s of Dutch and his boys scurrying back and forth across the White House lawn, leaping onto waiting helicopters and brooding tensely with each other across that big desk in the Oval Office.

Meese, Michael Deaver and James Baker, onetime campaign manager for George Bush and now secretary of the Treasury.

Jim Baker is one of the smarter boys in Washington, and he was one of the first to jump ship. He went out for lunch one day with then-Treasury Secretary Donald Regan, and after six or seven martinis they decided to trade jobs. Baker escaped from the White House, and Regan became Reagan's new chief of staff—but not for long; events soon caught up with him, and he was forced to resign in disgrace.

Deaver, once the ultimate *insider,* took a different route. He resigned to become a lobbyist, citing personal greed as his main reason, and he is now on trial in Washington for a grab bag of cheap crimes ranging from perjury and fraud to public drunkenness and relentless violations of the ethics code. His lawyers have chosen a unique defense strategy, claiming he was so hopelessly drunk during that period that he didn't know the difference between right and wrong.

It is basically a Wild Turkey defense, but it will set an interesting precedent if it works. There is a similar case pending in Colorado, involving a man who claims he snorted so much cocaine that he went totally insane and had no idea what he was doing when he went out on the street and chopped three or four people to death with a meat ax.

If either one of these manages to get his case assigned to one of the literally thousands of new judges appointed by Ed Meese, and somehow gets loose, we will all be in trouble.

In a generation of swine, Ed Meese from Oakland has somehow emerged as the boss pig—living testimony to George Orwell's classic statement in *Animal Farm:* "All swine are equal but some swine are more equal than others."

By incest, murder, suicide
Survives the sacred purple bird
Himself his father, son and bride
And his own Word

        —Howard Nemerov,
        "The Phoenix"

The Other George Bush

Skinner called from Washington last week and warned me that I was dangerously wrong and ignorant about George Bush. "I know you won't want to hear this," he said, "but George is an utterly different person from the one he appears to be—from the one you've been whipping on, for that matter. I thought you should know. . . ."

I put him on hold and said I would call him back after the Kentucky-Maryland game. I had given 5 points, and Kentucky was ahead by 7 with 18 seconds to go. . . . George Bush meant nothing to me, at that moment. The whole campaign was like the sound of some radio far up the street.

But Skinner persisted, for some reason. . . . He was trying to tell me something. He was saying that Bush was not what he *seemed* to be—that somewhere inside him were the seeds of a genuine *philosopher king*.

"He is smarter than Thomas Jefferson," Skinner said. "He has the potential to stand taller in history than both of the Roosevelts put together."

I was shocked. "You lying swine," I said. "Who paid you to say these things? Why are you calling me?"

"It's for your own good," he said. "I'm just trying to help you." . . . He took a call on one of his other lines, then came back to me in a blaze of disconnected gibberish.

"*Listen* to me," he was saying. "I was with him last night, all *alone*. We sat in front of his fireplace and burned big logs and listened to music and drank whiskey and he got a little weepy, but I told him not to worry about it, and he said he was the only living voice of Bobby Kennedy in American politics today."

"No," I said. "Don't tell me that swill. It's too horrible. I depend on you for more than that."

I laughed. It was crazy. Here was Gene Skinner—one of the meanest and most cynical hit men in politics—telling me that he'd spent the last two nights arguing with George Bush about the true meaning of Plato's Republic and the Parable of the Caves, smoking Djarum cigarettes and weeping distractedly while they kept playing and replaying old Leonard Cohen tunes on his old Nakamichi tape machine.

"Yeah," Skinner said, "he still carries that 350 with the Halliburton case, the one he's carried for years. . . . He *loves* music, really *high* rock 'n' roll. He has tapes of Alice Stuart that he made himself on the Nak."

Ye Gods, I thought. They've finally turned him; he's gone belly-up. How did he get my phone number?

"You hideous punk! Don't call me any more!" I yelled at him. "I'm moving to Hawaii next week. I know where you've been for the last two years. Stay away from me!"

"You fool!" he shouted. "Where were you when we were looking for you in New Orleans last week? We hung around for three days. George wanted to hook up with the Neville Brothers. We were traveling incognito." . . . and now he was telling me that Bush—half mad on cheap gin and hubris, with 16 states already locked up on Super Tuesday—showed up at the New Orleans airport on Sunday night with only one bodyguard and a black 928 Porsche with smoked windows and Argentine license plates.

It was hard to accept. Skinner was a professional, I knew—and Bush was a former director of the CIA. It was a strange mix; and especially strange, given Skinner's bizarre fix on Bush, which made me very uneasy.

"You know why he likes me?" he said. "He likes me because I know poems. He loves poetry. He can do 'Annabel Lee' from top to bottom." At that point his voice got blurry:

"It was many and many a year ago, in a kingdom by the sea. . . ." He paused for a minute, then went on in a very dreamy voice, which disturbed me. "And this maiden she lived with no other thought than to love and be loved by me. . . . I was a child and she was a child in this kingdom by the sea. But we loved with a love that was more than love—"

"That's enough," I said. "I can't stand it. The idea of George Bush cruising around New Orleans and quoting the works of Edgar Allen Poe is more than I can handle."

"That's nothing," Skinner replied. "He can sing every song that Bob Dylan ever wrote. He plays the Dobro. He has the second Dobro ever made—in its original case. Incredible, incredible."

I laughed harshly, but he seemed not to notice.

"And he loves animals," Skinner said. "Animals are the only thing he loves more than music."

"I saw him rescue a dead cat and try to bring it back to life," he said, "right out in the middle of Pennsylvania Avenue. He put his head right down on that animal's lips and blew his own breath down its throat. . . . People hooted and cheered at him and a big crowd gathered, but he kept right on.''

I felt sick and said nothing. Skinner rambled on, drifted from one demented story to another, like he was talking about the Maharishi. It made no sense at all.

None of it did, for that matter. George Bush was a mean crook from Texas. He had no friends and nobody in Washington wanted to be seen with him on the streets at night. There was something queasy about him, they said—a sense of something grown back into itself, like a dead animal. . . . It was impossible that he could be roaming around Washington or New Orleans at night, jabbering about Dylan Thomas and picking up dead cats.''

There was something very wrong about it, deeply wrong, even queer. . . . Yet Skinner seemed to believe these things, and he wanted *me* to believe them.

Why? It was like hearing that Ivan Boesky had written "The Rime of the Ancient Mariner," or that Ed Meese wakes up every morning and hurls a $100 bill across the Potomac.

I hung up the phone and felt crazy. Then I walked back to the hotel in the rain.

March 21, 1988

President Bush Will See You Now

"The very deep did rot: Oh Christ!
That ever this should be!
Yea, slimy things did crawl with legs
Upon the slimy sea"

—Samuel Taylor Coleridge,
"Rime of the Ancient Mariner"

This low-rent nightcrawling fire-sale of a presidential campaign has not taught us much about the nation we all call home—but every once in a while it hits a pure high note, a truly *original* flash.

They are not always *happy* or comforting, but that is not the point. They are the moments that make politics worthwhile—when you feel like you finally got paid back, in kind, for all the time and energy you've wasted on it.

One of these moments came around last night just before the Bush-Dukakis debate, when PBS put Barry Goldwater and George McGovern together by tube-link and asked them what they thought about the election.

The result was an eerie five minutes of *déjà vu* for a lot of people who never agreed on anything else in politics—except for a sudden realization that the two best and brightest and most honorable men to run for the presidency of the United States in the last 25 years were also the two who got beaten and trashed by the biggest margins since George Washington won a second term.

Goldwater held the record briefly, after he got flogged 62–38 percent by Lyndon Johnson in 1964. But George lost even bigger in 1972, when Richard Nixon beat him by a shocking 18 million votes.

History records these numbers mercilessly—but history also records that both Johnson and Nixon met a similar fate and were drummed out of Washington in a cloud of shame, defeat and disgrace. They both quit and slinked away.

Anyway, they are gone now, while McGovern and Goldwater are still with us and viewed by even their enemies as contemporary folk heroes. . . . When PBS wanted the *real thing* for their final pre-debate commentary, they called George and Barry.

It was a brilliant stroke of political journalism but it didn't do much for Get Out the Vote activists on either side.

McGovern dismissed the Democratic candidate as some kind of cheap robot, and Goldwater denounced Bush with such venom that George made a point of calling Goldwater a fool about halfway through his debate with Dukakis a few hours later. . . . Dukakis had the grace to not mention McGovern, but that was about the only thing he did right.

The first instant-reaction poll came from ABC, calling it 49–33 percent for Bush—which seemed like an honest count. George Bush stomped on the terra last night, and Dukakis made it easy for him.

He denied or apologized for just about everything he'd ever done in his life except showing up for the debate, which was clearly a fatal mistake.

Nobody summed it up better than a man from the *Atlanta Constitution* who said, "If it was a fight, it would have been *called*."

Ex Quizzo Nobium

That is political shorthand for the old trial lawyers' axiom that says "Never ask a question unless you already know the answer." It makes a mean kind of sense that most lawyers grasp instinctively, but Michael Dukakis—a Harvard Law graduate and a certified shrewd politician— has apparently not learned that lesson, and *school is out* for him now. There is no more time for learning. He is about to shoot the gap, and it will be a lonely experience.

Not since Evel Knievel tried to jump the Snake River Gorge has any high-rolling fool rushed out to The Brink so utterly unprepared.

About halfway into the debate, Dukakis was looking more and more like the incredible shrinking man. The fun was gone, and some of his staff people were seen moving nervously toward the exits.

My own notes on the argument are extremely dense and detailed, but there is no point in printing them now. It would be overkill, and I am not in the mood for it. . . .

I *hurt* for Dukakis last night, because I like the man and I believe he is a lot better than he comes across on TV—but it is hard to argue with the notion that anybody who can get into a high-dollar public argument with George Bush and come out looking like a mean dunce is probably not fit to be president of the United States.

To say that *Bush didn't win this election, Dukakis lost it* is a baleful judgment on both of them, but I think it is true.

It was Adlai Stevenson, among others, who said, "*In a democracy, people get the kind of government they deserve*." But there are some things that even smart people don't like to be right about, and for Adlai that is surely one of them.

He must have been spinning in his grave last night, stunned by Dukakis' embarrassing collapse.

And he was not alone. There are a lot of us lying out here in the weeds today, and we are not really whooping it up. . . . But what the hell? *Buy the ticket, take the ride*.

October 15, 1988

I Slit My Own Eyeballs

October 22, San Francisco

October is the cruelest month of any election year, but by then, the pain is so great that even the strong are like jelly and time has lost all meaning for anybody still involved in a political campaign. By that time, even candidates running unopposed have abandoned all hope of victory and live only for the day when they will finally be free to seek vengeance on all those treacherous bastards who once passed themselves off as loyal friends and allies and swore they were only in it because they all shared the same hopes and dreams. . . .

October in the politics business is like drowning in scum or trying to hang on through the final hour of a bastinado punishment. . . . The flesh is dying and the heart is full of hate: The winners are subpoenaed by divorce lawyers and the losers hole up in cheap motel rooms on the outskirts of town with a briefcase full of hypodermic needles and the certain knowledge that the next time their name gets in the newspapers will be when they are found dead and naked in a puddle of blood in the trunk of some filthy stolen car in an abandoned parking lot.

Others are not so lucky and are doomed, like Harold Stassen, to wallow for the rest of their lives in the backwaters of local politics, cheap crooks and relentless humiliating failure. By the time Halloween rolls around, most campaigns are bogged down in despair and paralyzed by a frantic mix of greed and desperation that comes with knowing that everything you have done or thought or worked for or believed in for the past two years was wrong and stupid.

There are never enough seats on the last train out of the station. . . .

November 6, Reno

November has finally come to an end and the Fat Lady is about to sing for a lot of people who will call it a hateful noise, even though they always swore they loved music. The campaign is over unless somebody gets assassinated, and even that probably wouldn't make much difference unless it was Jesse Jackson. . . . No riots would erupt if any of the others were croaked. You can't miss what you never had.

> *"The dog sucked his brains out,"*
> *the girl replied. "He's dead."*

The New Dumb

"How long, O Lord. . . . How long? Where will it end? The only possible good that can come of this wretched campaign is the ever-increasing likelihood that it will cause the Democratic Party to self-destruct."

—Fear & Loathing on the Campaign Trail, 1972

Sixteen years is plenty of time for even dumb people to learn just about anything they need to, especially when the difference between winning and losing is usually a matter of life or death, professionally, in the business of big-time politics. It is a question of enlightened self-interest —learn quick or die.

But there are exceptions as always like Joan of Arc, Lyndon LaRouche, and even Gary Hart—which is not really fair in Gary's case; it was not that he couldn't learn, he just had different priorities. They jeered and called him crazy when he quit, but polls taken immediately after the election had him as the Demo front-runner for 1992.

It was the kind of news that nobody wants to hear, like having your pre-marriage blood test handed back to you in a lead bag, or getting a job as the next sheriff of Sicily. . . . Richard Nixon might handle a horror like that, or maybe William Burroughs, but no other names come to mind. Some things are too ugly to even gossip about.

Gary was unavailable for comment on the '92 poll, and his former campaign manager, Bill Dixon, has long since moved to Bangkok. Other Democrats wept openly at the news, but most just stared blankly. "The front-runner for '92?" one asked. "Are you crazy? I'd rather have a truckload of pig entrails dumped in my front yard by some of those tattooed guys from Yakuza."

It is an ancient and honorable method of collecting debts in Japan, but not yet chic in this country. The Yakuza, however, are said to be infiltrating American cities at a rate that will soon make them the second most powerful political organization in this nation, behind only the Republican Party.

The Mafia ranks No. 3—followed by the Roman Catholic Church, the IRS, the U.S. Congress and the American Marijuana Growers' Association.

Indeed. There are many rooms in the mansion. James Angelton said that back when the CIA was still a ranking power. . . .

The Democratic Party is not even listed in the top 20, despite a No. 4 ranking two years ago. It was a shocking plunge.

"The Democrats shouldn't even be listed in the top 40," said political analyst Harold Conrad. "They have become the party of Losers."

That is probably wishful thinking—but at 10 to 1 it might float, even in Las Vegas. The last time a major political party self-destructed was in 1853, when the Whigs went belly-up despite the leadership of Henry Clay, Daniel Webster and John Quincy Adams. They had ceased to stand for anything except pure politics.

"They refused to learn," says Conrad. "They became the New Dumb, and then they died."

If that is the only issue, the Democrats appear to be doomed. They have not learned anything about presidential politics since 1960, and they have lost five out of the last six elections despite a consistently powerful showing in state and local elections. While Dukakis lost in 40 states, the Democratic Party added to its control of Congress with a net gain of five seats in the House and two in the Senate.

The dumb are never with us for long, and there is a lot of evidence to suggest that Republicans learn faster than Democrats....Consider the crude learning experience that fell like a huge snake around the neck of the national Republican Party in 1964, when they were forced to go public as the party of Dumb Brutes and Rich People, and then see themselves flogged in the general election by 16 million votes.

When Goldwater was forced to wallow in the horror of public defeat, many experts said he was not wallowing alone, that the whole Republican Party was wallowing with him. The GOP was doomed, like the Whigs, to a cheap and meaningless fate.

But not for long. Four years later, Richard Nixon came back from the dead and ran the Democrats out of power with a 500,000-vote victory over the wretched arch-liberal, Hubert Humphrey....

It was 1968—the Death Year—and this time it was the Democrats who ran amok. If the campaign had been conducted under the Rules of War— which it *was*; a *civil* war—thousands of hate-crazy young Democrats would have been tortured to death by their own kind, or killed in the streets like wild animals. Both Johnson and Humphrey would have been executed for treason.

We were all crazy, that year, and many people developed aggressive attitudes. When I packed my bags for Chicago, there was nothing unusual about including a Bell motorcycle helmet, yellow ski goggles, a new pair of Chuck Taylor All-Stars and a short billy club. Packing for Chicago was not like taking off for the Club Med.

The Democratic Party has never recovered from that convention. It is a wound that still festers, and these people are not quick healers. They have blown five out of six presidential elections since then, and their only victory came after a criminal Republican president was dragged out of the White House in a frenzy of shame.

It was no big trick to beat Gerald Ford in 1976. He was clearly Nixon's creature, and the GOP was massively disgraced. It was a friendly preacher from Georgia against a gang of crooks....And even then Carter blew a big lead and only won by 2 points.

Four years later he was crushed by Ronald Reagan, a goofy version of Goldwater, who ruled for two terms and then anointed his successor while Democrats embarrassed themselves once again.

Party Chairman Paul Kirk should be whipped like a red-headed stepchild, and the others should be deported to Pakistan. Any major opposition party dominated by the shaggy whores and failed dingbats not only cripples the two-party system, but insults the whole democracy.

November 22, 1988

Letter to the President

James Baker
c/o White House
Washington, D.C.

October 15, 1988

Congratulations on your great victory last night in Los Angeles. I have been on your side from the start, and this only confirms my conviction. When you came on board in New Orleans, I knew it was all over. Who else could have annihilated the whole Gender Gap in 72 hours? The Quayle move will go down in the history of political science as a Master Stroke. Even Frank Mankiewicz wept and said he was quitting politics forever.

I feel the same way, except that I will need work after the election and there is no place I'd rather work than the White House for the next eight years, especially with *you* in control. And that is inevitable, I think. I have admired the raw power and awesome consistency of your work for many years and I look forward to finally joining up with a winning team and putting my expertise to work.

You can consider the Drug Problem *solved*, for instance. Don't worry about it. George didn't *lose* that war, he was just biding his time and waiting for the right kind of help.... Which is *me*, James. I feel like Bo Jackson on his way to join the Raiders. We will kick more ass than anybody since Truman.

Don't worry. I know what I'm doing, and so will a lot of other people pretty soon. There will be grumbling, but only from the Wrong Ones. We have cleared the decks, James. We will march on a road of bones.

And speaking of bones, Jim—never mind all those crazy things I used to say about George Bush. Hell no! Remember that law about "sticks and stones can break my bones, but words can never hurt me."

You bet. I have it framed on the wall right in front of my desk.... Hell, words are only pearls before swine, anyway. Our job will be to make the swine break their teeth. We can turn them into impotent sloats by using their fear against them. That is the main principle of judo.

OK, Jim. That's about it, for now. Pls. give me a ring ASAP, so we can get a running start on this thing. I am chomping at the bit, as they say, and the drug situation is so grim that we *must* move at once and get a jump on the buggers before they see the election results and run for cover.

Our time has come, and I'm ready if you are. We will crush them like hot grapes.

With warmest regards, I remain yr. slavish admirer,

Dr. H.S. Thompson
c/o Archibald
Gen. Delivery
Perth, Australia

ABOUT THE AUTHOR

HUNTER S. THOMPSON's books include *Fear and Loathing in America, Screwjack, Hell's Angels, Fear and Loathing in Las Vegas, The Proud Highway, Better Than Sex,* and *The Rum Diary* and *Kingdom of Fear.* A contributor to various national and international publications, including a weekly sports column for espn.com, Thompson lives in a fortified compound near Aspen, Colorado.

Also available from
America's most notorious outlaw
HUNTER S. THOMPSON

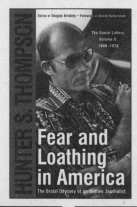

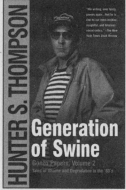

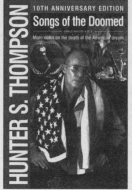

"There are only two adjectives writers care about anymore—'brilliant' and 'outrageous'—and Hunter Thompson has a freehold on both of them." —Tom Wolfe

Fear and Loathing in America
The Brutal Odyssey of an Outlaw Journalist
0-684-87316-8

Spanning the years between 1968 and 1976, these never-before-published letters show Thompson building his legend: running for sheriff in Aspen, Colorado; creating the seminal road book *Fear and Loathing in Las Vegas;* twisting political reporting to new heights for *Rolling Stone;* and making sense of it all in the landmark *Fear and Loathing: On the Campaign Trail '72.*

The Great Shark Hunt
Gonzo Papers, Volume 1
Strange Tales from a Strange Time
0-7432-5045-1

The first volume of Hunter S. Thompson's legendary *Gonzo Papers*. Pieces range from Thompson's *National Observer* days to famous entries from *Rolling Stone. Publishers Weekly* hailed it as "filled with moral outrage and fiendish humor" and *Cosmopolitan* called it "an indictment of everything shoddy, shifty, and just plain rotten that has afflicted our planet since the 1960s."

Generation of Swine
Gonzo Papers, Volume 2
Tales of Shame and Degradation in the '80s
0-7432-5044-3

The bestselling second volume, this collection of essays from Hunter S. Thompson's days as media critic at *The San Francisco Examiner* chronicles the social and political debauchery and decadence of the 1980s.

Songs of the Doomed
Gonzo Papers, Volume 3
More Notes on the Death of the American Dream
0-7432-4099-5

Spanning four decades, this extraordinary third volume covers high and hideous moments in Thompson's career, with original pieces from *The Rum Diary*, *Prince Jellyfish*, and *The Curse of Lono*, as well as memos to famous friends and coverage of the infamous Roxanne Pulitzer trial. In *Songs of the Doomed*, no one is safe from Thompson's savage wit and astute social commentary.

Kingdom of Fear
Loathsome Secrets of a Star-Crossed Child in the Final Days of the American Century
0-684-87324-9

Hunter S. Thompson's *New York Times* bestselling memoir: a hilarious, harrowing, historic chronicle of the making of the Gonzo journalist. **"Thompson's voice still jumps right off the page, as wild, vital and gonzo as ever."** *—The Washington Post*

The Rum Diary
A Novel
0-684-85647-6

A brilliantly tangled love story of jealousy, treachery, and violent alcoholic lust in the Caribbean boomtown that was San Juan, Puerto Rico, in the late 1950s.
"A great and an unexpected joy . . . reveals a young Hunter Thompson brimming with talent." *—The Philadelphia Inquirer*

Screwjack
A Short Story
0-684-87321-4 (hardcover)

A collection of three wild and outlandish short stories from literary legend Hunter S. Thompson—including rare and elusive lost classics.

SIMON & SCHUSTER
A VIACOM COMPANY